The Art and Science of

Vedic Counseling

David Frawley

Suhas Kshirsagar

MOTILAL BANARSIDASS PUBLISHERS
PRIVATE LIMITED • DELHI

First Indian Edition: Delhi, 2017

Published in arrangement with
LOTUS PRESS
P.O. Box 325, Twin Lakes, WI 53181 USA
lotuspress@lotuspress.com, www.lotuspress.com

ISBN: 978-81-208-4074-4

Also available at

MOTILAL BANARSIDASS
41 U.A. Bungalow Road, Jawahar Nagar, Delhi 110 007
8 Mahalaxmi Chamber, 22 Bhulabhai Desai Road, Mumbai 400 026
203 Royapettah High Road, Mylapore, Chennai 600 004
236, 9th Main III Block, Jayanagar, Bengaluru 560 011
8 Camac Street, Kolkata 700 017
Ashok Rajpath, Patna 800 004
Chowk, Varanasi 221 001

FOR SALE IN SOUTH ASIA ONLY

Library of Congress Number 2015959686

Printed in India
by RP Jain at NAB Printing Unit,
A-44, Naraina Industrial Area, Phase I, New Delhi–110028
and published by JP Jain for Motilal Banarsidass Publishers (P) Ltd.,
41 U.A. Bungalow Road, Jawahar Nagar, Delhi-110007

Table of Contents

Preface

We welcome the reader to the vast, dynamic and transformative field of Vedic counseling. This spiritual system of life-guidance can help you bring a greater consciousness, creative and happiness into all that you do.

The field of Vedic counseling covers the entire range of our life concerns from health to career and Self-realization. It is not a new invention but based upon the ancient Vedic system of India and its profound seer vision, with thousands of years of experience behind it. We can also call it "yogic counseling" as it reflects the philosophy and practice of Yoga on all levels.

Vedic counseling adds a new and deeper dimension to the modern practice of counseling that is relevant to everyone. The book is designed to address the needs of both counselors and their clients and can be used as a manual for right living in harmony with the universe as a whole. It emphasizes the role of Yoga and Ayurveda for both body and mind, stressing the importance of behavioral medicine and life-style therapies as a foundation for all other healing modalities.

THE BOOK HAS THREE PRIMARY AIMS.

- First is to bridge the gap between eastern and western forms of counseling and combine what is best in each.

- Second is to integrate the different forms of Vedic counseling, such as found in Yoga, Ayurveda, Jyotish and Vastu, noting the relevance of each.

- Third is to provide clear counseling skills for Vedic practitioners of all types, who may not be trained in these and can greatly benefit by them.

The book addresses the emerging field of Vedic Counseling as a guidebook for its application. While it can be easier to understand the book if one already has a background in Vedic thought, particularly previous study in Yoga or Ayurveda, one can gain much value from the book even if new to the subject. We have additional titles in these Vedic fields that can help.

The book is linked to special training programs for those who wish to pursue this profound subject further, including various counseling resources. The book includes several Sanskrit terms and has a detailed glossary to aid in understanding these.

We would like to thank the individuals and organizations that have helped in the inspiration and production for the book. Most notably is the foreword from Dr. Vasant Lad, who has guided the spread of Ayurveda in the West. Very important has been ongoing support from Dr. Deepak Chopra and the Chopra Center, who we have been working with for many years. We would like to thank all of our students and patients who have helped us understand how Vedic teachings work in daily life.

We have a special thanks goes to Megan Murphy and Nina Rogers for the beautiful and careful editing and layout, and to Tejasinha Sivalingam and Yogi Baba Prem for proofreading.

A note of highest appreciation goes our wives, Yogini Shambhavi Devi, who has written several books on Yoga and is a Vedic counselor, and Dr. Manisha Kshirsagar, who has authored several important books on Ayurveda as an Ayurvedic doctor herself.

May the book bring health, happiness and well-being to all!

Dr. David Frawley
Dr. Suhas Kshirsagar
Feb. 2016

Foreword

by Dr. Vasant Lad

Ayurveda is an ancient system of healing body, mind, and consciousness rooted in the timeless Vedic teachings. Ayurveda has been the main form of medicine practiced in India for the past five thousand years and its principles of healing are intimately related to the Vedas.

According to the Vedic system, the human being is a miniature of nature. Every individual is a unique expression of the universal consciousness, called *Purusha. Prakriti* is primordial matter and provides the substance for the creation. Before the creation of the universe, there was neither light nor darkness; no forms, colors or objects. It was a state of twilight, of cosmic presence and pure potential.

Creation of the Universe and the Human Being

Purusha and *Prakriti* as Spirit and nature were merged together in a pure expansive, all-inclusive state of awareness—the unmanifested state of the universe, an inseparable, expansive soup of cosmic plasma, before the big bang happened. This was the pure cosmic being with its vast immense mind.

Suddenly, within that state, the divine will arose, "I am one, I want to become many." At that moment, the big bang happened within the universal I-am-ness. There was an expression of primordial cosmic sound vibration known as AUM. The letter A represents the beginning, the letter U relates to sustenance, and the letter M is completion or ending. At the moment of the big bang, Purusha and *Prakriti* were separated for the purpose of creation. *Prakriti* is the divine mother, and within her womb, this beautiful little child, the universe, was born.

Within the heart of the universe began the pulsation of cosmic *prana* as the cosmic nectar of life. The pranic vibration within *Prakriti* began the process of cosmic evolution.

The first expression of Creation was *mahat*, cosmic intelligence.

Intelligence means to put everything in its right place, which is cosmic order. Before the expression of *mahat*, there was no sense of separation. However, within the core of *mahat*, the "I" (or ego) pulsated. That center of intelligence is "I am", which is ahamkara. Which literally means "I-former". It is the root cause of manifest expressions of consciousness, such as color, quality, and form.

In the human body, every cell is a center of awareness. This functional unit of the body has its own consciousness, a form of micro-*Purusha*. Every cell also has a *prakriti* or nature, which is its unique genetic code. Within every cell is *ahamkara*, the "I former that gives shape and qualities to the cell. Finally, every cell has a mind. That is why every single cell chooses its food.

Within cellular activity is a flow of life called *prana*, which is a flow of communication. There is a cellular intelligence, which is micro version of cosmic intelligence. All these are present within the DNA.

The Five Elements

In the cosmos, the expansive state of consciousness is space. There is a vast space outside the body and smaller spaces within the body, which hold life and intelligence. Space corresponds to nuclear energy. It is necessary for cellular communication. Space is freedom, lack of resistance.

The air element is the vibration and pulsation of the cosmic *prana* or universal life-force. This corresponds to electrical energy externally. Positively charged electrical particles are *prana*, while negatively charged particles correspond to *apana*, from which forces of attraction and repulsion arise and create expansion and contraction. Thus, all bodily movement is governed by the air element.

Because of the movement of cosmic air, heat is generated or the fire element. That is radiant energy. Fire governs color complexion, body temperature, digestion, absorption, and nutrition of the body and perception, judgment and volition in the mind.

Due to the radiant heat, consciousness melts into the water element. Water is a universal chemical solvent, which governs all biochemical activities in the body. Our body is eighty percent water, including plasma, serum, and cytoplasm. Water governs hydration and cellular nutrition, through the water-electrolyte balance.

The final expression of consciousness is the earth element. This is the solid ground for existence and relates to mechanical energy or physical energy. The cell membranes and all minerals are connected to earth element. It allows us to have boundaries in the body and the mind.

These universal factors of creation—*Purusha* (consciousness), *Prakriti*, Intelligence, Mind, Ego, and the five elements—are present in every human being. That is why the Ayurveda says that man is a miniature of the whole of nature.

THE THREE DOSHAS

The structure of the body is governed by the five great elements. The functional aspects of life are governed by the three fundamental organizing principles, which are the three doshas or biological humors: vata, pitta and kapha.

Vata is a biological combination of space and air, pitta is derived from fire and water, while kapha is an expression of water and earth. These three doshas, along with seven bodily tissues and three bodily waste-materials form the major constituents of the body.

At the time of conception, the predominant doshas from the father carried through the sperm, and the doshas from the mother present in the egg, are responsible for the nature of the individual constitution (birth *prakriti*). Every person has his or her own unique constitution.

Over time, the constitutional doshas undergo changes due to fluctuations in the diet, lifestyle, season, aging and environment. The altered status of the doshas is called *vikriti* or imbalance, the state of disease. *Prakriti* is order, whereas *vikriti* leads to disorder. In Ayurvedic clinical assessment, the Ayurvedic physician can detect the doshic constitution and its imbalances. To harmonize the person's constitution and its imbalances (*prakriti* and vikriti), is the basic paradigm of Ayurvedic treatment or *chikitsa*.

The Disease Process

Disease is born out of the interaction between the doshas and the bodily tissues. This definition of disease is quite significant and intimately connected to clinical assessment. The doshas undergo six stages in the disease process: accumulation, provocation, spread, manifestation, and differentiation (*sanchaya, prakopa, prasara, sthana samraya, vyakti* and *bheda*).

The first two stages of accumulation and provocation take place in the gastrointestinal tract, specifically at the main sites of the doshas: colon for vata, small intestine for pitta and stomach for kapha. If the causative factors behind the disease continue, the dosha then enters into the third stage of spread. During this stage, the doshas circulate throughout the body, seeking a place to hide. If there is any defective space within a tissue, due to weak digestion, genetic predisposition, previous trauma, or unresolved, repressed emotions, the dosha then enters into the tissue during the deposition stage and relocates there.

During this stage of deposition, the dosha not only enters into the tissue, the negative qualities of the aggravated dosha disturb or suppress the positive qualities of the tissue. This leads to the manifestation stage, where there is change in tissue function initially, or even changes in tissue structure at a later stage.

Ayurvedic Treatment

Ayurvedic treatment aims to skillfully separate the disease causing doshas from the affected tissues. The doshas can then return to the GI tract to be eliminated from the body. This is the primary purpose of Ayurvedic therapy.

In Ayurvedic literature, there are many forms of treatment. These include: *shodhana* (cleansing or detoxification), *shamana* (palliative measures), *rasayana* (rejuvenation), *vajikarana* (virilization) and balancing doshas through diet and lifestyle, healing through sacred sound (mantra), *daivavyapashara* (spiritual healing), healing through planetary energies (astro-therapy), *manas chikitsa* (psychotherapy) and *vastu dosha harana* (healing through directional energies).

Ayurveda is not only a philosophical science, it is a most practical art. An experienced and well-versed Ayurvedic physician is a good teacher in the client-practitioner relationship. An Ayurvedic physician is called a vaidya. *Vaidya* means someone with a profound knowledge of the body, mind, and consciousness, who uses his or her skills in diagnosis, including keen observation, tactile perception, and inquiry.

The Importance of Counseling

All varieties of Ayurvedic treatment can be greatly enhanced through proper counseling. Counseling is an ancient Vedic art of providing guidance and motivation, balancing the body, mind, and consciousness. *"The Art and Science of Vedic Counseling"* is an excellent work done by Dr David Frawley, also known as Vamadeva Shastri, and Dr Suhas Kshirsagar, a well-known Ayurvedic physician.

Dr David Frawley is one of the most highly honored Vedic scholars and teachers in the world today. "Vamadeva" means an expert in Vedic wisdom. In 2015, he received a prestigious Padma Bhushan award from the President of India for his lifelong service to the Vedic teachings. Dr Suhas Kshirsagar is a highly honored Ayurvedic doctor both in India and the United States. His depth of clinical knowledge and practical application of astrology, yoga, mantra, and meditation is unique and comprehensive.

Ayurvedic counseling requires flawless perception, clarity of sensory evaluation, and a good knowledge of Vedic principles. The skillful practitioner must enter into the heart of the patient. The patient's physical look and all details of appearance and facial expression have great significance for diagnostic purposes.

Never put your words in the mouth of the patient. The patient is the first authority, which means you must observe and listen to them carefully. Let the patient describe all signs and symptoms in his or her own words, as this helps in understanding which qualities and doshas are affected.

Try to understand the patient's diet and lifestyle, along with the environment in which the person lives. That helps the therapist determine the most important factors behind the disease. The causes of disease and suffering often lie within the diet and lifestyle of the person. A therapist can help the client change the way that he or she lives life, in order to reestablish balance. For this reason, a good client-practitioner relationship is absolutely necessary.

The field and scope of Vedic healing is vast. One can integrate Ayurveda with Vedic astrology, because planetary dispositions affect physical and mental health. For instance, during a Saturn period, a person will more likely come down with *vata* disorders, such as arthritis, rheumatism, or sciatica. Saturn can even cause serious illnesses such as stroke paralysis or neuromuscular dystrophy, or psychological problems like anxiety and depression. A Mars period of life causes pitta disorders, such as hives, rashes, urticaria, eczema or psoriasis, or psychological issues of conflict and anger. Dr Frawley and Dr Kshirsagar have beautifully elaborated the relationships between planets, individual nature and disease potential.

Vedic mantras and fire rituals serve to create a healing environment. The ancient Vedic directional science of *vastu shastra* has a great influence on relationships, health, and happiness. Each direction has a specific element and deity. Drs Frawley and Kshirsagar have indicated specific directional influences as a means of healing the person.

Sanskrit words have subtle vibrations that create powerful healing mantras. To pronounce these mantras properly, we need to bring a special discipline into our nervous system and good neuromuscular communication. Just by uttering Sanskrit words, which has a calming effect, the nervous system releases helpful neurotransmitters such as serotonin and melatonin. In this book, Dr Frawley and Dr Kshirsagar provide sacred mantras for body and mind.

Counseling consists of a friendly dialogue between the client and practitioner. It covers each stage from birth to the present day—the flow of the river of life. The practitioner will guide the client in every aspect of his or her existence. In Vedic counseling, the patient is inspired with the right motivation, intention, and attention, which then unfolds a deeper awareness that brings balance and healing on all levels.

"The Art and Science of Vedic Counseling" is the best counseling guide available for students, teachers, and practitioners of Ayurveda, Yoga, and related healing arts. The book is an ever-cherished collection of knowledge and wisdom and a practical, clinical reference. I highly recommend the book to all those who love Ayurveda.

Vasant Lad, B.A.M.&S., M.A.Sc, Ayurvedic Physician
Author of Ayurveda: Science of Self-Healing,
Textbook of Ayurveda series and more

Part I

Principles of Vedic Counseling

New Models of Counseling: A Vedic Perspective

The Counseling Renaissance

Today we are discovering numerous new and dynamic tools for understanding ourselves and bringing greater meaning into our lives, not simply at a physical level, but at deeper levels of consciousness. Our model of the human being is shifting from that of a separate individual fixed in one location in time and space to a global presence through the internet and information technology, and ultimately to a cosmic being through the universe as a whole. This means that we must radically adjust our educational system and view of life, to look at more expansive strategies to allow these new potentials to blossom in the optimal possible manner.

In this new expanded setting of the human being as information, energy and awareness, not simply as a mere physical body, we are also learning how to organize our lives in a broader and more transformational manner beyond the domain of physical necessity. We are now in communication with individuals and cultures throughout the world that were regarded as foreign and alien a mere generation ago a generation ago. Yet the world of nature is also appearing to us in a new light as we discern the intricate web of life through the ecology that links all human beings and all processes on the planet, from beneath the ground to the atmosphere above, as a single organic being.

We are looking for a greater connection with the entire planet and with the universe as a whole, that we are now coming to recognize as being pervaded by a unitary life and awareness. We are no longer content with older cultural models caught up in merely local, regional and nationalistic concerns that do not address all humanity, our full potentials, or the whole of life. We aspire to a higher awareness and a greater Self-realization as our ultimate goal, not merely material or intellectual achievements except as a support for a deeper inner growth.

To fill this new crucial need for conscious living, there is a whole new generation of counselors, therapists, coaches, doctors, gurus, and pandits from various backgrounds, trainings and traditions. Many helpful and innovative approaches to right living are becoming available, including new forms of physical and psychological healing, and a growing resurgence of traditional and native systems of medicine from all over the world. Older spiritual methods from natural healing to Yoga, mantra and meditation, as well as astrology, are coming back and becoming reformulated in the planetary age, carrying not just the insight of the past but secrets keys for the future of the planet.

Among these diverse and profound teachings, the ancient Vedic model from India, perhaps the oldest and most extensive, is emerging again and demonstrating its ongoing relevance and enduring power of creative renewal. The Vedic approach to life as an organic unfoldment of a unitary consciousness is returning through related Vedic disciplines of Yoga, Ayurveda, Vedic astrology, Vedanta, and Tantra, that have made their mark worldwide in recent decades. Millions have come into contact with one or more of these Vedic teachings, though few may know the complete Vedic system behind them. Yet that background Vedic system may hold greater depth, power and adaptability than any of its important branches.

The Vedic way of knowledge leads us to a new view of life-counseling, from physical and psychological well-being to unleashing our highest creativity and deepest awareness. The Vedic counseling model reflects a dynamic and transformative system of Self-realization, with special teachings and practices for all levels of our nature as body, senses, mind, prana, and consciousness. It is based upon the experience of thousands of years of great Yogis, rishis and sages from India, including the many great modern gurus who have brought their profound teachings to the West in recent decades. As such, the Vedic approach is both unique and universal, and presents us with extraordinary and powerful tools to enable us to shape our lives according to the highest Self-awareness. All those who are willing to study and apply this Vedic system with dedication and consistency, are bound to discover the greater reality and energy of the whole of life accessible to them in their every breath and behind every thought.

In the present book we will present a single foundational Vedic counseling model that encompasses all primary Vedic disciplines, in which they can be synthesized and used in their optimal integral and complementary manner. Vedic counseling rests upon a Vedic understanding of the nature of the human being and the nature of the greater universe. It requires recognizing an inner consciousness that guides all life from within - the inner guru or Divine presence, the Divine voice within us. It is not limited to ordinary knowledge through education, information, or outer systems and institutions, however helpful these may be.

Vedic Science of Consciousness

Vedic counseling is not just another form of counseling among many others, though it does have connections with the most dynamic and transformative counseling approaches available today. Vedic counseling rests upon a special view of the human being, life, nature and consciousness that can be very different than what we find in modern medicine. It reflects a profound yogic philosophy, psychology and cosmology interwoven together at the core of our being. This knowledge is not simply theoretical in nature but reflects a profound ascertainment of how the universe operates both externally and in our own psyche. Vedic counseling is rooted in the enduring wisdom of the cosmic mind, from which all recorded human knowledge is but a reflection or a shadow.

Vedic counseling is based upon the "Vedic laws of right living," which are also the "laws of Dharma,"- how to live in harmony with the greater conscious universe and with respect for the sacred nature of all life. These principles of dharma are lasting and enduring, as well as capable of being adapted to the unique needs and demands of every place, culture and individual.

Vedic counseling helps us establish what we could call a "Vedic life," which is a life in harmony with the universal dharma, not simply an unquestioned following of some ancient or modern code of conduct. A Vedic life links us to the universal life and asks us to honor all living beings. Vedic counseling is both a means of empowering our greater human potential and facilitating the unfoldment of the universal consciousness within us, which are intimately linked together. This greater potential that we have does not consist merely of new science and technology but of being able to create a "new human being" rooted in a higher consciousness that is one with all.

Vedic knowledge is part of an entire set of "Vedic sciences," and does not stand by itself. Vedic counseling helps us appreciate and access all these Vedic approaches along with their parallels in spiritual teachings and healing disciplines worldwide. Vedic sciences are yogic sciences of consciousness that rest upon a higher perception and deeper wisdom. Vedic sciences are not simply sciences of the external world rooted in ideas and information but ways of harnessing the forces of the inner world of awareness, which can take us beyond the limitations of time, space, and person.

Vedic sciences encompass all the ordinary sciences including physics, astronomy, geology, biology, medicine, and psychology. Vedic sciences do not exclude the knowledge and discoveries made by modern science, but seek to integrate these into a higher science of consciousness, in which they can be best understood and utilized. The Vedic view is that whatever knowledge we have externally of name, form or number is incomplete if we do not know our own inner essence, being and consciousness that are beyond all quantification. Vedic counseling teaches us how to access and live in our higher Self and being.

Vedic science is a "qualitative science" that reveals and unfolds the sacred and immeasurable - the essence of life. It is not another quantitative approach that examines things from the outside. As such, Vedic knowledge leads us to a quantum leap in awareness, a revolution in higher consciousness and a greater integration with the universe. Vedic counseling is one of its primary tools and expressions, if not its very foundation.

Vedic Technology of Accessing Higher Awareness

Vedic sciences have their own corresponding "Vedic technologies."

These consist of the tools and practices discovered by the Vedic sciences for accessing the inner world of consciousness, for working with the universal life and learning to use its powers that impact all levels of existence. These Vedic techniques reflect the full range of natural healing practices for body and mind, including diet, herbs, bodywork and lifestyle recommendations, along with special Yogic methods for unfolding higher capacities of prana, senses and awareness, including asana, pranayama, ritual, mantra and meditation. The range of potential recommendations in Vedic counseling is vast, comprehensive and covers all that we do in life.

This Vedic technology does not rest upon mere outer equipment, media devices or computers, though it can teach us how to use these in a more beneficial manner. Vedic technology is a technology of awareness that helps us work upon ourselves with the tools of our own mind and heart when they are open to the cosmic mind. We can access inner energies of body and mind through techniques like pranayama and mantra. We can develop inner senses, the inner eye and ear, which can reveal more about the nature of reality than our most sophisticated cameras and screens. There are group practices involving special gatherings, chanting, rituals or group meditation – a Vedic technology of higher social interaction or *satsanga*, allowing us to bring these higher energies into society as a whole.

The purpose of this inner Vedic technology is to provide tools that are rooted in our own awareness and in accessing cosmic energy, so that we need not be dependent upon outer technologies for our happiness. This inner technology includes how to access solar energy into the mind, pranic energy into the body, and the energy of peace into society.

Vedic Counselors and Vedic Sciences

A Vedic counselor is one who is trained in one or more of the Vedic sciences or Vedic ways of knowledge and their corresponding practices and technologies of higher awareness. A Vedic counselor brings to these Vedic teachings special counseling tools to communicate and share this knowledge with society as a whole, and to introduce it on an individual level for improving our lives overall. Such Vedic counseling skills are helpful, if not necessary, for all Vedic and Yoga teachers and therapists.

Many existing Vedic practitioners may already have a deep knowledge born of their own studies and practices, but they may lack the counseling skills necessary to communicate it properly and make it useful for others. Learning the art of Vedic counseling is an important aid in this regard for any Vedic practitioner. Vedic counseling is a vehicle for teaching the Vedic sciences and integrating them into life. A Vedic counselor is one who has both a background in the Vedic knowledge and knows how to share it in a meaningful and professional way with others.

This counseling dimension has at times been lacking in many Vedic teachers – whether in the field of Ayurveda, Vedic astrology, Yoga or meditation – who may think that passing on information and techniques is enough. Our purpose here is to show its relevance, importance, and practical means of application. We need to know how to develop a deep rapport with the client, or anything we give them, however profound, may not be accessible to them.

Integral Nature of Vedic Counseling

The Vedic view is of an integral knowledge of Self and universe, each reflected in the other, each having the potentials, faculties and sensitivities of the other. Vedic counseling provides the ultimate integrative model of counseling that can serve all counseling and teaching approaches for every type of person and circumstance.

Vedic counseling addresses the total human being as a reflection of the greater universe of matter, life, mind, and consciousness. It recognizes our entire individual nature as body, mind and spirit, including the workings of prana and the senses, and how these interconnect with a whole array of transformative universe of forces. Vedic counseling addresses all aspects of life from physical and psychological well-being, to career, prosperity, education, and one's spiritual path. Its concern is not only individual well-being but also that of the family, community, society and the world of nature.

Vedic counseling is the optimal system of total life-style counseling, helping us to ascertain the fabric and network of energy and intelligence that makes up the whole of existence. As such, Vedic counseling is not a specialization but a synthetic discipline. It helps us adapt and coordinate all that is helpful to our greater urge towards unity and wholeness. Vedic counseling does not exclude any helpful approach to greater harmony and well-being, but arranges these in a broader view based upon consciousness as the primary force in the universe. We will explore these teachings and approaches of Vedic Counseling in depth and detail as the book proceeds.

Ancient and Modern Counseling Approaches

Thousands of years ago, the ancient sages, seers and yogis did not possess the technological tools necessary to measure and quantify the physiological shifts that happen in response to psychological stimuli. They did however, deeply understand that mind, body and spirit are intimately related. Vedantic teachings go into great detail on the way each facet of our being influences and impacts the other. Brilliantly, the wisdom gleamed from these ancient texts is becoming progressively confirmed by modern science.

We now know that with every thought and emotion that passes through our field of consciousness, there is a corresponding biochemical shift in our physical bodies and brains. The recently coined term "molecules of emotion" refers to the cascade of neuropeptides that flood the body with each passing emotion. These molecules of emotion are chemical signals that allow neurons to communicate with each other in specific ways that influence the activity of the brain. In other words, the behavior of our brain changes dramatically as our emotions change. Our emotions act like drugs in the brain; they alter the neurochemical dynamics of our endocrine system. Emotions can store memories deep in our physiology, making it difficult to reverse long held traumas. Regardless of what effect they are having, it is clear that emotions are powerful forces that exist simultaneously both in our mind and body. We cannot dismiss them as merely subjective and look at physical health apart from them.

We have seen the astounding and often times devastating effects of stress hormones on the human mind and body. Emotions like fear, anxiety, or worry lead to an impending sense of danger, threat, or doom, which can lead to sudden, drastic and harmful responses. Collectively speaking, these feelings induce a state of being which we now refer to as "stress." Stress physiology is of tremendous importance in science today because of its prevalence in the modern lifestyle that is progressively out of harmony with the calm and support of nature. The deleterious effects of stress impact everything from insulin levels to infertility. High levels of fight-or-flight hormones like cortisol and adrenaline actually unravel and fray the end portions (telomeres) of our chromosomes.

Equally as amazing though, is how emotions like love and activities like laughter and having social support, induce the production of an enzyme called telomerase. This is the enzyme that repairs the destruction to the ends of our coiled DNA. The power of our emotions has far reaching effects, even down to the very biological code for our existence. We must learn how to take our emotions to a higher level of feeling and concern for others in order to go beyond their limitations.

The new field of "psychoneuroimmunology" was born out of science's appreciation for the dynamic relationship between the psyche and physical body. This interdisciplinary area of expertise is devoted to investigating the complex interactions between psychosocial processes and subsequent endocrine and immune responses. In other words, scientists are studying how the body's defense system responds to the state of our mental well-being. Intuitively, we have long known that when someone is depressed, grieving, or highly stressed they are much more likely to get sick or come down with various diseases. Now, science is doing the experimentation to show us the details of just how this happens.

Recently science has also taken great interest in meditation. Studies performed on meditating subjects show that a regular practice of meditation has a significant effect on reducing blood pressure, anxiety and depression, and also builds focus and concentration. At this point, the research is even showing that heart disease can be correlated with a *lack* of meditation! Those of us who practice meditation as a part of our daily routine can vouch for its stress-relieving qualities. It is deeply nourishing for our minds to have a moment in the day to "step off the roller coaster," so to speak. Meditating daily reminds our cardiovascular and nervous systems that they are safe to relax and unwind for a period in time. This trains our bodies to learn where the "off switch" for our agitated minds is located, and as a result, we are better able to manage our stress. In sum, there is no longer any doubt that the state of the mind and spirit affects the functioning of the body (and vice versa). Over and over again we find the practices of ancient wisdom such as meditation are, validated and substantiated by modern science.

There is a tendency in conventional western medicine to treat an isolated component of a disease. Say for instance someone is dealing with depression; the standard psychiatric method of treatment would be to give Prozac, or maybe another kind of selective serotonin reuptake inhibitor (SSRI). Here, there is a focus on the individual molecule that is involved in the problem. Too little serotonin equals too much depression. The answer then, is simply to increase the availability of that isolated component of the system - serotonin.

Ayurveda, on the other hand, takes a different approach. The solution is not merely to correct any one molecular deficiency. Rather, it is to remedy the reason why there is a deficit in "happy" neurotransmitters in the first place. Ayurveda may for instance, prescribe behavioral practices that will give rise to a positive emotion. That emotion then makes a corresponding physiological shift in the body. The biochemical changes that ensue encourage a new, positive neuropathway to develop, without the possible side effects of intrusive drugs.

Astoundingly, Ayurveda long ago inadvertently developed its behavioral rejuvenation program to take advantage of something we now refer to as neuroplasticity. Neuroplasticity is the idea that our neurons can become 'comfortable,' along a particular pattern of activity. They get used to running on the same track, over and over again, thinking the same thoughts, in the same way, with any given stimulus. However, with a change in behavior, environment, mind-set, or emotions, our brain circuits can actually change in a positive manner. We need not remain stuck in a certain way of operating forever. The point here is that we have the power to change our behavior, so that we can change our emotions and thus, their associated molecular pathways. Changing our attitude from the inside can be easier and more effective than taking a medicine from the outside.

The modern field of psychological and behavioral medicine is evolving and expanding both in regard to its basic philosophical underpinnings and its treatment modalities. There are many new innovative and effective systems of therapy being used today. Coincidentally, many of them mirror the foundational components of Ayurvedic behavioral rejuvenation and the Vedic codes of ethical and moral living.

One modern modality that shares many features with Vedic philosophy is transpersonal psychology, which has its roots in the great western psychologist C.G. Jung's encounter with eastern thought, including Yoga and Vedanta. While remaining part of modern psychology, transpersonal psychology branches out to integrate the more transcendent experiences of the human psyche. It studies subjects like higher states of consciousness, spirituality, personal transformation and human potential. It has been described as "beyond-ego psychology," which is essentially the essence of Ayurvedic and Yoga psychology. To support mental and physical well-being, Ayurveda also aims to reunite the divided self (ego) with the whole or universal Self (Spirit), in a process of spiritual realization through Yoga and meditation.

Another wonderful modern method of communication and conflict resolution is known as, Non-violent Communication (NVC). This modality is based on the principal of compassion and provides strategies to clear any form of violence from the heart and mind. It echoes the cardinal virtue of *ahimsa* (or non-violence) honored in the Yoga tradition. The basic assumption of Yoga is also shared by Vedantic philosophy – that we are all inherently good and compassionate by nature, if we can return to the core of our being. NVC purports that violent means of action or language are learned behaviors adopted in an attempt to meet basic human needs and can be unlearned and changed through behavioral modification.

Vedanta, the Yogic philosophy of the unity of all existence, validates the basic person and their emotions and needs, but goes a step further and imparts a spiritual component to the explanation of violence. It says that because our inmost nature is one with the Divine and the Universe as a whole, violence is a reflection of living in disconnection with our true Self, or our true nature. The remedy then, would be not be to find a way to get our tangible human needs met, but rather to ascend beyond them and become one with *Atman,* or Spirit. In this way, spiritual satisfaction can alter egoic desires and our needs in life become fundamentally changed. From the locus of a limited being living in self-ignorance, there is always desire, fear and attachment but with the knowing of "I am that" or "What I am is Brahman," there is absolute freedom and a sense of love for all. When this union happens there is no need to fix anything in our lives because everything is whole and enduring.

Another fascinating approach is Neuro-linguistic programming (NLP). This system of thinking investigates the connection between neurological processes, language and behavioral reprogramming. Proponents of this theory state that behavior is a collection of subjective sensory based experiences and thoughts (or language). Dysfunctional behavior can then be changed by altering the sensory and linguistic qualities of the experience. It becomes a matter of relearning rather than any emotional confrontation.

It is incredible to realize that thousands of years ago Ayurveda essentially utilized NLP through its therapy of daily behavioral recommendations. It explains attitudes to maximize and avoid, refining the language that is spoken continually through our minds. It also outlines practical, daily activities, which embed new sensory information into our biochemistry, thereby reprogramming our behavior.

Furthermore, Ayurveda employs that which is beyond language, and resonates at the sensory level of sound and hearing, the power of mantra. Mantras are special sounds that are repeated silently or aloud in order to bring the mind to a new state of awareness. These sounds are not words in the usual sense. They do not refer to anything specific in the physical world (for example, in the way that the word 'dog' refers to a four-legged animal). Instead they are resonate sounds that have a powerful spiritual impact by virtue of their energetic formation. They vibrate very deeply in the mind at the basic level where sound itself can have meaning that is separate from language. Mantras can be described as primordial, meaning "foundational" or "original," because their form is beyond human thought and reaches the state of pure consciousness.

Modern science has also accepted the idea that positive intention can and does have a real effect on our bodies. Research shows that settling into the heart and opening up to emotions like love and gratitude can actually alter the configuration of our DNA for the better. This means that if we genuinely feel an intention whole-heartedly, that we are actually having a profound impact on the essence of our physiological functioning, our DNA. If this is true, then doing things like spending time in *satsanga* (community) or participating in group therapy could also impact the conformation of our DNA. When we spend time in groups we're filled with emotions like compassion, understanding, empathy, love, gratitude, and connection. It makes sense that these potent emotions could have such a beneficial effect down to the level of the very code of our existence. We evolved to be in consistent connection with others, sharing life in bands and tribes. Spending so much time in isolation or at looking only at the face of our computer screen isn't natural or healthy for our minds and spirits.

Along the same lines, children should not be going through life without the presence of a positive role model. A non-profit organization that supports this value is *The Boys and Girls Club of America.* In this program, youngsters are provided same-sex role models who help them learn valuable life skills needed to navigate the tribulations of youth. Role models get kids outside, playing and moving their bodies and educate them about how to stay healthy. Unfortunately, however, many children today are born into homes that do not provide them with the proper stimulus, love, nurturing or code of conduct.

As we grow and learn, we need exposure to people who live an exemplary life and whose qualities we can safely emulate. Regardless of whether or not we had role models growing up though, as a mature adult we have the opportunity to seek out teachers, saints, gurus, or any admirable figure in our lives whose example we can trust and to whom we can align our behavior. This is important because we need to bolster positive behavioral changes in ourselves that will support the awareness of our own, innate higher consciousness. Role models can help guide and direct us on how we can do this in the face of the challenges of everyday life.

It is important to appreciate the overlap between modern psychology and Ayurveda's ancient behavioral healing programs. We can see the threads of truth that run between East and West and bridge the gap of time. These common truths have imparted positive behavioral changes throughout the ages and continue to do so today. Vedic science and modern science can thus support one another in their efforts to bring peace and harmony to the minds of anyone who suffers.

The Spiritual Art of Counseling

Counseling in its widest connotation has existed in one form or the other from time immemorial, starting with the family and the community in most human societies. In all traditional cultures the elders not only set the norms of behavior within the culture but also counsel the youth how to follow these norms and keep them relevant and meaningful in their daily activity. In India, parents and teachers regard counseling in the form of giving advice and guidance as one of their fundamental and most sacred duties. Respect for the elders by way of carrying on sacred traditions is part of the traditional way of life. Though we are moving away from this in the modern world where education is more a media event, in the end those who have the wisdom of experience still hold a place of honor.

There is an often repeated Vedic adage; *"Mata, Pita, Guru, Deva,"* meaning Mother, Father, Teacher, God. This reminds the young not only to honor their guides in life, but also their priority at various stages of life. The Mother is the first guru for the child, followed by the father, then by teachers in schools, but ultimately the Divinity that is our own inmost Self is the real teacher behind all teachers. The ancient stories of India are replete with depictions of counseling and guidance, both formal and informal. Elders were happy to take up the role of counselors as part of their place in society, and youth sought their guidance and worked hard to apply it. Many such incidents can be explained away as mere acts of casually "giving advice." However in most of those transactions, we can discern the scientific practice and ethics that are now developing in modern counseling techniques.

The most widely acknowledged counseling situation in the history of India is that of the dialogue between Lord Krishna and the warrior Arjuna on the battlefield of Kurukshetra, prior to a great battle. Whether this dialogue has all the characteristics of modern counseling can be looked at in greater detail. Clearly the account is one of asking the most deep and difficult questions and being directed to the most profound and transformative answers. Krishna does not assume responsibility for Arjuna, tell him what to do, or provide him a formula to follow. He systematically guides Arjuna to his own discovery of the truth so his intelligence can discern it for himself.

Many people question the relevance and suitability of modern counseling techniques and its ability to provide guidance relative to all the deeper issues of life. Modern counseling may get caught in the outer aspects of life, in personal psychology, materialist thinking, or simply promoting individual wants and desires at a commercial level. Yet as modern counseling methods take in a new knowledge of the unity of life and consciousness they may begin to resemble such ancient dialogues of great gurus and their disciples.

Counseling and Life-Guidance

Counseling is often a misunderstood concept. To the layman it appears to be an occasion when an expert in a field solves the problems for others less proficient. Most of us believe that there is an expert who has the ready-made solutions for all our problems. We just need to find out who they are and let them either solve the problem for us or provide us a formula to solve it for ourselves. Most professional counselors know that this expectation of having another person solve our lives problems for us is far from the truth. Without actually working on ourselves, including confronting our problems and understanding how we ourselves create them, we cannot change our lives in a fundamental way, no matter how wise or skilled our counselor.

The term "guidance" denotes explicit directions given by an informed person regarding an important aspect of life. An expert in career guidance can impart information regarding different career possibilities and the aptitude required in order to pursue these. He may also be able to tell the best available career options or job openings at any given time. In imparting such information, the career guide can provide information irrespective of the suitability of the client for the job, or whether that is the best job for the person to follow. However, he also has the option to test the suitability of the client using the appropriate job proficiency tests.

Counseling, on the other hand is more dynamic and looks at life as a whole. It aims to solve a clients' problems overall, not merely relative to one field or issue. Counseling is an interactive process between the counselor and the client in which solutions emerge as a joint venture between the two. It is a journey in self-discovery in which the optimal human potentials can arise and be developed.

Chief Characteristics of Counseling	
1 |	It is expected to be a process, the result of which will unfold over time.
2 |	Counseling is usually for normal people with common life problems, not for extreme cases that may require medical intervention.
3 |	It is essentially a dynamic interaction between the client and the counselor, where the interaction is the main factor, not any preconceived information passed between the two.
4 |	The client is expected to be honest, frank and forthright.
5 |	It is the duty of the counselor to keep confidentiality regarding the client and their life.
6 |	The counselor should show patience, warmth and sympathy while listening to the client's problems, trying to understand them as completely as possible.
7 |	The counselor is expected to be non-judgmental and non-critical, and not to harbor any preconceived notions.
8 |	The relationship between the client and the counselor is expected to be genuine and sincere, not merely commercial.
9 |	Counseling works best at the level of rapport and not at the level of transference. The counselor and client share a common humanity, rather than the counselor being looked upon as the problem solver.
10 |	The client's conscious motives are explored more so than their unconscious motives.

Counseling Perspectives

This orientation relative to counseling may change from counselor to counselor. There are differences in training, clients and settings, and expected goals of the counseling process. Yet the basic perspective of counseling remains the same, though the emphasis may vary. Common to these perspectives are the notions that:

- Counseling is aimed at helping people make meaningful choices and act upon them in a consistent manner.
- Counseling is a learning process, not a mere setting forth of rules or data.
- Counseling enables personality development and the improvement of character, a greater process of self-unfoldment that is unlimited.

We must remember that counseling is a professional relationship between a trained counselor and a receptive client. The counselor requires a certain type of training. The client has a degree of expectations based upon the nature of the counseling approach or the reputation of the counselor he is seeking.

Counseling is more intimate than medical examination that looks at physical conditions. It requires a direct dialogue between the counselor and client, not simply a performance of various tests or diagnostics, though these can be helpful. It is designed to take the client to a deeper level of self-understanding, so that either personal or relationship problems can be more easily resolved.

At times counseling may require working with more than one client at a time, as in the case of relationship counseling, or counseling employees at the work place. Counseling can be related to broader approaches of advice and management, as work with business management. Vedic counseling has a yet broader view because it brings in spiritual issues and broader human concerns, as well as having a broader base of counseling approaches through Ayurveda, Vedic Astrology and Yoga.

Theory and Practice of Counseling

Theory and practice always go hand in hand. Many trained counselors initially adhere to one specific theory of counseling when starting their career. However, even those who are strongly tied to one theory may change over time. This is because the client is the link between the theory and practice of counseling. When a person does not fit into the theory, the counselor is compelled to change his theory. This is one of the most demanding challenges of counseling. All theoretic approaches to counseling are merely provisional and cannot be applied rigidly. Knowledge, however authentic, must be adapted according to the nature, level and temperament of the client, as well as circumstances of the life-style, society and culture.

With Vedic counseling, counselors may expand their counseling methods over time, perhaps beginning with Ayurvedic life-style counseling but then finding a need to add Vedic astrology, or starting with Yogic recommendations and wishing to supplement that with Ayurveda for a better ability to deal with health based issues. Counselors should work to increase their avenues of counseling expertise, but yet keep the main interchange with the client free of any technicality that would be hard for the client to comprehend.

Counselors must keep their minds receptive and flexible and be capable of new insights and adaptations. Each individual is unique and must be appreciated. Individual clients with their differing temperaments have different problems, goals and aspirations. To believe that all clients would benefit from one type of counseling approach is unrealistic.

The counselor requires the appropriate tools to ascertain the nature of the individual, their specific needs and also what is possible at any given moment in time. Counseling must begin with an understanding of the individual as a whole, not with some model of disease or dysfunction. This requires not merely getting to know the person but having the adequate knowledge to determine their unique individual nature. Here Vedic counseling with its determination of different physical, psychological and spiritual types is quite relevant and can be very transformative. Each individual is a unique combination of universal forces of matter, life, mind and consciousness. The Vedic counselor has clear approaches and applications for all of these and various types of physical, psychological and spiritual typologies to consider.

Behavioral Medicine

Counseling as a healing practice can promote the deepest level of healing, which arises from properly understanding ourselves. This is a much greater and more enlightening experience than taking medicines, undergoing medical tests or receiving external therapies alone.

Counseling is part of "behavioral medicine," which can be said to be the essence of counseling. Counseling emphasizes our changes in life-style, which can be very simple or very challenging -from a change of diet to a change of our emotional response. Counseling rests upon a certain life-style or behavioral prescriptions for the person according to the specific nature of their relevant needs and problems.

The adept counselor does not simply talk to the client but recommends precise strategies and practical tools designed to change their behavior on a daily basis. Yet these strategies cannot be recommended in a mechanical manner or turned into rigid rules to be followed like a formula. They are recommended in an experiential manner, as a way for the client see if there is a better way to solve their problems and develop their higher potentials within.

The Vedic approach to counseling can be easily defined as behavioral medicine first and foremost. A true counselor, particularly in the Vedic sense, must be able to look at life and the person as a whole. He or she cannot be an expert in one field or subject alone. They must be able to get to the heart of the client, which is to understand their inner nature and purpose in life. Only when we reach this deepest level of motivation can there be lasting change for anyone. This can help us change our karma, our actions, reactions and the results.

What is Vedic Counseling? Primary Questions and Answers

In this chapter we will provide responses to key questions about Vedic counseling, its nature, application, value, and connection with other teachings and disciplines. These are meant to help the student understand the relevance of this profound system of Vedic life-guidance.

What is Vedic Counseling?

Vedic counseling is life guidance based upon the Vedic tradition of Self- knowledge and cosmic knowledge. Vedic counseling helps us determine our dharma in accord with the laws of nature and consciousness that work behind the visible universe. It enables us to access the unlimited wisdom, energy and vitality inherent in the cosmos. Vedic knowledge connects us to universal intelligence that helps us move beyond our human constraints.

We can define Vedic counseling as *dharmic guidance on right living, right action, right relationship, and right awareness.* Its basis is self-understanding and bringing us to a direct perception of the truth, not imposing a belief system, formula, or set of preconceptions upon anyone.

A Vedic counselor is a teacher of Vedic ways of knowledge. He or she can be defined as "Vedic educator," guiding others on Vedic ways of improving communication, social harmony, respect for nature, and inner realization. A Vedic counselor is a guide to higher living and deeper awareness.

What are the Components of Vedic Counseling?

Vedic counseling provides both practical guidance and a deeper perception to help us live with greater integrity, continuity and consistency. From simple matters of right diet for the body to right diet for the mind, from right exercise for the body to right expression for the mind,

Vedic counseling has tools to help us on all levels of our complex existence. These Vedic tools are gentle and non-invasive, helping us access the greater healing powers and potentials within our own nature. They extend to all the Vedic and yogic sciences and healing arts.

What is the Antiquity of Vedic Counseling?

Counseling has been an important part of all Vedic disciplines and teachings since their inception thousands of years ago by the great rishis and yogis of the Himalayas. This guiding role has taken many names and forms like: guru, pandit, acharya, or vaidya. These people could be found in each village or community and could provide guidance in all aspects of life. They could recommend healing practices, rituals, Yoga, mantra and meditation, all to help us overcome our difficulties and to promote overall well-being.

Such traditional teaching roles are being revised in a counseling model that is easier for people outside of India to understand and reflects the conditions of the modern world and its different guidance based disciplines and approaches. We have many specialist teachers, guides, counselors or coaches in the world today, in health, psychology and spiritual fields.

What Constitutes a Vedic Counselor?

A Vedic Counselor is an aware and compassionate guide who knows the core Vedic knowledge of universal unity, through the underlying principles and practices of Vedic philosophy and psychology. He or she is able to guide others at an individual levels on the principles and practices of dharmic living in a meaningful, creative, and adaptable manner. A Vedic counselor helps us unfold our lives as a way of Self-knowledge and Self-realization, uncovering greater capacities that link us to the universe as a whole and create harmony and abundance for all.

Specializations of Vedic Counselors

A Vedic counselor has an overall training in general life-counseling, centered on addressing psychological and spiritual issues. This is the foundation of all Vedic counseling approaches, and requires good counseling skills and communication ability. This includes an understanding of dharma, or our individual nature, and karma or our patterns of action.

In addition, a Vedic Counselor may follow one or more specializations in particular Vedic and yogic fields, including Yoga (Vedic Experimental/ Experiential Patterns), Ayurveda (Vedic medicine), Jyotish (Vedic Astrology) and Vastu (Vedic directional science). All Vedic sciences develop various aspects of the Vedic approach to life. Yoga provides practical tools to help us apply Vedic knowledge in order to change our consciousness. This means that Yoga in the broader sense is the most important aspect of Vedic counseling.

Those already practicing one of these specialized Vedic disciplines can benefit greatly by learning the core Vedic counselor knowledge that is common to all areas. Such benefit can extend to all those working in the healing, counseling and spiritual fields, who want to bring a rishi or seer vision into their work.

Vedic counseling reflects the different branches of the Vedic sciences. It is involved with the different branches of Yoga that constitute the practical side of the Vedic sciences.

Vedic Sciences	
Ayurveda	Vedic medicine for well-being body and mind
Vedic Astrology	Vedic science of time and energetic affects of cosmic bodies on the mind
Vastu	Vedic science of space and directional influences
Vedanta	Vedic philosophy of Self-awareness

Vedic Sciences	
Vedas	Prime Vedic sacred sound and rhythmic knowledge of the universe
Vedic Yoga	Vedic tools of Self-unfoldment and Self-realization

Yogic Specializations – Aspects of Classical Yoga	
Hatha Yoga	Vedic discipline of psycho-physical integration
Raja Yoga	Vedic discipline of mind power and will power
Jnana Yoga	Vedic direct knowledge approach to Self-realization
Bhakti Yoga	Vedic approach to union with the Divine through inner surrender
Karma Yoga	Vedic discipline of right action and altruism to all living beings
Mantra Yoga	Vedic discipline of consciousness development through sound, rhythm and repetition
Prana Yoga	Vedic discipline of higher life energy, breathing practices and energy healing

How are these Vedic fields related?

All Vedic specializations cross over to some degree as they share the same Vedic matrix of Self-knowledge. All are ways of deepening Self-awareness and recognition of universal law. Each has its particular place in the greater scheme of Vedic knowledge relative to different aspects of our nature and different facets of the greater world around us. We can draw benefit from each one of these.

What is the Relationship between Vedic Counseling and Yoga?

Vedic counseling always has a yogic or experiential application which directs us to a higher unity and synthesis of our energies. Each of the different Vedic sciences or ways of Vedic knowledge has practical applications, which is a kind of Yoga.

Vedic counseling reflects the Greater Yoga tradition that includes not only the physical Yoga of asanas and exercise, but also the spiritual Yoga of meditation, and related disciplines of Ayurveda and Vedic astrology. Yoga is a practical application; perhaps the most important tool of Vedic knowledge and Vedic counseling. Vedic counseling implies some sort of Yoga or integrative approach to developing all aspects of our nature.

A Vedic counselor should be a Yogi, one who practices Yoga and meditation, and has the awareness, skills and adaptability that Yoga brings. This power of Yoga or the Yoga Shakti of Vedic counseling extends to all aspects of life.

Yet Vedic counseling has a broader base and a greater variety of tools than the commonly understood as Yoga and, approaches available today, particularly those that are not rooted in the system of Vedic knowledge. Vedic counseling promotes an individual model of application and cannot be limited to en masse or group approaches. It trains the Yoga teacher to be a wise life counselor and not simply an exercise or fitness teacher.

Why Would One Go to a Vedic Counselor?

One should go to a Vedic counselor in order to access a deeper level of dharmic guidance to live a better life and develop an awareness of higher consciousness. The Vedic tradition has the benefit of thousands of years of experience and numerous Self-realized Yogis and sages to draw upon for its knowledge. It contains teachings for all types of individuals and all types of life-circumstances. As such, you can find the right teachings and practices for your unique nature and circumstances in life through the Vedic vision.

Why Should I seek to become a Vedic Counselor?

Training as a Vedic counselor enables you to provide the full wealth of Vedic guidance. Vedic counseling is part of a path of Self-knowledge and Self-realization that is the highest aim of life for every creature. A Vedic counselor is one of the most important spiritual occupations that one can take up. It provides an excellent foundation for any higher type of guidance, instruction or service. It helps ennoble the spirit and bring out our deepest potentials. It shows us how we can bring a transformative awareness into life in order to make our every thought and action reflect a greater meaning and relevance to the universe as a whole.

How does a Vedic Counselor Differ from other Counselors?

A Vedic counselor is rooted in a core knowledge of Sanatana Dharma with access to all the branches of Vedic and yogic knowledge that provide an unparalleled set of resources for right living. He or she has an understanding of the complete and integral human being from the physical body to pure consciousness, from individual to universal existence, along with the appropriate tools and practices to create harmony on each level.

Other counselors tend to be specialists relative to a particular aspect of body, mind or life experience and seldom are rooted in a full science of consciousness. Their tools tend to be limited to a particular field or only address one aspect of the human being.

Why Should I add Vedic Counseling to my Vedic Practice?

Many Vedic practitioners lack good counseling skills as well as an overall understanding of Vedic counseling models and resources. Those who learn such Vedic sciences as Ayurveda, Vastu or Vedic astrology, are not always taught good counseling skills like how to interact with clients and address their changing needs. In addition, they may not adequately know the foundation of dharma and karma or the interrelationship of all Vedic disciplines. They may get caught in technicalities or partial views. A study of Vedic counseling can aid in countering such limitations and provide a better foundation for practice.

With the background of Vedic counseling, you can be much more effective in your Vedic practice, whatever it may be. The Vedic counseling approach will improve and broaden your skills in guiding others. It will help you integrate your Vedic specialization into the greater scope of Vedic knowledge.

Is Vedic Counseling a type of Religious Knowledge?

Vedic counseling is a way of Self-knowledge and cosmic knowledge that includes all aspects of life and consciousness. It can accept any religious or non-religious approach that honors the universal laws of dharma. It can be approached from a scientific, philosophical or artistic angle as well, as an extension of deep thinking or creative intelligence. It does not rest upon belief or faith, but upon inner knowledge. It is relevant to all human beings and helps us understand the greater universe.

Vedic counseling does address the key issues of the spiritual life, including our ultimate destiny as a soul – how to come into a living contact with the Divine or universal consciousness, whatever one wishes to call this power of immortality.

What Kind of Training is Required to Become a Vedic Counselor?

Vedic counseling rests upon inner knowledge gained through meditation, mantra, study and practice relative to Vedic philosophies and disciplines. It requires developing special counseling skills that address the inner being of a person, not simply the outer personality. It requires as much training as any important healing or counseling discipline, but a training that flows in harmony with life and nature, not one that is a product of mere books or classrooms. Vedic counseling training includes study of teachings, application of techniques, and learning Vedic models of diagnosis and treatment.

How Much Time Does it Require to Become a Vedic counselor?

Vedic counseling is part of an on-going pursuit of Self-knowledge, so its training never comes to an end. It is not a role or job that one takes up temporarily but an understanding of our true purpose as human beings, which is to bring a greater consciousness into the world. One should expect to take at least two years of initial study as well as several years in practice. Some degree of specialization may be developed over time, which can take additional time to master.

What Courses are Available in Vedic Counseling?

The main courses on Vedic counseling occur relative to specializations of the Vedic sciences of Yoga, Ayurveda and Vedic astrology. Such Vedic practitioners may receive some training in counseling, but it is not always sufficient or complete. That is why we are introducing a *specific Vedic counseling approach in* this book to fill in this gap. We also have with the book a special course in Vedic Counseling that can be relevant to everyone in Vedic or counseling fields.

Can Vedic Counseling be used with non-Vedic counseling methods?

Vedic counseling can aid with any genuine approach to guidance. There are many new and old systems from throughout the world, particularly from natural healing traditions that work well on a Vedic foundation. Vedic counseling is inclusive of all our higher aspirations regardless of name and form or place and time or origin. Yet the Vedic approach provides a broad-based, integral and structured system that has withstood the tests of millenniums of application.

Should we view Vedic Counseling as a Medical Practice?

Vedic counseling is an approach to integral healing and optimal well-being for body, mind and consciousness. It includes all aspects of medicine as part of a greater life knowledge that embraces our entire existence. Ayurveda is the specialized Vedic branch for healing and medical treatment that is the foundation of Vedic counseling. Vedic counseling is more psychological and spiritual in nature, helping us to manage our mind, life and daily activities, but rests upon Ayurveda for its recommendations.

How is Vedic Counseling Related to Ecology?

Vedic counseling emphasizes an ecological management of all our resources, externally and internally. The Vedic view regards the universe as a single organic whole rooted in consciousness at a universal level. It sees that the entire universe dwells in each creature, with the whole dwelling in each part. Vedic counseling honors the earth and asks us to develop a deeper planetary awareness.

The Vedic Art of Higher Investigation

Counseling implies a pursuit of knowledge, not theoretically but at the level of life experience. The counselor seeks to guide the client and the client seeks to gain relevant insights from the counselor. This means that in order to understand any system of counseling, we must first become familiar with its approach to the learning process.

To approach Vedic counseling, we need to understand the Vedic way of thinking, questioning and investigation. The Vedic way of knowledge can be very different from the ordinary way we think today, in which we are largely gathering information about the external world through our senses and various scientific instruments based upon them. The Vedic way of knowledge requires that we first question what we think we know and move beyond our ordinary knowledge to a new way of insight, deeper perception and higher consciousness.

"Vedic thinking " is a way of thinking in harmony with the movement of awareness within ourselves and in the greater universe. It requires a process of observation and examination of life as a whole, moment by moment. Vedic thinking is not what we would call "thought" in the ordinary sense of the word, which consists of reactions based upon memory and which is rooted in past conditioning. Vedic thinking is not a dry logical or academic discipline, but rather requires receptivity to the nature of existence and its movement on many different levels at once. Vedic thinking is contemplative and meditative, not seeking immediate results but looking to abide in a greater consciousness and state of being that itself provides the solution to all problems.

Vedic thinking is rooted in the "Vedic art of investigation," which is an inquiry into the inner truth, above and beyond all outer appearances. The Vedic art of investigation enables us to understand the nature of reality, including our own true nature, prior to any words or concepts used to describe it. The Vedic approach is not one of mere belief or formula but requires that we discover the truth of life for ourselves - that we learn to see things as they are. This makes it more difficult to learn than other approaches but also more powerful to apply.

The Vedic view is not simply to analyze or dissect life into discrete phenomenon, as we tend to do today, but to synthesize our perception into an integral awareness of the whole. The Vedic mind has a profound insight into the universe and the intricate processes through which it operates, at physical, psychological and spiritual levels. This Vedic way of seeing is rooted in an inner way of perception that rests upon the practice of introspective meditation.

To understand this Vedic art of investigation, we must first examine our ordinary sense of self and world, which usually keeps us limited to the surface of existence. We must expand this self-focus and learn to embrace the entire universe within ourselves. This means to cease viewing our problems as personal, but look to the greater movement of life, which will dissolve our problems if we are willing to let them go.

The World of Appearances or Maya

The Vedic view begins with helping us to understand the outer world in which we live. We are all confronted with a world that is difficult to comprehend, that contains many different objects and creatures, which have their own realities and considerations that may be different from our own. There are many sides to everything and our initial views about anything may not prove to be correct or complete in the long run.

We live in a world of manifold appearances, which come to us based upon the action of our five senses. Each sense provides us with a different type of data about the world. We try to synthesize the discrete information that the senses present us into an overall understanding of the objects and events in the outer world. However, the information that the senses provide us is not always clear or conclusive and can require further examination in order to determine what it really indicates.

The external appearances of name and form derived from the senses do not show us the complete truth of things and are not entirely reliable. The senses are limited in their scope and provide a one-sided view of the world that must be supplemented with additional views in order to allow us to function adequately in life. The senses not only reveal, but in their partial and superficial nature also conceal. There usually remains something more important behind the scenes that rules over and controls what we actually see.

Appearances must be interpreted and investigated in order to find out what is really behind them. This realm of mere appearance is what is called *Maya,* often translated, though not entirely accurately so, as illusion. Maya does not mean that the world is false in the sense that the world has no meaning or reality behind it. Maya means that appearances cannot unthinkingly be trusted and must be investigated further in order to discover what they really mean.

Ever since we were born we have been learning how to interpret the world and discover more about it. We have learned how to organize our sensory impressions into intelligible patterns so that we can move, talk, work, and relate to one another. As children we had to first learn how to focus our senses, learn language, name things, think for ourselves, and eventually become capable of making independent decisions. Even as adults we must constantly refine how we interpret our world as we receive more accurate information and experiences about the nature of the vast and changing realm of life.

We learn early on in life that "things are not always what they appear to be" – that the package and its content, or the advertising and what you actually get, may not be the same. Whether it is shopping for food or seeking a new job or relationship, we must investigate appearances and try to find out their true worth. For another example, in relationship, we may realize that how someone might appear to us on a first meeting may not be how they really are should we come to live with or work with them on a regular basis. We can multiply these examples a thousand times. These dominate our lives which consist of ever trying to adjust to what the world is and its demands.

Appearances consist of various snapshots taken by the mind, limited views in time, and surface views in space that can be distorted or manipulated. When we go to buy things, for example, we realize that the appearance of the item, particularly according to its packaging and the propaganda about it, may not be true relative to its real contents.

We cannot trust appearances as accurate, though we cannot dismiss them altogether as unreal either. When we see a building burning down, we need not doubt what our senses tell us, but few perceptions are so clear and determinative. What is important is to accept the practical value of the senses but understand their inherent limitations for determining the ultimate issues and values of life. These rest upon a deeper examination of life, including questioning the reality of the external world as it normally appears to us.

Behind Appearances

Appearances reflect various qualities, energies and karmas through which they affect us. We must learn the nature of these in order to navigate through the complex set of forces that constitutes the outer world. Vedic thought provides us various ways of understanding the qualities of nature through such factors as doshas, gunas, elements, chakras, karmas and levels of existence that we will discuss in detail later in the book.

There are inner dimensions or essences behind things that we can discover and learn to use in order to change apparent reality into a higher existence. We can learn to move into deeper dimensions of Self-awareness inwardly and higher realms of experience and perception outwardly. A Vedic counselor helps us perceive the inherent limitations of the realm of appearances and shows us how to discern the deeper truth, so that we can act according to our true nature, rather than be deceived by the show of appearances in the outer world.

The Role of Language

All our knowledge is rooted in language, which provides a vehicle for holding and developing what we know and turning it into enduring memory patterns. Yet the languages of the world vary significantly both in terms of style and meaning. Language not only promotes knowledge but can also sustain prejudices and misperceptions, such as we find in propaganda and advertising. Words not only hold knowledge and information, but also carry emotions and intentions that can be positive or negative, distorting what we see.

We must be very careful in terms of the words we use and how we understand their meaning. We should use words with consciousness and clarity to promote light and understanding, not to evoke blind emotion or promote conflict and division. This requires that our communication occurs through consciousness, not through an intention to influence or control.

Vedic counseling provides an important place for language and helps us use our words in a creative and lucid manner, so that we do not simply carry on unquestioned stereotypes and preconceptions. Even common terms like "I", "other," "world" or "reality" are seldom defined properly in order to eliminate potential miscommunication.

When people use the same words but with different meanings or different intents many unnecessary problems arise. Vedic counseling employs certain key Sanskrit terms to aid in this precision of meaning. It directs us to the use of mantra in order to make the words we use more effective and harmonious. It takes us towards a mantric use of language that in turn brings us to a meditative state of mind. Part of the work of any Vedic counselor is bringing clarity to the words and thoughts of the client.

World of Reality: Self or Brahman

The world of reality – the eternal and infinite realm of pure being and consciousness called *Brahman* in Vedic thought– is always present as the ground of existence and the origin of our own mind and prana. If we but learn the art of turning within, we can in an instant move beyond all Maya, doubt and confusion to the certainty of the inner truth.

Brahman or absolute reality ultimately transcends all words and concepts. It is accessible through the language of mantra and by the process of meditation. Reality includes all appearances but transcends them, like the ocean that includes all waves but is not limited to them. Brahman is the ground of being that we must contact in order to find lasting peace and happiness in this ever-changing world.

Of course, this idea of discovering the ultimate reality of the universe is very different than ordinary counseling concerns and can seem far removed from our personal lives. Yet we must remember that our true Self or Atman, our inner nature as pure consciousness, is one with reality. Getting the big picture, as it were, can help us move beyond many of our problems that are based upon getting caught in the outer details of life.

A simple relevant practice is to bring a sense of vastness into our thought and awareness.
The counselor should work to bring a greater space into the mind and heart and a broader perspective on life, in which our problems can dissolve of their own accord, and we will seek to work for the greater good of all.
Often the solution to a problem is to transcend it into a higher and broader realm of existence.
We must move from darkness to light, which is from a narrow, limited and divided awareness, to one that has no barriers and constrictions.

Counseling as Inner Investigation

Though we all learn to investigate the workings of the outer world, we seldom learn how to investigate the inner world of our own minds. While we learn not to gullibly accept outer appearances as true, we often naively accept as true what we think we are, or what others have told us that we are. Our lives rest upon an incomplete knowledge of who we are and what our full capacities may be.

The problem is that we have not adequately investigated the fundamental factors of our lives. This is not about what might be the true worth of our property, but about what is behind the outer appearances of our own body and mind. We have not adequately investigated who we really are or what we really want. We have accepted social stereotypes about ourselves and have not searched out our deeper unique potentials. Though we continue to investigate external reality, we fail to properly investigate internal reality, starting with our own daily processes of sleep and waking. We take who we really are to be our name, job, memory, or social identity, though these change throughout the course of life.

Once we learn to investigate our inner reality we can discover greater potentials of well-being, creativity, and higher consciousness. These are latent and can only be developed by cultivating them in the right manner. We can learn to let go of habits, addictions, compulsions, fears and desires.

We must cultivate the proper introspection in order to find out who we really are and the truth of the ground of our being. This is not a matter of self-criticism but of questioning how our minds, emotions and senses work, freeing ourselves from mechanical and compulsive patterns born of a lack of awareness. Vedic counseling helps us uncover and manifest our deeper potentials in life, in which our true happiness lies.

Vedic counseling is an experiential discipline in which we learn to reclaim power over our lives through directly perceiving the nature of our own reality. This rests upon proper self-observation, which is allied with inner investigation. True investigation is not simply interrogation but observation, learning to examine our world with detachment and see how it works apart from our own preconceptions or desires. It involves holding to the consciousness of the witness or seer within us.

A Vedic counselor should set in motion a deeper process of investigation in the client. It is not enough to provide them ready-made answers from the outside. A Vedic counselor works to awaken the deeper intelligence in a person, which is overall to empower them and make them independent.

Vedic counseling rests upon the Vedic art of investigation. Vedic counseling teaches us the Vedic way of thinking, analysis, and inquiry. This begins with a more accurate examination of the factors of our lives, inwardly and outwardly. It leads to following out the fundamental questions in life, which we can only answer for ourselves. No book, media or external person can do this for us. The Vedic counselor works to help awaken that inner intelligence within each person.

Prime Questions of Vedic Counseling

Counseling rests upon primary concerns and questions of life. The Vedic counselor will initiate a process of self-examination in the client, not simply provide ready-made answers. Unless we have first resolved the fundamental questions of life, the peripheral issues cannot be adequately addressed. This questioning must go to the fundamental or eternal questions of life. Often we are not asking deep enough questions and so the answers we get are not complete and transformational.

First we must properly pose these questions and create a space in our minds in order to reflect upon them in an enduring manner. The proper formulation of the question suggests the answer. The goal is not to quickly answer questions but to understand the full depth of what they may imply. These are questions to live with, meditate upon and cultivate with great care and attention.

The Question of Who We Really Are

- Who am I? is the ultimate question that gives rise to all other questions and concerns. If we do not know who we are then anything else we may do becomes problematical. Each person can formulate such fundamental questions in a way that is most meaningful for them.

- What is your true reality? – Is there any independent reality within you or are we just reflections of the external world?

- What is your real identity? – Is our identity outer or inner as body, mind or consciousness?

- Are you the body and its organs or are these but your instruments of physical life, relative to which you stand behind as an enduring power of awareness?

- Are you the mind and its thoughts or are these but instruments of your shifting mental expression behind which you have a deeper and lasting identity?

- Where does your true and lasting happiness dwell? – Do you need external happiness and gratification or can you find your ultimate contentment in your own nature?

Vedic counseling is a way of Self-knowledge. It does not consist of merely providing us information from the outside. It is meant to stimulate our own inner processes of knowing. Ultimately pure knowledge is our own nature. This self-discovery process is the real process of Vedic treatment. Self-discovery is self-healing, in which our greater universal Self is revealed.

Understanding Self, Nature and Universe:

The Science of Vedanta

Each system of counseling reflects a certain worldview, which includes an idea of the nature, capacity and purpose of the human being. This background worldview reflects how the system of counseling will determine the main issues it addresses and the primary strategies it employs. If we understand the worldview behind the counseling approach, we will be better understand its nature and its efficacy.

Modern systems of counseling reflect current physical and psychological models of human life, rooted in modern systems of thought over the last few centuries. These view the human being primarily according to socio-economic considerations and to a personal model of happiness rooted in success in the material world. They take a limited view of the person as a physical being, as a complex of memories, or according to some social role or vocation.

Vedic counseling is based upon a very different model of the human being, of life and the purpose of existence. It is both challenging and potentially transformative relative to other counseling models. The Vedic view addresses the spiritual essence of a person and all aspects of our being that has many layers, dimensions and hidden potentials. In this regard we have many selves, several roles and different personas in life, with an eternal and immutable soul hidden behind these, seeking to emerge and manifest itself. We must learn how to work with all the myriad aspects of our manifestation in a creative and harmonious manner.

Vedic counseling rests upon the Vedantic view of the nature of reality and the greater human being of body, mind and consciousness. A study of the prime principles of Vedanta is essential for any Vedic counseling. *Vedic counseling is also Vedantic counseling and is part of the Vedantic path of Self-knowledge.*

Basic Principles of Vedanta
Nature of Self – Purusha, Atman

Your true personhood or subjectivity lies in pure consciousness or the witness state; not in body and mind that are but your outer means of expression. Your own deepest consciousness unites you with all beings and with the entire universe. The universe constitutes a single organic being that is one with your true Self. This higher realization of Self as the *Purusha* is the goal of Yoga practice. True counseling means speaking to the inner Self and helping it awaken and take mastery over its outer existence.

Your true Self is the light of awareness, not any outer identity or memory based experience. The core of your sense of Self is the same sense of Self that dwells in all creatures and pervades all of existence as the underlying Self-awareness behind the entire universe. Your true Self is a state of pure identity that is identical in all things and can experience itself in everything. Vedic counseling addresses the I behind the I, the inner Self behind the outer ego.

Brahman, Unitary Reality

There is a supreme reality behind all existence, which we can access through our own deeper awareness. Everything we see is part of it, though it is not limited to anything and is beyond all name and form. This transcendent being or *Brahman* in Vedic thought, is the Self-being behind all processes and entities in the universe. All that we can experience are but waves and currents in the ocean of Brahman, which dwells within our own hearts.

Our journey in life is a movement back from the surface differentiations of the outer world to that inner essence of unity. All of us are seeking unity, whether through knowledge, relationship or action. Once we consciously seek unity through Yoga and meditation, we can overcome all our individual and social problems. That unity is the nature of existence itself, which is peace and bliss.

Nature of the Individual Soul – Integral Model of the Human Being

The Vedic integral model of the human being is defined according to the "five koshas" or five layers of the soul, the three bodies and the seven levels of existence or cosmic reality. We will refer to these throughout the book.

Five Sheaths or coverings of the soul		
1 |	Annamaya kosha	Matter, food, physical reality
2 |	Pranamaya kosha	Breath energy, life, the vital force
3 |	Manomaya kosha	Information, programming, conditioning, sensory inputs
4 |	Vijnanamaya kosha	Buddhi, intelligence, discernment, wisdom
5 |	Anandamaya kosha	Bliss, love, unity consciousness

Healing must reach the deeper layers or koshas to be lasting and effective. The following are the healing factors for each kosha.

1 |	Annamaya kosha	Right diet and nutrition
2 |	Pranamaya kosha	Pranayama and right exercise
3 |	Manomaya kosha	Right sensory impressions, accurate information
4 |	Vijnanamaya kosha	Right judgment, true knowledge, wisdom
5 |	Anandamaya kosha	Right relationships, inspiration, devotion

These five koshas or sheaths form three bodies, with our inner being as the fourth principle beyond them:

Physical	Food sheath	Waking state
Subtle	Mental sheath	Dream state
Causal	Bliss	Deep sleep state
Soul	Ever wakeful state of awareness, beyond koshas and bodies	

The pranic sheath or energy principle mediates between the physical and subtle bodies. The intelligence sheath mediates between the subtle and causal bodies.

Seven Levels of Existance		
1 |	**Anna**	Matter, food, physical reality
2 |	**Prana**	Energy, life
3 |	**Manas**	Information, programming, conditioning
4 |	**Vijnana**	Buddhi - intelligence
5 |	**Ananda**	Bliss, love
6 |	**Chit**	Consciousness
7 |	**Sat**	Being

The five sheaths relate to the first five of the seven levels of existence in the universe. Being-Consciousness-Bliss exist as our true nature beyond all five sheaths - our inner nature beyond body and mind. They constitute the nature of the soul and are deathless and eternal. Note that the higher aspect of Ananda or bliss relates to our inner nature. The lower aspect of Ananda relates to our outer body and mind through the five sheaths.

We must understand life on all these seven different levels. The same forces that work on one level work on others, though in different ways. Vedic counseling has seven levels based upon these seven aspects of our nature. Its approach considers all seven - their specific energetics, functions and capacities. Disharmony on one level will likely be mirrored on the others. Similarly, creating harmony on one level will have its effects upon the others. For example, if we create harmony at the deepest level of being then harmony will be developed on all seven levels.

Vedic counseling addresses the integral human being who is of consciousness in manifestation. It looks to the whole person, which includes our spiritual essence as the primary reality. It considers all levels and layers of our being and their particularly energies, capacities and requirements. We can work from the outer factors like body and prana in order to reach the inner factors of being, consciousness and bliss. Or we can work from the inner factors using our higher consciousness to help us master our outer instruments. Where we begin depends upon the receptivity of the person and the karmas active within them.

Beyond Information Technology

Today we pride ourselves on our information technology and look to it to lead us to a better life. We have moved beyond matter as our primary reality to subtler levels of energy and information. We are accessing more extensive forms of energy and information, with new computers to process these for us. Yet whether this information age ends up ennobling our souls and enhancing our deeper sensitivities remains in doubt.

We not only use computers to improve our lives, we are also seeking happiness through the new enjoyments that our technology provides, which is replacing our direct interaction with people and with the world of nature. We are functioning more like computers ourselves and losing our inner dimension of creativity. We are moving into virtual and Facebook realities in which our actual self is hidden behind a media persona.

The Vedic view is that matter, energy and information form only the lower three principles of the seven rungs of existence. All three remain on an outer level, which is largely a product of external conditioning and caught up in habit and impulse. They cannot take us to the higher realms. In other words, information, however helpful it may be, is not enough to reach a higher level of awareness. Information can also easily be distorted into advertising and propaganda.

Vedic counseling aims at awakening the four higher cosmic principles of intelligence, bliss, consciousness and being. These principles generally develop in a progressive manner, starting with the awakening of a higher intelligence within us that can be defined as our ability to discern the truth from the falsehood, the real from the unreal, the eternal from the transient. This deeper intelligence leads us to lasting bliss, infinite awareness and eternal being.

Information, we should clearly note, is not intelligence. Information consists of data that can be held even in a machine. Information can be helpful but it is not in itself creative or aware. Intelligence is rooted in direct perception and is capable of immediate decisions and clear action rooted in the present. The awakening of intelligence requires looking beyond information, names and forms to the background energy and awareness. It requires direct perception and unmediated experience. Information is a quantitative factor of data accumulation. Intelligence is a qualitative factor of higher discernment.

Vedic counseling addresses the inner Self or eternal aspect of our being that dwells behind our other concerns. It is not aimed at our outer personality, but tries to adjust and harmonize our outer personality with our inner being. It teaches us that true well-being is only possible if we are linked to our inner Self. Vedic counseling is a way of Self-knowledge. This Self-knowledge is also a cosmic knowledge and connects us to this higher realm of Being-Consciousness-Bliss.

Body and Mind as Instruments not as Self

We can describe our human nature in a simple threefold manner as consciousness, mind and body. Consciousness is our true nature or inner Self that is beyond time and change. Mind and body are instruments of its expression, which constantly changes. We are more than these instruments. We are the being and awareness behind them.

The body consists of tissues, organs, fluids and systems that are physical in nature and change radically over the aging process. The mind consists of sensations, emotions, thoughts, memories and tendencies that are subtle energy patterns, and change every moment. Consciousness is of the nature of pure awareness and Self-being complete in its own nature, timeless and immutable. Our continuity of being and Self rests upon an inner consciousness, not our outer instruments of body and mind.

Whatever is an instrument is not who you really are, whether it is your automobile, your computer, your body, or your mind. Our well-being in life requires mastery over our instruments, not letting them rule over us. Just as we should not let our car tell us where to drive, we should not let our desires and emotions born of the body and mind direct as to what to do. Our actions should rest upon the inner decision born of our highest intelligence.

We must understand the nature of our instruments and how to use them properly. Vedic counseling teaches us how to master the energies and capacities of body and mind. We need to have right nutrition and expression for both body and mind. If we treat our instruments poorly, they also will prevent us from accessing our deeper nature, as well as cause disease and disharmony. Yet we can only find happiness and truth within, not through our instruments, which have no consciousness of their own.

Nature and Its Powers

The world of nature consists of various substances, qualities and actions that follow certain laws and processes. Nature has tremendous variety and diversity yet reflects underlying unitary seed powers. Science and technology have unfolded new powers of nature externally, but there are greater powers that remain to be found internally, including direct ways of knowing and doing, connecting to the universe as a whole. To discover these we need to know how nature operates at a deeper level. This is what Vedic philosophies teach us.

Prakriti and the Three Gunas

The origin of the world of nature lies in the power of consciousness itself or *Chit-Shakti*. This sets in motion the power of division and differentiation called *Maya*, through which the One appears as many. Maya manifests as *Prakriti,* an organic process of unfoldment of the various levels of mind, body and prana.

Nature is an organic system that follows precise laws and processes that promote a greater unfoldment of life and consciousness, starting with the inanimate world. Nature is called Prakriti in Sanskrit meaning the "original power of action." We need to understand Prakriti on its various levels of body, energy, mind and soul. Yet behind the manifest forms of Prakriti dwells a higher or Divine Nature, *Para Prakriti,* which reflects our inner nature as pure consciousness.

Prakriti as defined by the three *Mahagunas* or "great qualities" of *sattva, rajas* and *tamas,* which can be related to the three powers of light, energy and matter, or of mind, life and matter. Understanding the three gunas is the key to working with nature and her powers.

Sattva	Light	Mind	Heaven	Harmony
Rajas	Energy	Life	Atmosphere	Agitation
Tamas	Matter	Body	Earth	Inertia

Prakriti is a natural state of harmony but can fall into disharmony or *Vikriti* through wrong application. Vedic counseling helps us move from Vikriti to Prakriti or from any imbalances that we may have to the natural state of balance on all levels. It directs us to our true nature of pure consciousness beyond the laws and formations of nature, which can only be accessed by the calm mind.

Duality and Unity

All of life consists of various dualistic, complementary, and contrasting forces. These include light and darkness, attraction and repulsion, fire and water, male and female. Learning how to work with and transcend the forces of duality is the key to true harmony in life. This means learning how to balance dualities, resolve conflict, and understand different opposing points of view.

Shiva and Shakti, perhaps the prime duality of Vedic thought, as consciousness and its power, embody the ultimate transformative polarity of the cosmic duality. They encompass action and inaction, expansion and contraction, stillness and dynamic movement, male and female. Each is rooted in the other, supports and turns into the other. We must balance these dualities within ourselves in the body, senses, pranas and mind, extending to our spiritual capacity.

Duality is the basis of all the energies of life, which arise through the union of opposites. Yet non-duality or pure unity is the foundation through which all dualities can function and become integrated. Non-duality is the basis of duality and all dualities can be resolved into non-duality, without losing their essence.

Without an underlying unity there could not be any dualistic forces or any connection between them. This unity allows dualistic energies to interact and to eventually be resolved. All duality is ultimately a seeking of unity. But that unity can only arise when both sides of dualistic energies are understood.

Vedic counseling directs us to a unitary and non-dualistic view of life. Through this unitary view we can access the inherent forces of unity and transformation within ourselves and in our environment. We must learn how to cultivate non-duality, which means moving beyond conflicting opposites of all types. We do this by finding the point of balance behind all dualities, from which they manifest and into which they must eventually return.

Part II

Living according to Your Dharma

Karmic Reckoning: Taking Control of Your Life

The first thing Vedic counseling teaches us is that our lives are a product of our own action or karma. Who we are and what we experience, both individually and collectively, is the result of forces that we ourselves have set in motion and for which we are ultimately responsible We are responsible for ourselves and to some extent for the world as a whole. This assumption of "karmic responsibility" is the basis of all deeper yogic practices as well as our ability to gain freedom in life overall.

The universe is our own co-creation that we have participated in along with the great creative forces of nature. There is no God to blame for the condition of the world apart from ourselves. The state of society is similarly our own co-creation along with all other people. There is no person or group to blame for the state of society apart from ourselves. Above all, we as individuals are the result of our own thought and action, not the result of what other people have done to us. There is no one to blame or to try to get even with.

This realm of karma remains a work in progress with changes happening at every moment. We must remain vigilantly aware of its constant development and direct it towards the highest good. We cannot claim ignorance as an excuse for achieving wrong outcomes in life.

Recognizing that our lives are a creation of our own karma means that we must first take responsibility for who we are and learn to act in a way that insures we achieve what we are really striving for. We cannot place the responsibility for who we are on anyone, though we all have to assume a degree of mutual responsibility for all that occurs in our lives.

Life is action, which is karma. Life is never static or completed. Life consists of forces that are ever changing and reshaping themselves in various ways, undergoing regular renewal and transformation. While these forces in life cannot be destroyed, we can alter their level and degree of manifestation, sometimes in a radical manner. To do this we must be consciousness at every moment of the type of forces in play around us. We must remain wakefully aware at every instant, not as a state of stress but as a state of receptivity to the vast movement of life.

We must also recognize that placed behind visible causes and their apparent effects in the world today are yet subtler forces of karma shaping them in powerful currents, with links to other times, places and aspects of the greater universe. The karma in our world is linked to the karma in other worlds, including those beyond the physical that we may not know.

Karmic Counseling

The key Vedic law of life is the law of karma, which shows the interdependence of all creatures and actions in the universe. Though karma is a common term today, it is seldom understood in its proper light. Vedic counseling requires understanding our karma in life, which is different for each person, and which is regularly changing. This requires recognizing the law of karma and how it works, which can be very subtle.

Vedic counseling is largely a *karmic counseling*, designed to help us become aware of our karma and manage it in a positive manner. It helps us know the nature of the karmic forces that we must deal with and provides the tools that can help us modify and ultimately transcend karma altogether. Vedic counseling rests upon an understanding of the karma of a person and an ability to improve it in a way that is beneficial to the inner being.

Life is a *karmic reality* that we must recognize, honor and respect. Behind everything that we see or experience are karmic currents that are shaping our future and our world. There are tremendous powers that we are linked to, which can be far stronger than anything we can set in motion ourselves. If we do not act with awareness, we can get involved in forces that take us in a very different direction than where we wish to go, like jumping into the powerful stream that will go only the way that it is flowing. Though the effects of karma do not always manifest immediately, they can be very hard to overcome once they have been set in motion.

Karma as Cause and Effect

The law of Karma indicates that there is an inviolable relationship of cause and effect in regard to all actions in the universe. As is the cause, so is the effect: as you sow, so shall you reap. This seems very simple at first, yet that is only the beginning of how karma works.

The Vedic law of karma is not merely a physical law but an ethical and spiritual law. Everything we do sets in motion various forces that have certain consequences and results that can either be beneficial or harmful. While we can easily see cause and effect relative to material forces, it is harder to observe on a subtle level.

The ultimate result of the law of karma is that our present actions in our current life reflect actions done in past lives that we do not remember. This causes us to come into certain experiences in life that we feel are not the result of anything that we ourselves have actually done or are responsible for. For this reason, karma and its effects can be hard to discern. The chain of karma connects us not only to our own past lives but also to the karmas of all living beings.

Karma, we must clearly note, is not a matter of reward and punishment for good or bad deeds. It is simply a movement in natural forces. If you put your hand into a fire, you will get burned. It is not a matter of morality. Yet there are laws relating to the mind and soul as well that are ethical in nature. For example, if we create anger, which is a fiery force, it can burn not only others but also ourselves. We need not cover karma over in a veil of judgments but should try to determine how the forces of karma work on an objective level, not according to the will of another person or the whim of a deity.

Karma, Destiny and Free Will

Karma means action and refers to the results of our previous deeds. It does not mean destiny or indicate that our lives are predetermined. The past projects an influence that can be very powerful but life in the present can modify that in various directions. There is always room for the new.

The law of karma means that each of our actions has consequences that we should be aware of, not only for the present but also for the future.

The law of karma means that we are free to create our own destiny in life. There are, however, three important correlates to this idea that serve to qualify it.

Karma and Time	We create our destiny in the field of time, which means that who we are today is a result of what we did yesterday, extending into previous lives that we have forgotten. The shadow of past life karmas hangs over us and must be understood.
Karma and Dharma	We create our destiny in the field of universal law. For example, we are free to put our hand into a fire or not, but we are not free to put our hand into a fire and not get burned. This means that if we violate universal laws that we will suffer. Unfortunately, the results of certain actions manifest only after time and so our immediate reaction may be incorrect. When we come down with an illness, for example, it may be the result of wrong actions over a long period of time, like eating of too many sweets may lead to diabetes.
Collective nature of Karma	We are co-creators of karma. We as individuals live in a certain era and cultural field that affects our actions. For example, someone with a certain career potential in our society today may have a different career than if they were born a thousand years ago. Similarly, we can be affected by collective karmas extending to major social changes, innovations or conflicts.

Assuming Karmic Responsibility for Your Life

The foundation for all Vedic counseling is that we must first assume responsibility for our own lives. Only when we assume responsibility for ourselves in life can we effectively change who we are and alter how we live in a harmonious manner.

One of the biggest obstacles to change in life is that we do not accept responsibility, particularly for the difficulties that come to us. We want to make others responsible, whether it is our family, friends, society or the world as a whole. Yet in blaming others, we give away our own power and deprive ourselves of the motivation necessary to improve our lives. We are not victims and cannot blame others for our condition in life, even though the actions of other people do affect us. The attitude of being a victim weakens us, inhibits positive change and gets us caught in the past.

Once we accept our karmic responsibility in life, we are able to forgive others and let go of the past. We can make positive changes in the present moment. We recognize that we are responsible for the world in which we live. Accepting our responsibility for our karma allows us to take control of our lives and make meaningful and lasting changes. It provides a great relief and opens up a new horizon of transformation.

Karma and Desire

Sometimes we feel that we should be free to do what we want and to fulfill our desires whatever they may be. This attitude is naïve and draws us into conflict and suffering. True freedom is not the ability to get what we want, but the freedom not to need anything external for our internal happiness and well-being. Desire is a form of want and dependency that binds us to various objects and actions. It is not a self-aware motivation but an attraction from the outside that binds us to the outside.

We have duties and responsibilities in life, which if we do not fulfill we will experience pain and cause greater karmic entanglements. A good rule is to fulfill our duties first and then go after the pursuit of our desires, but only those desires that take us to greater awareness and creativity, which are the deeper wishes of our immortal soul.

Manage and Transcend Your Karma

Vedic counseling can be defined as *karmic management*. It teaches us how to understand the nature of our karma and set in motion better karmic outcomes. It helps us create sattvic or harmonious karma in order to help us move beyond karma that is dominated by rajas and tamas, the forces of agitation and inertia in life.

We can improve our karma but only if we know what our karma is, how it works, and what are the main tools and times of action that we can work with in order to affect. This is what a Vedic counselor can help us with.

Yet the goal of all karmic management is not simply to help us get what we want, or to further our actions in the realm of desire. It is to further the unfolding of our higher awareness that leads us beyond karmic bondage to the external world and into the creative response of Self-awareness.

Karma and Time

To determine our karma, we must carefully examine the nature of the forces that we are setting in motion and their long term consequences. Negative effects may manifest only after time, which may at times be years or even decades. For example, wrong diet may not result in significant health problems until after the age of forty. For another example, negative thoughts that we have in a relationship may build over time and bring it to an end some months or years in the future. Having no immediate negative effect for wrong thoughts or wrong actions is no sign that there are no consequences.

Understanding karma implies understanding the nature of time. Time unfolds according to certain rhythms and presents us with different challenges and opportunities moment by moment. We need to be aware of the movement of our karma through time during the day, the month and the year, from childhood to old age, in this life, and according to past life influences. Learn the movement of time and karma within you, your inner karmic and biological clock. Vedic astrology can help you to do this.

Time, conditioning and karma are all bound together and part of the cycle of birth and death. We can move beyond time and karma only by contacting our eternal essence – the Self beyond karma, as the essence of our consciousness that is the witness of the mind. There are several keys to do this. Perhaps most important is to learn to witness your karma. Observe your actions with detachment in order to find out where they are taking you. Step back from the compulsive stream of action and try to determine the best thing to do and the best time to act. Give up automatic reactive patterns for creative awareness. Karma is an outward reality only. Your inner awareness can stand beyond. The best way to work with, manage, transform and transcend karma is through developing a greater Self-awareness.

Note that your true nature is beyond action. Action only occurs through your association with your sense and motor organs, and with various instruments and objects in the external world. Much of your time is spent in an action free state of awareness or rest. This reflects your true nature beyond time and action.

Karma Yoga

Karmic responsibility leads us naturally to *Karma Yoga* or action for the good of all. A Vedic life begins with Karma Yoga. Karma Yoga is not simply selfless service to a good cause. It is action rooted in an awareness of one's higher nature as an immortal soul, as well as others. Such action is an expression of consciousness, not following the reactive patterns of the mind.

Action done as Karma Yoga frees us from bondage to karma. Karma Yoga takes us beyond time and the influence of the past. It takes us beyond the seeking of mere favorable results and outcomes for ourselves to promoting the good of all. Yet action done as Karma Yoga is also more efficient as the personal factor is taken out that distorts our efforts with selfish considerations and wrong judgments.

Using Karma Yoga to manage and transcend karma is the Vedic way of action. Karma without Yoga is binding, while Karma Yoga is liberating. Karma Yoga implies action as a way of discovering unity and integration. Karma Yoga means that our life should be a service to the whole of life, not simply a seeking of gain for our personal self. Yet Karma Yoga means serving the divine or higher consciousness, not simply working for the sake of others and their desires.

Karma Yoga helps us reduce tamas or the quality of inertia, darkness and ignorance in our minds and hearts. It helps break through deep-seated traumas and lead us from personal sorrow to compassion for all living beings. Karma Yoga is an important treatment recommendation for many issues and helps cleanse our minds and hearts.

Karma Yoga and Ritual

Karma Yoga is not just service; it is action in harmony with the whole of life. Action in harmony with the whole of life can be defined as a ritual or as "sacred action." To take control of our karma requires following the right daily routine and life-style, which implies a daily ritual. Whether it is eating, sleeping, working, or exercising – all daily activities become more karmically beneficial if we do them in a sacred or sacramental manner.

Adding some degree of ritual to our lives is helpful, whether it is lighting incense, candles, chanting, or prayer. There is an entire art to it, making our actions reflect a deeper aspiration and greater reverence for the beauty and grace behind all life.

Karma and Astrology

For determining our karma, Vedic astrology and your Vedic birth chart is particularly important. Vedic astrology is the ultimate science of karma. Yet a good teacher can also help you understand your past life karmas directly. Additionally it can occur by understanding your actions and desires in a state of deep introspection.

Dharma, Artha, Kama and Moksha: The Four Great Goals of Life

Dharma is the foundation of Vedic counseling, which can also be called "dharmic counseling." This begins with an investigation into what our true dharma in life is and how it relates to the universal Dharma. But dharma is not just of one type only. Dharma refers to the right way of action and awareness on all levels of our being and our entire interaction with the whole of life. The way of Dharma is subtle and many sided. It cannot be reduced to a mere formula or routine but requires constant adaptation to the movement of life at every moment.

There is a famous Sanskrit statement from the *Mahabharata* that "Dharma protects those who protect Dharma." If we do not follow the way of dharma our lives can easily fall under forces of ignorance, disintegration and imbalance. Dharma is our greatest protection in life.

Physical and Psychological Health and Well-Being

Basic health and well-being for body and mind, what is called *Arogya* in Sanskrit, is the foundation of all our other pursuits in life. If we are physically unwell we may not have the energy to pursue the other goals of life, even if we may have the talent or capacity to do so. Similarly, if we are psychologically unwell, our perception and motivation can be impaired. We can make wrong judgments that can cause us to deviate from our true path.

This fact of the primacy of health provides a special importance to Ayurveda in Vedic counseling, particularly Ayurveda's foundation of right life-style practices for body and mind. Ayurvedic living is the foundation of dharma for physical and psychological balance and harmony. Ayurvedic living is the foundation of dharmic living. Ayurvedic counseling is the foundation of dharmic and Vedic counseling.

Our duty for health and well-being however, is not simply personal but extends to our family, community, nation, humanity and nature. It implies a seeking to alleviate all suffering and disharmony in the world.

The Four Great Dharmas

There are four aspects of Dharma as mentioned in Vedic texts. The four Dharmas or ways of life, are also referred to as the four *Purusharthas* or goals of human life. While commonly known they are seldom deeply understood.

Dharma	Living according to our inner purpose
Artha	Establishing goals and values that promote it
Kama	Finding happiness in what we do based upon our Dharma
Moksha	Gaining the freedom of consciousness

Dharma Artha, Kama and Moksha are called the four Dharmas. We can also refer to them as Artha Dharma, Kama Dharma and Moksha Dharma.

The Primary Dharma of One's Nature

Our primary dharma should rest upon and be part of the universal dharma, of which our soul is one manifestation. Dharma in this deeper sense should be the foundation of our goals, enjoyment and seeking of freedom. However, this is not always the case, particularly today. Modern society usually places wealth or pleasure, aspects of Artha and Kama, before Dharma. Unless our actions are rooted in Dharma, an adharmic pursuit of the goals of life will not bring happiness or peace.

For a dharmic life, one must first ascertain our primary dharma as an individual soul. This consists of one's personal dharma, one's social dharma and one's duty to the universe as a whole. It is the purpose that we have come into this life in order to fulfill and reflects our karmas from previous lives. It is our duty as a Divine soul.

Dharma differs according to individual. Our individual dharma or svadharma is reflected in our doshas, gunas and karmas, as well as our unique capacities in life. It is usually reflected in our vocation and in our spiritual path. Ayurveda and Vedic astrology can help in determining it. A Vedic counselor should learn this ascertainment of individual dharma as his primary or first task. We may have the dharma of an artist, an entrepreneur, a healer, a yogi or any number of possibilities.

Artha Dharma – Goals and Abundance

Artha refers to the pursuit of the goals and resources of life in a dharmic way. The non-dharmic pursuit of wealth and property is not covered here.

We must be very clear and careful as to the goals that we set for ourselves in life. The nature of the goal determines the nature of our striving and the type of energy that we will be creating. Dharmic goals are inclusive and considerate, not isolating or promoting of conflict. Adharmic goals are those based upon violence, selfishness or division. They cannot take us to a meaningful and happy life. Dharmic goals promote dharma. They are goals that help the world overall.

Artha implies wealth and abundance, including money. Vedic thought, we should note, is not against the accumulation of wealth. But it is important that wealth belongs to the Divine force, which means that it is used to promote higher causes, not just personal enjoyment. To win wealth for the Divine is a great occupation to have and we should honor those who support Dharma with wealth used for the good of all. There should be abundance for everyone and this is possible when we cease trying to take things only for ourselves.

Kama Dharma

Kama Dharma refers to the pursuit of enjoyment, happiness, well-being and bliss through Dharma (not just to any pursuit of desire). It does not encourage us to run after a life of enjoyment only.

We have many modes and avenues of enjoyment available for us. We should seek those enjoyments that are ennobling to our spirit and help us develop a deeper taste, refinement and sensitivity, avoiding desires that wear us out or make us feel dull and heavy in the end.

We should learn to discriminate between the pursuit of desire and the pursuit of Self-realization. Not all desires reflect our real needs, capacities or highest goals. Adharmic kama is the pursuit of desire for its own sake, pursuing self-indulgence and dissipation. It is desire that is against dharma and promotes conflict.

Happiness is our very nature. Bliss is our birthright. Our own Self-awareness is Ananda. But we can only experience this happiness in our outer life once we are root in right dharma and the right use of our resources.

Moksha Dharma

Moksha refers to the pursuit of liberation and higher spiritual knowledge through dharma. It does not include the non-dharmic pursuit of religion, in which we are only seeking to convert others to a belief, or the pursuit of the spiritual life through escaping the world and not honoring one's duties.

We are all seeking freedom in life in various ways and like to have a greater space around us. Yet true freedom is not simply the freedom to get what we want but freedom from the pain and burden of desire, the freedom from outer or worldly compulsions. True freedom can only be found in Self-awareness. It is not the freedom to do but the freedom to be. Freedom from desire brings the highest happiness. The ability to get what we want only breeds further wants.

The traditional means of pursuing Moksha Dharma is Yoga in the broader sense of principles and practices that develop Self-realization, primarily meditation. Freedom is the nature of consciousness, which is like unbounded space. We should not tie ourselves down by the power of attachment. To let go is the highest form of freedom. To be free in our awareness is to be one with all.

Integrality of the Four Dharmas

The four dharmas are not separate but form an integral whole rooted in each other. A proper dharmic orientation in life leads us to seeking dharmic goals and the right use of our wealth and resources. This grants lasting happiness and directs us to the freedom of the soul. Similarly, the spiritual life provides happiness (kama), right organization of resources (artha), and fulfillment of duty (dharma).

Understanding your Individual Karma and Dharma

Karma and dharma are inherently linked together. We develop and transcend karma through dharma. Our karma or action, should be dharmic or in harmony with the great laws of life. Our dharma similarly must manifest in our karma or action. This creates two simple principles of dharmic action to follow.

Avoiding adharmic-karma	Avoid actions that do not support your life purpose or the good of all.
Cultivating dharmic-karma	Let your actions reflect your dharma. Walk your talk and put your values and principles into manifestation.

All dharmic action is a kind of Karma Yoga. Dharma begins with service to oneself and service to the whole of life. Karma Yoga is the way of Yajna, or making sacred. This supports Dharma. Working for and serving others is a way of inner healing and bringing out our deeper capacities.

Cultivating Higher Values

Dharmic living rests upon a value based education in which we promote enduring and universal values that benefit everyone. Dharma implies that we are ever striving towards something higher, seeking to unfold a higher consciousness in life. It requires effort on our part to improve our lives that directs us to a sadhana or spiritual practice.

Pursuing our dharma means that we are not just doing what we want to do but rather that we are pursuing a way of excellence in which we ever seek to grow, develop and transcend our previous limitations. Dharma means seeking the highest, not following what is convenient. Only when we achieve something new, extraordinary or beyond our previous capacities can we truly feel happy and fulfilled.

Examination of Dharma

Part of knowing who we are requires understanding our dharma and discovering our highest purpose in life. Our life has a kind of mission that we must first fulfill. We need to know what this is in order to act in the most responsible and efficacious manner. Note a few key dharmic questions below.

- What is your real purpose in life? – not just short term goals or desires, but what you wish to achieve in your life as a whole and leave as your legacy.

- What is your real purpose in this particular life and incarnation? – What is your background as a soul with many births?

- What is your proper role in society? – How can you help others and help uplift humanity, without compromising your own inner purpose?

- What constitutes your true individuality? – Not merely what is unusual or special about you, but what is your unique essence that does not change throughout your life?

- Where does your true and lasting happiness dwell? – as apart from where we may derive the most pleasure or feel the most comfortable.

Discovering Your Inner Light: Developing Your Agni or Inner Flame

A counselor is always working to light the flame of wisdom in the client. His work is not simply to provide information but to bring in the higher light for all to see. Counseling is not just examining human potentials but unfolding the Divine light of awareness.

Our inner flame can be shared and transmitted, just as one candle can light another. This transmission of the light is one of our highest duties. In all counseling procedures we are striving to bring more light, to illumine what is obscure, dark, uncertain or problematical.

A Vedic counselor should be a giver of light perhaps more than anything else. The inner light gives true knowledge, not any conceptual or rational analysis. The main solution to our problems does not reside in an idea or formula but in an ability to access a greater light within and around us. Vedic counseling is part of a greater search for enlightenment.

The Vedic view of the cosmos is of a universe of consciousness, light and energy. This is described symbolically as *Agni* in Vedic thought, which means fire, particularly as the power of transformation. The Vedic concept of Agni extends to all aspects of light, life, intelligence and consciousness. It reflects the inherent light giving power at the very ground of existence. An understanding of Agni is key to the Vedic view of life, evolution, health, well-being and liberation.

Agni also represents the individual soul or divine consciousness within us that is hidden in the body like fire latent within wood. The individual human being is a particularized manifestation of Agni as the universal power of life, light and consciousness. In our soul or essence we are a flame of Divine light and aspiration.

The Vedic view of the universe is that of a cosmic fire. The Vedic mind regards the universal process as a series of fire offerings unfolding different levels of transformation of energy and light. Vedic practice consists of working with different forms, aspects and levels of Agni, in body, mind and consciousness, nature and the Godhead.

Developing Your Inner Flame

Each one of us is a light being, seeking enlightenment, taking birth here on Earth in order to spread the light of awareness. The pursuit of enlightenment should be our primary goal and purpose. Vedic counseling helps us to develop our inner light and connect it with the greater light of all life.

Agni represents our primary power of will, motivation and aspiration to the higher truth. Cultivating our Agni allows us to develop the optimal energization of our faculties towards what we consider to be the highest goal in life. We are all individual flames seeking to expand into the full and comprehensive light - the spiritual Sun of truth.

One of the main aspects of Vedic counseling, perhaps its very foundation, is awakening the higher Agni or spiritual motivation in a person - sharing the Divine flame. Vedic counseling begins with contacting our inner Agni and bringing it to the front of our awareness. This requires lighting our inner fire, which means helping each person to develop his or her own inner light. Once our inner light is functioning, we can have clear judgment, peaceful emotions, and create a harmonious life-style that can manifest our highest potentials.

The orientation of our inner fire is different for each person and may vary at different times. What inspires us or what energizes our higher light cannot be reduced to a formula. We must understand the rhythms of the sacred fire of our soul and learn how to adapt to them as our life moves on various levels. Similarly, a counselor must know how to awaken that inner flame in the client and help it grow and sustain itself throughout all the difficulties of life. Awakening the inner flame provides the knowledge and the inspiration, the insight and the motivation, to take us forward to Self-realization.

Agni as the Counselor

Agni is the guiding force in the universe, the innate cosmic mind or intelligence of nature. Agni represents the inner guide and guru, which is the guiding flame within us, seated in our inmost heart and core of our being. The Vedic counselor represents Agni for the client. He or she is meant to shed the inner light to help the person deal with the problems born of darkness and ignorance. The counselor should function like a steady and inextinguishable flame.

Counseling is a type of initiation or entrance into the inner world of light. The Vedic counselor works to reflect the universal power of Agni back onto the client, not simply to project human opinions upon them. He or she should continually cultivate and sustain their own inner flame. This requires a life of meditation, contemplation, deep thinking and profound care for the welfare of all. The counselor is the inner Agni for the client, helping them to discover their inner light and balance all the powers of light within body and mind.

Vedic Counseling as Inner Empowerment

Vedic counseling seeks to empower us inwardly in order to manifest our highest potential. It does not breed dependency on the counselor or on external forms of guidance. It directs us towards self-mastery. It strives to develop independence, authenticity and clarity within each person. Once the light of the counselor is transmitted to the client, the client will have a direct means of illuminating his or her own life.

Different Levels of Agni as our Inner Fire

There are many forms of Agni within us that we need to learn about in order to develop our higher light and happiness.

Digestive Fire in the Body

The digestive fire or Jatharagni is the basis of the physical body and its well-being. It dwells in the navel and the small intestine. It is a material fire that converts solid and liquid food into the energy and tissues necessarily for physical health and sustenance. It also sustains the immune system. Right care for the digestive fire is the key to physical health and well-being.

Pranagni or Life-Fire

Pranagni is the fire of the breath that sustains our respiration and circulation, extending to the mind and senses. It is a gaseous fire dwelling in the lungs and heart. It nourishes the mind and the sense organs and gives energy and skill to the motor organs. It also sustains psychological immunity. Right care of the Pranagni or the vital fire, is the key to vitality and an aid to strength of the senses and motor organs.

Agni of the Outer Mind

The Agni of the outer mind is our power to digest sensory impressions. Sensory impressions comprise the subtle elements. These subtle elements build up the mind and the subtle body and aid in our psychological well-being. Subtle Elements are Earth – smell, Water – taste, Fire – sight, Air – touch, Ether – sound. We should make sure to have the proper wholesome and natural impressions that provide true sustenance to the mind.

Agni of the Outer Mind

The fire of our intelligence is what allows us to discern truth from falsehood, the real from the unreal, the Self from the non-self, the eternal from the transient. Connected to dharma and higher values, it allows us to digest our experience and turn it into wisdom.

Agni of Awareness

The fire of awareness is the ultimate form of fire in the universe. It allows us to be aware of the eternal and the infinite. The fire of awareness allows us to digest and burn up all our karmas and samskaras in life, leading us to the supreme light beyond all darkness. It is the flame of our inner Self and higher nature.

Four States of Agni

All forms of Agni have four states:

1 | **Low**	Burning poorly or incomplete, in which the flame may go out or create smoke, weak digestion.
2 | **High**	Burning too high, in which the fuel may be exhausted and the fire eventually goes out or consumes itself.
3 | **Irregular**	Burning erratically, alternately low and high,
4 | **Balanced**	Burning consistently, with the right fuel level, healthy digestion.

Taking our Agnis to a balanced state is a key to achieving balance in life.

These four states of Agni generally reflect the three doshas of Ayurveda:

1 | **Low**	More common in Kapha or watery types in which the fuel may be excess or moist, inhibiting the fire.
2 | **High**	More common in Pitta, fire types or fiery conditions.
3 | **Irregular**	More common in Vata or air types, like a changing wind that blows a fire in different ways.
4 | **Balanced**	The state of health and balance

The Light of Being

Being is the highest and most original form of light, but also the subtlest and easiest to overlook. The light of Being is clear and transparent, hidden behind all that we see. It sheds light upon all things in the sense of making them apparent. The light of being is the light of presence that pervades all things. The light of being is the light of space or the light behind space. The light of being is the ground of existence and the most original form of Agni.

The counselor should function like the light of being, providing a transparent presence in which the client can perceive his or her true nature. Yet the counselor should be able to provide a hotter fire and power of purification as necessary to remove deep-seated blockages and traumas. Counseling is part of an ancient fire alchemy of inner transformation.

Discovering Lasting Happiness and Total Well-Being: Finding Your Bliss or Ananda

All life arises from bliss or *ananda* and must eventually return to it. We are all seeking lasting happiness and well-being in life both for ourselves and for those who are close to us. This fact reflects the bliss that is the nature of all existence.

Yet we do not always seek happiness in the right way or in an enduring manner. We run after the transient enjoyments of the external world and lose the everlasting happiness that dwells within us. Often what we seek to provide us happiness ends up causing us pain and sorrow instead. We must learn where true and lasting happiness abides and not just run after superficial enjoyments that leave us feeling empty in the end.

Most of us seek guidance because our lives are in some way unfulfilling or incomplete. Understanding the nature of happiness and helping others to achieve it is an important part of any counseling approach, which should ultimately be a sharing of joy.

Vedic counseling teaches that our ultimate happiness and well-being lies within our own consciousness. It cannot be produced by anything external. The pursuit of happiness inevitably leads to sorrow because it places happiness outside of ourselves. Rather than pursuing happiness on the outside, we should be givers of happiness from within; then happiness will always be ours and will come to us from all things in life.

GOING BEYOND DEPENDENCY AND ADDICTION

The mind inherently becomes dependent upon or addicted to whatever provides its greatest source of stimulation, attention or enjoyment. Unless we choose our sources of happiness carefully, our minds can easily become addicted to inferior pleasures, if not drugs. Once an addiction is created, it is very hard to overcome, as it has become embedded in the fabric of the mind.

Addiction is a major problem in the modern world. It may be a simple food or sugar addiction, or extend to alcohol or drugs. It may be an addiction to certain forms of entertainment, sex, or even abusive relationships. Addiction arises from inner unrest and unhappiness. It is part of the compulsive movement of the mind to find some refuge apart from the stress of life, or to get caught in some repetitive action in which it can lose itself.

Perhaps the most obvious addiction is that to drugs. We use recreational drugs like cannabis and medicinal drugs like anti-depressants, to avoid sorrow in life and to make us feel better. This drug taking approach easily breeds dependency and throws us into inertia that leads to eventual sorrow. Yet it is part of our life-style that causes us to look on the outside for fulfillment in life. In encouraging the pursuit of sensation as happiness, our society easily makes us vulnerable to addictions which usually involve the most powerful sensations (like alcohol).

The Pursuit of Ananda

The way forward in life is to seek higher, more internal and lasting forms of happiness, not simply to try to content ourselves with being unhappy. This requires a deeper search and investigation into where real happiness lies, which is one of the most important factors of self-examination. There are higher forms of peace and bliss that we can develop through Yoga and meditation. But we must have subtlety of mind and refinement of our nature to be able to appreciate and discover these. They cannot come to us without working on ourselves and moving beyond our internal emptiness.

Most of us seek our happiness and enjoyment through the five senses, particularly sensations of sight and sound. There is nothing wrong with this, but there are proper and improper ways to use the senses. Our greatest sense of well-being arises through using our senses in an artistic and contemplative manner, seeking a more refined sensory perception, such as we find in the beauty of nature. Unfortunately, we often instead go after violent and dramatic sensations that occupy the mind and distract us from other problems, but provide us no lasting peace or contentment.

Art has a beauty that transcends outer utilitarian concerns. It lifts our perception to a higher level in which we can contact eternal truths and universal principles. Yet greater than possessing beautiful objects of art is becoming a creative person who can live in the creative state. This is to possess a natural refinement in ones nature, attitude and expression. To be creative is to look at life anew at every moment, to be able to contact the unique essence that dwells in each thing. In that state of creative intelligence, we can find beauty everywhere and we will never become bored.

Love and Relationship

Probably the main form of happiness in life that we seek is through intimate one-to-one relationships. Similarly, our main form of unhappiness usually derives from personal conflict with others. The ultimate happiness then is to be related deeply to all, which is to be at peace with all. This is to see our Self in all beings and all beings within ourselves.

The problem is that we confuse enjoyment and pleasure in relationship with true love and happiness. The demand for pleasure breeds expectation that causes frustration and conflict. Love, on the other hand, does not demand pleasure but inspires us to greater efforts at communion on the level of the heart.

Relationship counseling is one of the most important aspects of any counseling practice. It may involve working with both partners in a relationship or only one. Each human being is different and relationship compels us to see the world in a different light than if we were just living alone. Counseling itself is a kind of a relationship and requires the right connection and rapport. This is only possible if the counselor has a true sense of empathy for others.

Devotion and Compassion

Devotion and compassion are the two complementary Divine attitudes of deeper relationship. Devotion consists of finding meaning and happiness in our relationship with a greater consciousness, spirit or divinity. It causes us to look beyond the human to the transcendent. Devotion generates the highest upward aspiration towards transformation that is perhaps the most ennobling of all emotions.

Compassion means finding happiness in the well-being of others, extending to the well-being of the entire universe. It does not mean to pity anyone but to have a commonality of feeling with the whole of life. Compassion means affirming that every living being is inherently blissful, free and full of light and seeking to awaken that inner sense of fullness within all. Encouraging devotion and compassion aids in all manner of emotional healing. A counselor should have both, a higher devotion and a broader compassion.

Higher Awareness

True happiness is a state of awareness, not an outer achievement or acquisition. Such higher awareness has the power to sustain our sense of well-being even through difficulties and suffering externally. It is not even disturbed or bothered by death. If our happiness is within, it can never be taken away. If we have this internal happiness, we will not only find happiness externally but also create it for everyone.

Peace of Mind

True happiness begins with peace of mind, not with getting what we want. Peace of mind in turn rests upon inner stillness and surrender. It is not an achievement or even an idea. Peace of mind is rooted in discovering the peace that is inherent in life, which is there in all of nature and is a quality of existence itself. To find happiness we must first develop peace within. This requires we let go of anger, hatred, worry and desire and surrender to the Divine presence behind all.

Ananda or bliss is rooted in peace or shanti. It is not a dualistic emotion, a high that must inevitably be followed by a low. Ananda is the fullness of feeling that allows us to discover meaning in all things.

Ananda means that we approach each experience in life wholeheartedly and strive to grasp its essence. Such inner joy does not necessarily require a dramatic outer expression and is often best held in a loving silence.

Samadhi

Samadhi is the yogic state of inner happiness that arises through equipoise and balance of mind – the bliss of being and consciousness. Directing us to that inner bliss is the goal of a Vedic counselor. Samadhi is not a mere state of trance or altered awareness; it is the state of complete clarity, calm and composure in life. To approach Samadhi we need to first put our lives in balance. We are all seeking samadhi but it can only be achieved in a lasting manner through Yoga and meditation.

Degrees and Type of Happiness

Happiness in the ordinary sense is of many types and exists to different degrees and for different durations. We need to understand the different types of happiness that we are seeking and their place in finding lasting happiness and freedom from all sorrow. Some of what we think will bring us happiness will in fact more likely bring us pain.

Happiness can generally be described as inner or outer, with inner happiness being of a spiritual nature and outer happiness being of a material nature. The two overlap to some degree. Outer factors of happiness are more tangible. Inner factors are more personal and subjective. But only the inner happiness is enduring.

Outer Happiness	
Health and Physical Well-being	This is the foundation of all outer happiness. Unless we are physically healthy and strong, we will not have the energy to do anything else.

Outer Happiness	
Wealth and Prosperity	This is the basis of comfort in life, allowing us to accomplish many things and not come under the control of other people.
Property and House	This involves not merely owning a home, but arranging it so it is pleasing.
Relationship	This is the basis of all emotional happiness, but it is not the same for everyone. Some people can be happy alone, while others are gregarious. Some people prefer one-to-one relationship; others rely on a group of friends. Relationship needs change with time and the aging process. Marriage is important here as are children.
Career Success	This consists of having the type of job that one wishes to do and be paid sufficiently for one's efforts, including honor and dignity in what we do.

Inner Happiness	
Psychological Well-being	This is determined by how happy and content we feel inside ourselves. Outer success can support it, but even those who are very successful are often psychologically unhappy, restless or aggressive. The true measure of our psychological well-being is how enduring it is in the face of external difficulties.
Happiness through Selfless action	Happiness gained through helping others and uplifting the world is always more than happiness gained by our own personal assertion.
Creativity	This is our ability to spontaneously produce new ideas, perceptions, feelings and experiences - not merely works of art, though these are also part of it.

Inner Happiness	
Mental Power	Control of our own minds is one of the main factors for creating happiness and removing sorrow. If our minds are not in our own power, someone else is likely to manipulate them for their benefit, which may be our detriment! True mental power is not just being clever or educated, but being in control of our attention.
Divine Love	Love of nature, the Spirit, God, the Divine as Father or Mother, is a source of great internal happiness, which cannot be removed by outer factors. Divine love alone endures beyond death.
Love as Consciousness	This is happiness through unitary awareness. If all is one, there is nothing else that can be a cause for sorrow.
Inner Peace, Being and connections to the eternal	This is the ultimate happiness that is the ground of all existence.

Happiness Index

We can prepare an index of how happy we are. Yet we are usually not as happy as we would like to be, nor are we as unhappy as we sometimes think we are. The problem is that whatever we pursue, like a wild animal, it runs away from us. The pursuit of happiness means that we are always *pursuing* happiness and never catch it. The ultimate state is to find the happiness inherent in our own nature, in being itself. We should not seek happiness for ourselves; rather we should seek to share happiness with everyone.

We should carefully examine where we are seeking happiness and to what degree it can be found there. Where do we think happiness really resides and how can we achieve it? It is better to be a giver of happiness to all than to be one who seeks happiness out of a state of want. In our commercial age we are victims of externally induced desires that have little relevance for our inner being. True happiness must be intrinsic. Whatever is gained can be lost. The ultimate happiness dwells in no longer seeking happiness but in being content with the nature of reality, in which there is no division.

Managing your Prana, Spirit and Vital Energy

Each one of us is a spirit, not simply a body or mind. Our basic nature is energy and consciousness that activate our body and mind from within. This power of our spirit makes our bodies and minds either strong or weak. Only if we cultivate a strong spirit can whatever else we attempt be effective. This important fact enters into counseling. Counseling is not just about showing us a better way to physical or emotional well-being. It must aim at awakening and raising our inner spirit.

A strong body or sharp mind is not enough. We need a strong spirit to be really happy and to achieve our highest goals. A defeatist attitude will not help us, in which we let even little disturbances, delays and uncertainties upset us and makes us want to quit. Today when we depend on external stimulation and entertainment for happiness, our spirits are often weak. We have low motivation and low self-esteem and easily collapse before difficulties, rather than taking them as challenges for deeper growth. A strong spirit can work wonders even with a weak body.

Counseling consists of instilling a more powerful and positive spirit in the client, who is often weighed down by the stress, responsibility and complexity of life, and feels like giving up. Vedic counseling aims at raising the highest spirit in the person, which is the attitude of our inner consciousness not limited by time and space. Developing the spirit is part of any spiritual counseling. It means encouraging a certain daring, fearlessness and sense of adventure in the client.

The spirit is a like a power of the air or wind, called Vayu in Vedic thought. Vayu has no form but gives energy to all forms. It is invisible but makes all visible changes occur. It is the power of action in the universe, through which the movement of time proceeds. If we are aligned with the universal power, there is no limit as to what we can do. To sustain our deeper spirit we must learn to sustain a positive energy and attitude in all that we do. We must learn to access the universal spirit. Our limited bodies and minds cannot do much unless a higher power is moving them.

Yet this spirit is not simply an intangible factor; it is a reflection of our own Prana and vital energy, and whether this is expansive or contractive. It reflects our will power and motivation, whether we are willing to really make an effort in life or would just rather drift along. Most of us are dominated by desire, envy or jealousy and try to copy or imitate others. We lack a positive will power to do something unique on our own. Will power is not just about getting what we want. It means being in control of ourselves, which implies control of the mind and senses. It means our ability to direct and guide what the body and the mind do by the power of the spirit.

Right Management of Our Internal Energy

Our spirit is indicated by our energy and how we use it. One of the keys to a happy and successful life is right management of our energy. This includes being able not only to best use the energy that we already have but also to be able to access new and more creative forms of energy. The highest energy comes from within, from the power of our own consciousness.

Often our problems in life are not owing to wrong outer circumstances. They rest upon having insufficient energy to operate in the optimal manner. Any counselor should always question the client as to his or her state of energy, meaning not only physical energy, but also emotional, mental, creative and spiritual energy. Do we have the energy to achieve our goals? A lack of energy in turn often rests upon lack of motivation or inability to focus. It is not necessarily from weak health or low vitality, though at times it may be.

There are many ways that we can lose energy. These begin with wrong life-style practices such as poor dietary habits, lack of exercise, wrong breathing problems, sedentary life-style, self-indulgence, stress and worry. Without improving the management of our energy, we will not be able to succeed in our actions, however right or appropriate these may be. Of course, emotional problems can drain our energy, but lack of energy can also allow emotional issues like depression to continue.

Vedic counseling takes an energetic approach, helping us ascertain the nature and consequences of the forces that we are setting in motion.

This rests upon the energetic pattern of the person, though the vital forces, doshas and elements within their particular nature. Secondarily, it requires recommendations on how to improve and better manage our energy. These begin with diet and exercise but extend to our prime attitudes, values and beliefs.

PRANA: THE KEY TO THE ENERGIES OF LIFE

Prana is the Sanskrit term for energy. It is usually defined in terms of the breath and our vital energy overall, but extends to our deeper spirit. We need adequate prana to function and additional prana for enhanced performance in any field. Our inmost spirit and immortal nature is the deepest level of prana within us.

Our technology allows us access to new outer forms of energy and to operate more powerful forms of equipment. Additionally we need new forces of creativity, intelligence and consciousness. If the person who is operating the equipment is weak, it does not matter how powerful the equipment may be.

OUR NATURAL ENERGY SOURCES

First we need to take an overview of our natural energy sources. These can be categorized in a simple way relative to the primary aspects of our nature:

PHYSICAL	Through food and beverages, which can be enhanced with herbs and supplements.
SENSES	Both through natural use of the senses and media devices to enhance them. Yet while natural sources of sensory impressions renew the mind and nervous system, artificial sources tend to deplete them.

Vital Energy	Primarily through the breath, which can be enhanced by Pranayama practices, extending to our ability to draw in the healing forces of nature.
Positive Emotions	Including caring, love and encouragement from others, extending to our connection to the Divine within. Negative thinking, on the other hand, reduces our vitality.
Good Thoughts and Positive Attitudes	Including concepts, ideas, ideals, principles and values, whether from teachers, friends, well-wishers or our own practices of contemplation and meditation.
Our own will power	Which includes connecting to the Divine will and universal power of motivation.

The energy we take in on these different levels can be sattvic, rajasic or tamasic, meaning that we can also take in negative or disturbed energy that can deplete us. Sattvic energy is peaceful, refined and uplifting. Rajasic energy is stimulating but agitating and irritating. Tamasic energy is depleting and depressing and gets us caught in inertia.

Our Natural Energy Expressions

Complementary to the ways that we take energy in are ways that we express our energy. If expression is more than input, then we may lose energy.

Physical	Mainly through the motor organs, especially the vocal organs, hands and feet. We lose the greatest amount of our energy through wrong use of the vocal organs.
Emotions	Which may be positive, as love or negative, as fear, anger and attachment. Negative emotions cause long term energy blockage and energy loss.
Thoughts	Including thoughts that we hold within and those that we express through speaking or writing. Our thoughts hold subtle patterns of energy and action that influence all that we do.

The energy we express can also be sattvic, rajasic or tamasic, or either helpful or harmful to others. If our energy expression is sattvic or harmonious it links us up with the positive energy in others. If it is rajasic, it promotes unnecessary activity that is depleting in the long run. If it is tamasic it gets us caught in conflict and attachment. A good rule is that we should always cultivate a sattvic prana by having a spiritual motivation in life and by acting with courtesy, respect and humility.

Pranayama

The main Vedic and Yogic tool for working with our energy is pranayama, which consists of yogic breathing practices along with other ways of enhancing or monitoring our internal energies, including the cultivation of will power.

Vedic counseling teaches people how to breathe properly. We often hold and sustain negative thoughts and emotions in our breath and through it in our lungs, hearts and nervous systems. Wrong or inadequate breathing leads to stagnate or disturbed thought patterns that result in wrong decisions and the creation of difficult karmas.

Breathing practices begin with a detached observation of the breath and work into special techniques of developing a higher or unitary prana. We learn to how energize our breath in a positive way through positive thoughts, attitudes and good wishes, including prayers and mantras. Pranayama can be used to purify the mind and heart. You can learn to breathe your problems away, letting go of negativity with exhalation.

So'ham Pranayama

Breathe in deeply, mentally reciting the prana mantra ***"So."*** *Then relax the body and mind on the exhalation with the prana mantra* ***"Ham."*** *You can use the breath to let go of stress, tension, trauma, or negative emotions down to the subconscious level. Otherwise the breath reinforces negative patterns.*

Accessing Unlimited and Timeless Energy Sources

Forces of infinity and eternity embrace our lives on every side; such as we can easily feel in the earth and from the sky. They are beyond all diminution or exhaustion from our human realm. There is an immortal Prana within us, which belongs to our soul that never dies. We must learn to access that inner Prana of unity by embracing our interdependence with the entire universe.

It is important that we develop internal sources of energy, vitality, creativity and transformation, so that we are not dependent upon external sources. If we can create our own energy through awareness itself we can access all the powers of the universe. This requires Yoga and meditation at a deep level of opening the heart.

Developing Will-power

Will power is the basis of all other powers that we may have. It rests upon our ability not to be dominated by the mind, prana, senses or body. When our senses dominate us we lose our energy externally and come under the control of the external world. When we have will power then we direct our body, mind and senses to a higher goal regardless of any disturbances that may be happening around us. The supreme will power belongs to consciousness, not to the ego or personal self. That supreme will power arises through aligning ourselves with the Divine will and inherent power of existence.

There are many powers that we can access through life, mind and consciousness, both in nature and within ourselves. The power of consciousness (Chit-Shakti) is the highest force that we can develop. It can control all other forces from within.

Power Points of Transformation

There are special power points and matrixes of transformation in body, mind and nature. Marmas are such power points on the body. They are 108 points discussed in Ayurvedic medicine as the most important. Chakras are also such special power centers in the mind and subtle body. They are conduits to higher forces and are activated by Yogic practices.

There are many transformative locations, or sacred points in nature that are special sacred sites. Some examples are: high mountains, waterfalls, caves and grottos, special lakes, the confluence of rivers, special plants and rocks. Additionally, there are powerful moments in time, like the sunrise, sunset, new moon, full moon, solstices, equinoxes, eclipses and seasonal conjunctions. It is important that we learn how to access these things by linking our limited energy with higher power sources. This way we can move or progress to a higher level of manifestation.

Sexuality: the Complementary Powers of Shiva and Shakti

Our sexuality is one of the prime determinatives of our behavior, extending to how we speak, how we dress and to the main emotional issues that we have in life, which often revolve around relationship. Sexuality is a key component of whether we feel happy or sad, complete or incomplete. We are organic beings and need to be true to the capacities that nature has given us. Male and female qualities have natural places and roles both within and around us, yet they also have higher capacities that may need to be manifested for the full unfoldment of our potentials.

Counseling commonly involves how to deal with our nature as male or female, which extends to roles as husband and wife, son or daughter, brother or sister, or friends and partners of various types. There are masculine and feminine energies and capacities within each one of us that we must recognize and honor. These energies are not entirely fixed and have variations over time and different levels of functioning.

Vedic counseling defines the masculine and feminine aspects of our nature in a broad way, with regard to their karmic and yogic implications, as universal energies. Unless we work with the personal, social and spiritual aspects of male and female energy together, our lives will likely remain out of balance. An inability to work with the creative energies of the psyche overall gets us caught in relationship conflicts and sexual compulsions.

For Women – Developing Shakti

Women are more likely to be open to counseling than men because their nature is more socially minded and they are more receptive to the advice of others. Men tend to think they need to do everything for themselves and seldom want to listen to anyone. The majority of counseling clients are likely to be women. Yet counseling is also a field in which women can excel, as they have an innate ability to care for, nurture, guide and heal and can thus make natural counselors.

Women have their own issues relative to work, family, children, self-expression and spirituality that can be very different from those of men. For them, personal feelings may be more important than outer practicalities. Some of these issues may require a female counselor in order to adequately deal with them. There are woman counselors who specialize in woman's issues for this reason. Yet men can provide helpful guidance for women, as women can for men, if they understand the balance of forces in life and the value of each.

Our current society, in spite of its efforts to promote equality between the sexes, remains largely dominated by lower masculine values of assertion, achievement, domination, and control. We value outer accomplishments over inner feelings. This often puts women at a disadvantage. It may cause them to seek fulfillment in assertive masculine behavior patterns that may not suit them in the long run. While women should be granted equality with men, there should be a corresponding recognition of the value of female qualities and energies in the general social fabric.

On the other hand, women often suffer from not expressing themselves, from not doing what they want to do, or from feeling suppressed. They often put the needs of others above their own. They are more likely to feel a conflict between work and family roles, and sacrifice their work for their families. Women more commonly define themselves in terms of their relationships more so than men. They are more likely to emphasize emotional fulfillment, rather than just outer success. There are many special powers, qualities and capacities in the woman's nature that should be better developed in society, including a greater honoring of their roles in society.

Women have an innate power and energy in life, starting with the ability to give birth to and nourish the child. This begins with motherhood and child rearing at an outer level but has many inner ramifications, extending to an ability to work with the creative forces of nature, the Earth and the Goddess. This feminine power is called Shakti in yogic thought and is the key to energy, will power and transcendence in the *universe as a whole.*

If that Shakti is lacking or is misplaced, then women can suffer, even if other things in life are going well for them. On the other hand, when that Shakti is properly cultivated, it can overcome all other problems. Counseling women as to the nature of their Shakti and how to use it is central to any Vedic or yogic form of counseling.

Different Goddesses, notably different forms of Shiva's consort, symbolize the cosmic feminine power in transformational ways. She has many names as Kali, Durga, Uma, Parvati, Sundari and Gauri, reflecting her various roles in life and powers in the universe. Women need to learn how to recognize and access their own inherent Shakti and inner Goddess, rather than let themselves be controlled from the outside.

Shakti is executive power or the power of intention, decision and motivation. This leads to the power of administration and management as its expression. Shakti is not necessarily an overt or work power or a force of labor. This power of Shakti begins with a power of receptivity and an ability to nourish. Shakti is the power born of peace, openness and sharing, which has a special capacity for self-renewal. For women, cultivating the power of Shakti is an important tool for dealing with all the issues of life. There are special Shaktis or forms of feminine grace and inspiration in healing, art, Yoga and spirituality.

Developing Shakti in its authentic sense is required to help women deal with their concerns in life. A true Vedic and Yogic counselor should be able to help women clients connect to and develop their own inner Shakti. Yet this often depends upon a positive role model, the influence of a female teacher who has an awakened Shakti and can share it with other women – or with a model of the Divine Feminine energy through the great deities and women gurus of history.

For Men – Developing the Power of Shiva

Shiva is the Vedic and Yogic prototype of higher masculine energy, not simply the image of a good father, leader, brother or friend, but the cosmic masculine force that upholds the universe as a whole and allows our energy to ascend and to expand to the infinite and eternal. Shiva is the counterpart of Shakti. Shiva represents the capacity to hold Shakti. Shakti empowers Shiva and Shiva empowers Shakti.

Men also have their issues of energy and vitality, which increase as they get older. Men have responsibilities and high expectations to meet, whether at an individual level, with friends, family, community or society as a whole. These reflect a certain image of male energy and power in the world. At a deeper level, men have certain spiritual potentials and capacities. Yet to access these requires the right attitudes and actions. These can be defined in Vedic terms as cultivating our Shiva nature, which is the image of Lord Shiva as the great yogi.

Shiva stands for steadiness, stillness, calmness, and composure – the spiritual qualities of the higher male energy. Male energy when spiritualized loses its restless, aggressive, competitive and hotheaded nature. Crude or unrefined male energy, on the other hand, has often been the bane of humanity causing so much war and conflict in the world.

Shiva or the higher masculine force can be different than what our culture emulates as male energy, particularly through its violent action movies and its ruthless executive types. The Shiva being does not work through aggression but is not timid either. Shiva is not reckless but adventurous. The higher masculine force is detached and does not react. It has no buttons that can be pushed. It is cool and calm, not hot headed and unstable. It rejoices in upholding peace and harmony not in disrupting others or causing harm.

Only that Shiva state of mind can hold and develop Shakti as energy. It can carry the most powerful energies because it does not seek to control them but allows them to unfold according to a higher law of consciousness. Shiva has the cool and calm to hold the fire and transformative force of Shakti.

Men today are often confused about their nature. They have a crude aggressive male image on one side, and on the other, a rejection of male energy because of that harsh image. They need to be aware of higher masculine energies such as Lord Shiva typifies. The cosmic masculine energy is the power to protect and uphold dharma or universal law, not the effort to promote oneself or to gain power and prestige in the outer world.

The highest form of the male energy is the great Yogi, such as Lord Shiva represents. Similarly, the highest form of the female energy is the Yogini, such as Shiva's consort Parvati represents. It is these higher goals we should seek in our human relationships. We should remember the image of *Ardhanareshvara*, in which the right half of the body is Shiva and the left half is Shakti, each in its full development but as two sides of the same organic reality. We must learn to give each of these two forces its own place but also recognize their inherent mutuality and complementarity.

Part III

The Practice of Vedic Counseling

Necessary Qualities of a Good Counselor

Knowledge is indeed powerful but its impact is limited if it cannot be conveyed or shared. The purpose of gaining knowledge is to turn it into relevant information that can be received and have an impact on the world. This transduces raw knowledge into effective communication and is the art and science of counseling.

Powerful communication occurs when there is a solid relationship between the speaker and listener. Therefore, developing a clear, sincere, professional and trusting relationship with your client is the foundation necessary to convey the message you need. The role of the Vedic counselor is to be able to communicate on any number of spiritual, psychological or physical topics. The proper relationship is needed to set the stage for these kinds of substantial conversations and to ensure compliance with the subsequent recommendations.

The responsibility for creating this positive environment resides primarily with the counselor. It is up to you to cultivate the skills and qualities necessary to build meaningful communication with your clients. The following attributes are outlined for you as a guide to practice and gain proficiency in Vedic counseling.

Eye Contact

"The eyes are the windows to the soul." This is a timeless phrase we are all familiar with because it is so true. The light in the eyes mirrors the light in the soul. As a counselor, it is important to make eye contact with your patient. Looking intently into their eyes so you can see the deeper, subtler layers of their reality. You may detect a twinge of pain behind their anger, or perhaps a note of guilt when they share their life story. These nuances may never be out rightly revealed by the patient, but can be discerned within the subtle expressions of their eyes.

For the patient, eye contact is equally as valuable. When a counselor maintains steady eye contact with them, they begin to feel their story is genuinely valuable and is worthy of being heard. The patient senses that the counselor is completely present when he maintains eye contact. This sets the foundation for a healing relationship to develop.

Positive, Reinforcing Body Language

Actions really do speak louder than words. As humans we've developed a keen ability to interpret the subtle cues of body language. The way we position our bodies reveals the state of our subconscious mind. It is clear when someone is not interested in a conversation. Their body may be positioned away from the speaker and their eyes may dart around the room, looking for another occupation. Similarly, it is obvious when someone is getting defensive or angry in an interaction. They may hold their hands on their hips or cross their arms defiantly over their chest. Likewise, if someone is ashamed for instance, their head will be looking downward, their back and shoulders will be hunched over and their legs squeezed tightly together. Intuitively we all know what these postures communicate because we evolved to be able to interpret them. Therefore, since body language is such a powerful tool to communicate, it is important the counselor is aware of both his own body language and that of his client's as well.

The counselor's body language must be positive, inclusive and engaging. It needs to reinforce the message that you are invested in your patient's case. Generally, this means keeping your body positioned in the patient's direction with your arms and chest gently open. This communicates a stance of acceptance and tolerance. Similarly, if your patient has just shared something important with you, you may find yourself slightly leaning forward, or gently holding your patient's hand for a moment if they begin to cry. All of these gestures naturally reinforce your dedication to deeply listening and caring for the patient.

Honesty

The patient needs to feel that their counselor is honest. Be honest about who you are and how helpful you can really be. Do not create unrealistic expectations for your patient's progress. Admit to what you can and cannot realistically offer them. In addition, be aware if there is a temptation to make more money off of the client by selling them a product. First of all, this is an ulterior motive that the patient will sense and furthermore, it morality is questionable. Your pure, honest intention to heal the patient must take precedence over any agenda of your own. If not, trust will immediately be broken. Your client will see that your personal motives are top priority instead of the progress of their healing.

Most importantly, look deeply within yourself to make sure your intentions for practicing Vedic counseling are honest. This is the fundamental quality to any moral, ethical and healing relationship. It is an absolute necessity in upholding the integrity of both professional and personal relations.

Sincerity

The counselor must find in their heart the energy and capacity to cultivate sincerity in each and every interaction with their patients. This means that as a counselor you are not just showing up for work and mechanically doing your job; instead you are putting your heart into it. When you do this, you are naturally investing in the success of your patients. You begin to truly care for their well-being, much as you would for a dear, old friend. Your patients will feel your sincerity and take comfort in your genuine care.

Compassion

Look upon others with a feeling of commonality. Having experienced yourself the many difficulties inherent in human life, you can appreciate the context around your patient's trials and tribulations. Each person comes to the table with a unique story and set of life circumstances and karmas. Knowing their history and where they are coming from is the doorway to compassion. Having compassion means to be in a state of non-blaming and non-judgment. Naturally, this feeling cultivates forgiveness and mercy. With compassion you are never looking down upon anyone, but rather seeing each person as a counterpart of your own self. Compassion it is a powerful sentiment that your patients will feel emanating from you. They know when you have authentic concern and empathy for their sufferings and misfortunes. They can sense when, instead of casting judgment upon them, they are viewed with the tenderness of compassion.

Trust

The patient needs to be able to trust in the character of their counselor. A new patient rightfully may want to know whether or not their counselor upholds high moral and ethical standards in their practice. They also need to know that their practitioner is reliable and won't leave them stranded when they're in need. Simply by virtue of maintaining a consistent, competent, and honest character, you can build trust with your client. It is your job as a counselor to ensure the patient in every possible way that you are a person of high integrity in whom they may confidently place their trust.

Faith

When patients come to you for help because they are lost or ill, they are making themselves vulnerable. They are acknowledging that they can't do it all themselves and need guidance and support from you. This means that they are placing their faith in you to lead them toward higher well-being. To uphold this faith, it is important that the counselor likewise, have faith in his patient. The patient needs to feel that someone believes in him and knows that it is possible for him to heal. When this happens, the counselor's faith in his patient is able to transform into the patient's faith in himself. One faith supports the other, and the end result is a self-perpetuating positive, hopeful, and healing outlook.

ACTIVE LISTENING

Listen with an open mind and heart. Do not interrupt or become impatient even if the client may be scattered. Instead, engage the client with active listening. Active listening means making a conscious effort to make sure you've thoroughly understood what your patient is telling you. It can help both you and your patient to stay focused on what is most important. Ways to do this are by vocally re-stating (paraphrasing) what you, as the listener, think you've just heard. This way the speaker can confirm or deny that you've correctly understood their point of view. By default, this process also allows you to gain clarity on any information that you may have misunderstood. In the same way, it provides an opportunity to probe deeper into the patient's experience. Furthermore, when the patient hears his own sentiments reflected back to him by another person, he is sometimes able to gain a new perspective on his own story. Overall, the end result is that the patient feels validated and affirmed when he hears the counselor articulate his story and listen deeply and actively.

NON-JUDGMENT

Do not judge or condemn. Instead, take a moment to observe and bear witness to what is really going on in the context of your client's life. Whenever judgment is present we cannot see a person in their true, spiritual nature. We are unable to offer them compassion because we do not stop to understand where they could be coming from. Our judgment clouds the truth. In judgement, we only feel criticism and an equally false sense of superiority. We begin to see things as divided - one thing as "good" and the other as "bad." When judgment is present, whatever the mind deems as "bad" is interpreted to be repulsive, disgusting, shameful and less-than. For instance, if judgment is present because you personally subscribe to a vegetarian diet and your client does not, you may find his choice to eat meat revolting. Yet if compassion is at the root of your approach, you will patiently remember that it is not your place to venomously impose your personal values upon your patient. If a vegetarian diet is indicated for your client's health however, you could professionally recommend it without the presence of your personal judgment tainting your suggestion. There is a difference in offering guidance from a place of understanding than from a place of judgment. It is your job as the counselor to check yourself to make sure you are coming from the right place.

Positive and Confident Demeanor

As the counselor, you take on a role of authority. The patient is coming to you for advice on whatever ails them. You must rest assured in the value and efficacy of the advice you offer your client. When you speak with a tone of confidence and relay a positive attitude, you bestow upon the patient the gift of hope. Continually instill your confidence in their recovery by reassuring them about their progress. If your patient is struggling with negative thinking, it is your job to be a beacon of light. They will need encouragement and acknowledgement for even the smallest improvements that they have made. With this confirmation, they will feel better about themselves and their progress. They'll be able to relax because they know you are at the helm, so to speak, and they are optimistic about the direction you're headed with them on board.

Confidentiality

Maintaining confidentiality is crucial to uphold the professional dynamic between counselor and patient. Confidentiality means keeping all interaction with your clients private, except if there is a need to share information with other professionals. If confidentiality is broken, there is a breach between personal and professional relations, which is unethical. When a patient shares their personal story, they are only sharing it with you – not your spouse, neighbors or colleagues. They need to be able to trust that talking with you is a safe space to open up about the vulnerable condition of their mind, body or spirit. By sharing their personal and private details with you, your patient places their trust in you as their confidante. Upholding confidentiality then, is a cornerstone to any professional, ethical and healing relationship.

Empathy

When we are sincerely engaged and listening compassionately to a patient, the feeling of empathy naturally arises. Empathy is the ability to share in the emotions of another as if they were your own. When you listen empathetically to your patient you "put yourself in their shoes" and can feel what they feel. There is a fine line however, between being empathic and being co-dependent. While it is possible to have empathy for your patient's experiences, and even feel the pain of their suffering, it is important to remember not to take that on as your own burden. Their journey is something only they can ultimately take responsibility for in their own way. Maintaining this boundary is professionally necessary so that the practitioner does not "burn out." Along with the proper mindfulness however, it can be a beautiful and intimate phenomenon which allows your heart to open and really connect with the experience of another human being. Then, seeing how fully you understand and how deeply you care, your client's trust in you will grow.

Tang

TANG stands for Therapeutic Affirmative Noises and Grunts. These are non-verbal sounds made to let your client know that you are listening while they are speaking. Without needing to interrupt the client and say anything, the counselor can make slight sounds that affirm that he or she is actively listening. Even the smallest affirmative noise can encourage the client to continue along their line of thinking to further express themselves. Using TANG is an effective way to tell your client that you really care about what they are saying.

Knowledge

A patient comes to you because they believe that your knowledge and background can help them. They are seeking to be assisted by virtue of the insight you can offer. Therefore, your education must be adequate for the service you are providing and for the knowledge that you are expected to offer. If your knowledge falls short in certain areas, it is your responsibility to honestly concede and refer your patient elsewhere. In the case that your knowledge is sufficient however, you may explain your understanding to the patient in a manner that is accessible to them.

Also, all practitioners need continuing education no matter how knowledgeable they may be. Take advantage of the many opportunities to acquire new information. There are countless workshops, seminars and classes at your disposal through the Internet or in person. It is important for you to have the latest information on the different issues that your client presents. This may require significant research or further investigation on your part, but it is your duty as a clinician to never stop learning.

Deep Understanding

As a Vedic counselor, your primary aim should be to fully understand your patient as a whole being so that you can best determine the pathogenesis and prognosis of their disease. Develop a sense of the physical, psychological and spiritual nature of the person. To do this, you must accurately assess your patient's *physical and mental constitution,* as well as their *quality of awareness.* From this vantage point, you will know what your patient's inherent tendencies are and which course of treatment will be most tolerable and suitable. It is equally important to gain a detailed understanding of their day-to-day lives to figure out what behavior or environmental factors may have contributed to their illness. In short, only with a thorough assessment and deep understanding can the root cause of disease be identified and the correct treatment administered.

Communication

When addressing your patient, you must use language in which a mutual, clear and concise understanding can arise. Without mutual understanding, true communication is not possible. Miscommunication occurs when one person interprets the other person's words to mean something different than what they are intending. Sometimes assumptions are made and great misunderstandings with serious consequences can arise. To avoid this, it is important that the counselor speak clearly and logically. Be explicit in your recommendations to make sure that you and your patient are on the same page. Then, do not be afraid to ask your patient if they are following you, or check to make sure they have grasped what you're meaning.

Communicate with your patient in a simple, practical language that can be easily understood. Use language that is appropriate for your patient's age range, cultural and educational background. When a common lingo is used between patient and counselor, understanding is inherent behind the words and miscommunication is less likely to occur. It is also important for the counselor to make sure that he or she understands their patient well. Cultivate active listening in order to confirm and summarize the points your patient makes. Take time to listen with your full attention, looking into your patient's eyes and noticing their body language. All of these things will help ensure that you are accurately interpreting what your client is saying. It should be top priority for counselor and patient to develop mutual and positive communication with one another.

Patience

As a counselor, your training allows you to determine the best possible route for your client to heal themselves. Many times however, they are not able to fully or promptly follow your direction. The time you feel would be reasonable for your client to achieve certain milestones may be quite different from the reality. The fact is that they may have only been able to accomplish one half or one quarter of what you initially recommended. The bottom line is that your agenda and timeline for the client's success needs to come second to the pace they set and the things they're actually able to accomplish. This requires patience on the part of the counselor. It can be frustrating to see potential that is not realized due to lack of compliance. Try adopting a step-by-step approach, not looking too far ahead, like traveling on a long journey.

If we remember to breathe into a space of compassion, patience can be cultivated. When the presence of patience is with you, there is an acceptance of the situation as it is that naturally happens. No longer do you need to rush the client along their journey towards better health, and you don't have to regret that they haven't accomplished something either. As a result, your clients can see that you have patience with their imperfections. They will appreciate your willingness to meet them without judgment, exactly where they are at, and to help them move forward from that point with clarity and consistency.

Discipline

Be capable of providing clear guidelines and do not allow deviation from the primary principals of your patient's treatment. Sometimes, when compliance to recommendations is faulty, a certain level of disciplinary action is needed to motivate the patient to make better choices. Discipline in this sense, is referring to the tactic which will work to instill drive and will power into mind of the patient from within theirself To find the right discipline, you must work within the parameters of your patient's psychological and physical constitution.

For instance, someone with a Vata or airy constitution according to Ayurveda, may need a gentle but firm boundary drawn in order to activate their own discipline. This can actually feel soothing to a Vata person because they are given a container to encompass their erratic energy. A Pitta or fiery person, may develop discipline if a solid goal is laid out before them and a reward for its accomplishment is clearly in sight. Pitta people are naturally more goal-oriented, so this line of discipline works well with their constitutional proclivity. A Kapha or watery type, may need to find their motivation and discipline through being reminded of the consequences of *not* following the recommendation. This type of person needs extra reason to drive his more sluggish energy into action. All in all, it is the job of the counselor is to find the right tactic that will best inspire their client to follow through with their own treatment plan.

Prioritization

As a trained Vedic counselor it is easy to see all the many treatment modalities that could help a patient who comes to you in need. It is impossible, however, to give each person every single remedy that could help them. If given all options, the patient would undoubtedly become overwhelmed. There needs to be a process of prioritization in order to choose the right modality to address the person's chief complaint. Although many therapies might be helpful to the patient, there are usually a few that would make the most marked and immediate impact on the patient's condition. With only a few items to focus on, the patient is more likely to succeed and see results.

First, the practitioner should address the primary issues – these are the far reaching, most detrimental problems that have the strongest deleterious effect on the patient. They are often connected to the root cause of the imbalance and must therefore be the first to be managed. Following this, the secondary issues can be addressed. Usually these are the symptoms that stem from the greater source of the problem.

In order to select which medicine is most appropriate for which person, the counselor must take into account their patient's family, work, social and private life. They must determine which causes of disease precipitated their illness and thus, which form of treatment is most indicated. On top of this, there needs to be consideration for the person's biological and psychological makeup, as well as a review of their mental strength. This way the treatment selected will be appropriate for the person's physical and mental stamina and will address the root cause of their disease.

Experience

The practitioner needs to develop experience in their field. Nothing is more valuable than practical experience correctly informing prescription. What you witness in clinical practice will give you anecdotal evidence about what really works and what doesn't. While a certain medicine may theoretically meet your client's needs, your practical experience may tell you otherwise. Over time, you begin to have confidence in particular therapies because of how you've seen them work in your patients. Plus, when you witness healing based on what you recommend, you become more self-assured which gives you a stronger healing presence for your patients.

Another type of necessary experience to have as a Vedic counselor is that of personally living a Vedic life. Practicing what you preach is key here. When we have experienced the difficulties that come with implementing lifestyle, dietary, spiritual or behavioral changes, we can offer empathy as well as practical advice to our patients.

Professional Clinical Practice

If a Vedic counselor is to practice clinically, she must adopt a professional mentality. She will need to begin to treat her services as a professional occupation rather than a side hobby or pastime. This entails abiding by all legal, moral and ethical standards for a professional business in the field of health care. Proper boundaries and responsibilities include: getting a business license, filing taxes, managing finances, honoring scope of practice, protecting patient confidentiality, wearing professional attire, communicating with professional demeanor and setting up an office where your certifications are visible.

Furthermore, the operation of the business itself is a reflection of the professional character of the owner. If a counselor's staff is treated with fairness and respect and her finances are stable and office is well kept, it is clear that she is responsible and takes her business seriously. She also is more likely to have a good, professional reputation in the community. Her patients can be reassured in the competency of their practitioner's business operation and from there, a sense of trust and security are developed.

Note Taking

In a professional practice it is legally and practically important to take good notes. For the counselor, it gives a trail to follow, so that you can refer back to your client's history. You can see how they responded to certain treatments, how their condition has changed or improved, and what you recommended to them in the past. Clearly this is needed to catch you up to speed on their progress and to inform you on the direction of your current visit.

Sometimes it is even valuable to encourage the client to keep a diary of their own that reflects their interaction with you. This allows them to have a written reminder of the things they learned during their visit, as well as any benefits they may have gleamed from their treatments.

The legal component of note taking is crucial. As a health care provider, you must have meticulous records of your client's complaints, your resulting recommendations, and their responses to treatment. Without this, you could potentially become legally liable for something outside of your range of responsibility. In other words, proper and detailed note taking serves as insurance for the integrity of your health care practice.

Timing

When someone comes to see you, they are committing their time, energy and money to working with you. It is your responsibility then, to put forth an equal effort to make yourself fully available to them. If they arrive to your office and see that you are in a great hurry because you are running late, they will feel rushed and on edge themselves. Your agitation will disturb the connection you are able to make with the patient because they will see that you are not able to be fully present with them. It is pivotal to accept the necessity of time for healing. You cannot squeeze a meaningful, healing conversation into five minutes, so you must allow ample time for each patient to be truly seen and heard. To do this, make sure that your schedule is not overbooked. Every patient is a priority and the way you manage your time should reflect that belief.

Leadership

In the counseling relationship, there needs to be a healthy appreciation of the dynamic between the patient and counselor. The patient is there to receive the guidance and wisdom of the counselor. The counselor is there to bestow their knowledge and assistance upon the patient. This means that the counselor needs to clearly establish himself in this role. He can do this by making sure that he is the one directing the trajectory of the conversation and treatment, and not his patient.

Sometimes when first beginning to practice counseling, it is easy for the counselor to let go of authority and mistakenly allow the patient to direct them. When this happens the therapeutic relationship becomes tainted because there is an inappropriate role reversal. Instead, it is up to the counselor to step confidently into his stance of leadership and assume responsibility for directing the course of conversation.

Observation

Fully tap into your senses when observing your patient. By doing this, you will begin to look at everything comprehensively and see your patient as a dynamic, living being, communicating to you in every way. To cultivate this skill, try tuning into what your senses of sight, hearing, smell and touch reveal to you.

When you shake your patient's hand, is it cold or hot? Maybe you notice they have an odor that could indicate the presence of toxins, or perhaps you see in their face that they are exhausted and defeated. Notice how the person walks. Is their gait quick and erratic, or slow and soft? Do they hold themselves with confidence and pride or insecurity and shame? Then, listen to the sound of their voice. Is it high pitched and fast, or low and slow? All of these observations will grant you valuable information about the nature of your client, and their current status of health. So learn to keenly observe with your senses and you will find a whole new way of seeing your patient.

Tools

Ayurvedic treatments are designed to empower the patient. Ayurveda has an inherent trust that the patient will return home to their private lives and by the force of their own self-discipline, implement the recommendations properly prescribed to them. Some people, however, need help in order to break a cycle of pain or negative emotion. Their body and mind may not be in a state to embrace the necessary behavioral modifications. In this case, it is valuable to have tools at your disposal that you can use to directly intervene and arrest a pattern of dysfunction in its tracks.

Therapies like bodywork, acupuncture, aromatherapy, energetic healing or massage, all engage the healing power of the senses. Pleasurable sensory information like the feeling of a warm, herb-infused massage oil on the skin, release chemicals that are natural pain relievers and mood enhancers. When the senses are stimulated the mind can sink into the body and become grounded, making it less fearful of the future or angry about the past. These tactics can help reconstruct a foundation of strength for your patient so that they can eventually independently implement their own healing regimen at home.

Encouragement

Sometimes the road to healing is arduous. It can be painstakingly difficult to change long held habits and beliefs. Making dietary, lifestyle, spiritual and psychological changes puts the patient at their growing edge. At any opportunity, therefore, it is important to give the patient praise for their efforts and progress. If the grand scheme of things seems daunting and unachievable to your client, point out the little wins and successes they've accomplished along the way.

However slight they may be, minor changes like a more positive attitude, an increased awareness in the body, or the adoption of a one minute meditation practice, all deserve to be applauded. Your client should be commended because they're doing their best to eliminate the cause of their suffering instead of taking a pill to cover up their symptoms. The latter option is far easier and more common in our society, but your patient is choosing to take the road less traveled when they work with you. They are therefore, well deserving of praise, encouragement and your absolute faith in their abilities.

Ethical Principals and Morals

As a Vedic counselor, you must have a strong moral and ethical orientation. Having a foundation in moral principles will positively influence all areas of your professional and personal life. A good example of an ancient system of such higher values is the *Yamas* and *Niyamas* of Yoga. These guidelines are pillars of strength you can lean on when faced with any moral or ethical dilemma.

Spiritual Practice

"Walking the talk" is of the utmost importance in Vedic counseling. In order to be a channel for healing wisdom, you yourself must practice its discipline. Developing a spiritual *sadhana*, or practice, is essential to the continual development of your mind, body and Spirit. To use Vedic counseling with grace, your mind must be aligned with Spirit so that you can genuinely offer compassion, sincerity, patience and hope to all those you work with.

In addition, morally, it would be irresponsible for you to ask your patient to practice proper dietary, lifestyle or spiritual regimes if you did not yourself. You cannot counsel others to do what you yourself are unwilling to do. Plus, your patients assume and trust that you're recommending these things because you have personal experience with them and know they work. To them, you are a role model and it is your duty to live an exemplary life.

Intuition

Part of Vedic counseling is reading between the lines and momentarily letting go of the mind's interpretation and ongoing analysis. Intuition is the ability to perceive something immediately, without the need for conscious reasoning. It is a phenomenon that lies outside of logic and evidence, and is based on instinctive feelings, or "hits" about what is really going on. The skilled practitioner knows to listen in the moments of silence and allow her intuition to come forward. Here she is not relying on external information to get feedback, but rather, she is referring to the inner voice of her intuition.

The practice of meditation heightens internal awareness and teaches the practitioner to tune into subtle energies. When the counselor has a connection with her spiritual Self, she can become a channel for the energy of *Atman*. This allows her to see the heart of the client and their inner potential as a divine being. Clearly, the wisdom that emerges from this space is priceless and invaluable to the progress of healing.

It takes a lifetime of learning to master all of these qualities. However, if you focus first and foremost on the components of spiritual evolution, compassion, deep listening and sincerity, you will bring your practice and your life to a new level. Your interactions with clients will be warm and heartfelt and you will enjoy the process of counseling more than ever before.

Lastly, there is a flow and rhythm to the art of counseling. Without the proper sequencing of events, a consultation can easily feel disjointed, awkward, or choppy. Following this discussion there is a reference table outlining the nine practical steps you need to ensure a smooth and successful counseling experience.

1 | Meet & Greet

Respectfully and warmly introduce yourself. Make your client feel comfortable in your presence. You may like to offer them a glass of warm water or tea, and ask if they need to use the restroom before you begin your work together. Overall, make your first conversation with your patient lighthearted. Avoid immediately speaking about their health concern or why they made an appointment to see you. Instead, ask them about their travel to your office, the weather, or some other topic that is not too serious.

2 | Observe

All the while, clearly observe your client. Tap into their auric field and use your senses to keenly gather information. Are they healthy or unhealthy? Where is their energy currently? Notice their gait, physical stature and posture, facial expressions, tone of voice, etc.

3 | Investigate

At this point, you and your client should be comfortably settled. Now it is time to go over their paperwork and ask more questions to probe deeper into the cause of their imbalance. Look through their history and listen fully and attentively to their story. What sorts of concerns have they suffered from in the past? What is the timeline of major events in their life? Find out what could have precipitated their illness.

4 | Situate

Next, situate your client within the larger context of their lives by using Jyotish, Vedic astrology. With the help of your client's natal chart, you'll be able to determine the backdrop to their life. By looking at their planetary periods, current life transits, and the strength of their planets, you'll see what is coloring and animating their life experience. You also may be able to see why they're dealing with the crisis they're in and when they'll most likely be able to recover.

5 | Examine

If you are an Ayurvedic Practitioner, at this point you may take the opportunity to feel your client's pulse. Begin by closing your eyes and saying a silent prayer or mantra before you proceed. You may ask your client to close their eyes, so that you both can be in mindful concentration during the assessment. After taking your notes on the pulse, kindly ask your client to expose their tongue for another diagnostic exam. Once that is complete, it is time for the collection of objective data on the client's vitals: height, weight, respiratory rate, and blood pressure. Finally, conclude with a physical exam. Palpate any organs that are of concern and look at areas on the body that may be swollen, tender or uncomfortable.

6 | Conclude

By this time you should have a clear idea about your client's physical and psychological nature, as well as their disease and mental strength. Naturally then, the pathogenesis behind your patient's main complaint should also be evident. With this information combined, you'll be able to formulate a treatment plan that will be most effective for your client's unique needs.

7 | Explain

In plain, clear words explain your findings to your patient in a way that they can easily understand. Relay your conclusions about their condition and why you think they are suffering. Then, lay out the details and timeline of the treatment plan you suggest they undergo in order to restore their sense of well-being.

8 | Counsel

Now, zoom out and give your patient a view of the grand scheme of things. This often entails reflecting to them the psycho-spiritual components of their disease and healing processes. Then, gently lead them into a mindfulness technique that they can follow during the duration of your work together.

9 | Inspire

Leave your patient with words of encouragement and inspiration. They should know that you have faith in their ability to succeed. Schedule a follow up and remind them that you'll be there for them in between visits should anything urgent arise. In this way, your patient can feel secure knowing that you're available and ready to help. Finally, end the consultation on a high note so your patient leaves motivated to reclaim their health.

The Unique Orientation of Vedic Counseling

Vedic knowledge provides a complete guide to right living and higher awareness. Vedic counseling shows us how to achieve this for both the individual and the society. Vedic life counseling teaches us how to live and think in harmony with nature, science and consciousness. Its goal is the full integration of the individual with all humanity, nature and the Divine.

Vedic counseling is a special and extraordinary form of counseling that is yogic in nature and links us to cosmic knowledge. The practice of Vedic counseling does not just consist of suggesting helpful ideas or strategies for the client; it requires the counselor bring in a higher wisdom and energy. This requires first that the counselor is able to personally connect to the Cosmic Mind through the power of meditation and mantra.

The Vedic counselor needs to consider the individual overall, not simply as a physical being but as a Divine soul or center of universal consciousness. This has several steps.

Jivatman	Ascertain the Individual Nature and Karma as a Soul	This requires deep insight and can take a great deal of time and interaction to determine. The astrological chart can be particularly helpful.
Manasika Prakriti	Determine the nature of the individual mind	This requires psychological knowledge based upon Yoga and Vedanta, including the three gunas of sattva, rajas and tamas.
Sharirika Prakriti	Determine the nature of the body and its energy	This is mainly an Ayurvedic consideration, through the doshas or biological humors and their correlations.

Integrative Counseling

The Vedic life counseling model takes an integrated approach looking at the entire being of body, mind and consciousness. It examines the whole of life, rather than one part only. It is not simply career counseling, health consultations or pain management. Vedic counseling integrates several levels of guidance, with Ayurveda for healing, Yoga for awareness and Vedic astrology for karma.

Vedic counseling looks at the individual in the context of their greater relationships and is not limited to the person only. Vedic counseling aims at maximum integration with humanity, nature, and the universal consciousness. Our inner fragmentation is the root of our problems in life, through which we lose consistency and fall into confusion. Greater consciousness brings in greater wholeness and consistency into all that we do.

◈	Integrating body, mind and consciousness at an individual level
◈	Integrating individual, family and community at a collective level
◈	Integrating humanity, nature and the Divine at a cosmic level

Vedic knowledge provides us with a model of the integral human being and eternal human soul, with the three bodies, five sheaths and seven chakras, which we will address as our discussion proceeds.

Requirements of a Vedic Counselor

A Vedic counselor has a high level of requirements and must be on a continual journey of self-discovery. He should follow a Vedic life-style and a life of Yoga, meditation, non-violence, and compassion for all. He must have a good knowledge of the Vedic teachings, as well as good counseling skills. A Vedic life-style rests upon a Vedic view of life and the adaptation of Vedic values. It involves promoting Vedic life-enhancement practices and being connected to Vedic communities.

Vedic counseling is a "master discipline" that requires knowledge of the several related branches of Vedic knowledge, Yoga, counseling and healing. A Vedic counselor we could say is a "doctor for the soul." Generally one should have at least three years of study and practice to begin to function as a qualified Vedic counselor. Yet the insights of Vedic counseling begin at a simple level of self-help and can be made relevant to everyone.

Vedic Counseling and the Role of the Guru

The Vedic counselor is a life-style guru, not simply an expert in one field or another. But he should remain first of all a teacher and not become an object of worship or transference. He or she should provide right guidance without breeding dependency. His goal is to aid in the conscious movement of life, not to become the focus of attention himself. A Vedic counselor should be a spiritual friend and well-wisher. There should be no efforts to influence, control or dominate in Vedic counseling. The process is open and voluntary and should be done with grace and respect, allowing the client the space and the freedom to respond. The Vedic counselor will never interfere with the life or decisions of the client, but aim at providing helpful knowledge and practices, giving the client the space and time to adapt these in an individually meaningful manner.

Creating Sacred Time and Space

Vedic counseling helps us develop sacred space and time as the matrix of transformation and transcendence. This is the basis of Vedic astrology and Vastu, as the Vedic sciences of time and the directions of space. Right orientation to the planets in time and to the directions in space can allow us to access higher currents of energy and awareness.

We need to learn the art of creating sacred time and space. This is part of the practice of Vedic rituals and empowerments. Once sacred time and space are created unexpected transformations, if not miracles can occur. Sacred space requires an awareness and an intention in order to develop it. One must dedicate a certain portion of the home to it, and sanctify it with mantras, rituals and sacred objects. Sacred space arises when we are no longer defining space by the mind and can enter into the deeper space of the heart.

For counseling to truly work, the factor of time must be well understood. Healing occurs in sacred time, which is not chronological time or the counting of the clock. It is a qualitative time that arises when we are attentive in the present moment without distraction. To enter into sacred time, we must be willing to forget the outer chronological time, which also means to let go of our past

Determining Vedic Typologies

A counselor, like a doctor, requires an appropriate system of diagnosis in order to adequately ascertain the nature of imbalances. Most counselors today follow a psychological approach and use emotional terms such as stress management, anger management or countering depressing.

Any system of diagnosis is a reflection of a system of medicine and a view of the human being. Vedic diagnosis reflects Vedic systems of knowledge, healing and spirituality. These provide us with clear delineations to work with. Vedic systems provide several very well defined individual typologies, and a differentiation of disease syndromes for body and mind based upon them. The essence of any counseling process consists of determining the unique nature, energetics and aptitude of the individual human being. Each person is different both in inherent capacities and in their place in the cycle of time. Without understanding the uniqueness of each person, we cannot help them in a fundamental manner.

Vedic thought provides us with more important systems of typology for determining individual constitution and stage of development than any counseling system available. These typologies occur on several levels and in several disciplines and afford us with important tools of diagnosis and treatment measures.

Vedic typologies begin with three primary determinative factors of doshas, gunas and karmas that all Vedic counselors should learn. We will explain these in detail as the book proceeds.

◈	Three doshas of Vata, Pitta and Kapha or biological humors for the body
◈	Three gunas of sattva, rajas and tamas for the mind.
◈	Karmas for the soul or inner consciousness.

These three factors overlap extensively and should be looked at as a whole. In addition there are other Vedic typologies, particularly through Vedic astrology that we will outline later. Considerations are always two-fold in diagnosis – aiming to determining both the individual energetic type (Prakriti) and its current disease imbalances or pathologies (Vikriti).

Vedic Counseling Assessments

All counseling results in certain assessments of the client, both in terms of their nature and imbalances. Vedic typologies are part of the assessment of the person, but are more than any ordinary assessment. They cover all aspects of our nature. An assessment is a diagnosis, as it were, but is not strictly medical or disease oriented in regard to the factors that it is concerned with.

The Vedic approach begins with a general assessment of the person, including the reasons why they have sought counseling guidance, the specific issues they may have, and what may be hidden at a yet deeper level. Assessments include physical, psychological and spiritual factors. These are rooted in an assessment of the dharma of the person and of their karma, such as discussed earlier. They can include extensive forms of physical and psychological examination and diagnosis.

Vedic Counseling Therapies

Any assessment or diagnosis leads to certain recommendations or treatment measures and the prescription of various Vedic tools, methods, or life-style changes. These begin with new ways of learning and a deeper seeking of Self-knowledge, particularly through mantra and meditation. Vedic tools of healing reflect the different branches of Vedic knowledge and the different approaches of Vedic healing.

Ayurveda	Ayurveda has a broad range of physical treatment recommendations that begin on a life-style level with dietary factors and life-styles issues, including daily and seasonal health regimens. It extends to herbs, massage, special detoxification methods of Pancha Karma, and special rejuvenative or Rasayana measures.
Yoga	Yoga provides a broad range of Yogic approaches, Asana, pranayama, mantra and meditation for body, mind and consciousness.
Vedic Astrology {Jyotish}	Vedic astrology is based upon a detailed and systematic study of the birth chart, karmas and planetary periods, possible recommendations of ritualistic, yogic or Ayurvedic methods.
Vedic directional science {Vastu}	Vastu is the study of directional influences in the house, workplace and sacred space, with recommendations to improve these in a transformational manner for our well-being.

Counseling Approaches and Strategies

A good counselor needs to have a number of strategies for counseling. The same method or approach will not work on every client or for every session of the same client. Have many tools in your practice but at the same time remember that a good rapport is necessary for any specific recommendations. There are a few types of strategies listed below that can help.

Get in the Door Strategy

Start with whatever aspect of life or a particular problem that the client may be open to addressing. Some people may be more open to working on diet, others on exercise, and perhaps others on meditation. Find out from the client where they would most like to start to work on themselves. Yet try to inspire the client, not intimidate them.

Address the Chief Complaint or Main Problem in Life

Address what is most bothering the client at the present moment, as they define it, but use that issue in order to go deeper into the causes of the problem. You may focus on the particular disease or disharmony the client may have. Most clients will have a "chief compliant" or primary problem, an acute condition that needs to be addressed first or they will not be open to looking at other issues.

Provide an Overall Life Examination

Do an overall examination of the life of the person, the different aspects of their life and nature, and the various problems they may have. This is like a doctor doing an overall physical for a patient. It can include a general study of the life of the person. It can examine prime Vedic typologies like doshas and gunas and provide general life-style guidance and recommendations.

Specific Counseling Issues

There are a few topical issues to address in all counseling concerns and Vedic views.

Generally people come in for counseling when they have pain, suffering or problems to deal with; only a few will come in for general guidance or life improvement, though we can orient everyone in that direction as well. These types of suffering will usually concern physical or psychological issues, work or relationship concerns.

Dealing with the Complications of Physical Diseases

People come in for counseling when they are feeling unwell. This often occurs when the usual disease treatments are not working or if the disease is slow to resolve itself, as in the case of many chronic conditions. Whereas counseling usually addresses more life-style or psychological issues, physical concerns are always there, particularly given the Ayurvedic component of Vedic counseling.

The counselor should seek to determine how much the physical problem is rooted in physical, psychological or spiritual issues. Sometimes psychological problems may be rooted in physical problems, like low vitality or inadequate sleep that disturbs the mind. The physical problem should never be looked at in isolation from the whole person.

Dealing with Psychological Pain and Depression

Counseling is mainly a psychological tool resorted to for dealing with common psychological problems. It is best to start with counseling rather than medications in dealing with psychological issues, though each case must be examined carefully. Most of our problems are rooted in wrong attitudes and behavior that can be changed through counseling, not merely through medication.

Depression is a symptom, not necessarily a disease in its own right, and reflects low mental or vital energy. The counselor should not simply seek to end the state of depression for the patient but determine its cause. The cause may be a need to change in life, like a change of career to something to make the life more engaging and creative.

Pain is also a symptom and one must understand what the pain is indicating in terms of potential deeper imbalances. Pain may be telling us that we need to change our work, diet or exercise patterns. Taking a pain killer and continuing on as we have been is only avoiding the problem.

Getting to the Root of the Problem

One must always get the client to examine what is actually making them unwell or unhappy. Sometimes there are deeper problems behind the outer problems that the client wants to address. Someone, for example, may be wanting some career counseling, but there may be deeper emotional issues or lack of spiritual focus in life. We must always be willing to look deeper. Counseling involves a lot of unraveling and moving to progressively deeper layers.

Dealing with Trauma and Abuse

When there are significant deep-seated problems and negative karmas, one must take a very slow, gentle and compassionate approach. Abuse of various kinds occurs in the life of most people, and most people can be abusive to others at one time or another. But this is much worse in the case of children. Violence greatly disturbs the psyche and takes great effort and patience to remove. There are many kinds of post-traumatic stress disorders. Getting the client to live in the present is very important, which means being willing to let go of negative memories.

Dealing with Addictions

In the case of addictions, one need not challenge the addiction directly, label or condemn it. All addictions reflect a lack of control of the mind, which may rest upon poor education, difficult upbringing, or trauma. The important thing is to help build a new life-style, habits, interests and desires in the client, including awakening a higher aspiration towards spiritual growth.

Relationship Issues

When relationship issues exist it is better to work with both partners if possible - first separately and then together. Conflict resolution is best done with both parties together. Relationship issues create the strongest emotions and require a building of trust and confidence. The counselor should not be perceived as partial to one party or another in the relationship situation, and must act with detachment and compassion.

Work Issues

Work issues usually reflect deeper issues of dharma, as well as how to adjust to our changing workplace, including the stresses that can arise between different people in the work place. If a person is not happy at work, all of life is affected, extending to health and relationships. The counselor should make sure that each person knows his or her dharma.

Spiritual Issues

These usually rest upon first knowing ones higher capacities. It is not just a matter of choosing a guru or technique. Counselors need to respect any spiritual path that a person may already be following and not interfere. If we do not have a spiritual path in life we will likely suffer from psychological problems and make wrong decisions or get lost in lesser goals. Establishing a spiritual goal in life is one of the main foundation principles of Vedic counseling.

Regular Counseling

A true Vedic counselor is a guide and friend for all issues of life for the long term. To have such a guide for regular consultancy in life is very important. Do not go from counselor to counselor but seek to deepen your relationship with any good Vedic counselor you may meet. Weekly sessions for a period of several months may be necessary.

Do Not Try to Do Too Much too quickly

The counselor should be willing to take time and not hurry the client. First get to know them and let them reveal to you what it is that is behind their outer personality. Do not recommend too many things for the client to do. Set in motion a long term learning process and go from one key point to another. If the person is in a state of uncertainty, panic or confusion, first develop patience and peace in dealing with them.

Recommending Specific Vedic Disciplines

From general counseling approaches you may need to direct the client to specific Vedic counseling methods, techniques or treatments. This can be determined either owing to the receptivity of the client or according to what is best for their case and condition. If a client has a special interest in one of the other Vedic disciplines that is a good sign to bring it into the dialogue.

Generally, we move from overall Vedic counseling first to Ayurveda for right orientation of health and well-being for body and mind, then to Yoga for deeper spiritual practices. Vedic astrology is important for long term karmic indications and background orientation. Vastu has its place in providing a right foundation in which Vedic practices can work. These come in at a secondary level.

Specific Concerns for Different Vedic Disciplines

Each Vedic discipline has its special counseling issues that are best addressed by more specific books in these fields. Below we have indicated a few important points.

Yoga Strategies

Start where the client is receptive, from asana to meditation, but emphasize a yogic and Vedic life-style to support the practice such as explained in the yamas and niyamas. Define Yoga for the client as an inner state of peace, not the performance of complicated asanas.

Make sure that the patient is physically and emotionally grounded before suggesting subtle meditation or energy techniques. Aim at harmony and well-being in our ordinary state of consciousness before seeking to go beyond that.

Help promote and sustain a regular Yoga practice or sadhana for the person, however simple. Recommend regular Yoga classes but combined with regular one-to-one consultations with a Vedic counselor on deeper issues, along with ones daily practice. Emphasize daily pranayama for developing the inner power to heal. Emphasize daily meditation to relax and balance the mind. Recommend time alone or in nature contemplating the universal powers. Do not turn Yoga just into a practice but encourage study and contemplation of Yoga philosophy as well.

AYURVEDIC STRATEGIES

Address any acute issues that may be there in the person causing pain. If these require recommending the person to a more advanced practitioner or doctor, please do not hesitate to do so. Do not attempt any treatment beyond your capacity and experience, particularly if fever, inflammation or bleeding is involved.

Deal with Vata dosha imbalances first as it is the most disturbing overall, particularly at a psychological level. Vata disturbs the nervous, digestion, sleep and emotions in a fundamental manner. If Vata is agitated even at a superficial level, one cannot go deeper in the treatment, as the person will be distracted and disturbed.

Correct and balance the digestion and digestive fire (Agni) before making major dietary changes. If our digestive power is weak, we may not be able to handle or assimilate even the foods and herbs that are good for us. Right use of spices and proper dietary regimen is important here.

Look to long term doshic balancing with strategies that are implemented slowly and consistently over time. This may include special seasonal detoxification (Pancha Karma) and rejuvenation (Rasayana) measures. Regular massage can be helpful, along with the proper use of Ayurvedic oils.

Vedic Astrology Strategies

First look into the main issues the client is seeking to address. Address any difficult transits or on-going positions of planets along with planetary periods. Then you can examine the issues of the birth chart. You can do a prashna or question based chart as needed.

Afflictions caused by Saturn and Rahu may cause depression or volatility that can make it difficult for the other potentials within the chart to manifest. If these impact the ascendant they can affect the health and stability. If they impact the Moon, emotional and psychological issues will come out. If they impact the Sun, vitality and self-confidence can be harmed.

Besides the basic birth chart, you can examine the annual chart, current transits, and specific questions of the client as these may arise, if you have the training to do so. Astrology has many options in this regard.

Vastu Strategies

Examine to what extent the person is vulnerable at the level of Vastu or the directional influences dominant in life – particularly for explaining why issues addressed by other counseling methods may not be getting resolved in the normal way.

First look at the location in which a person is living and the degree of positive natural influences accessible. Urban and apartment living have their special challenges. Then examine the overall Vastu orientation of the house for the person and his family. Then you can look into specific issues of how the placements in the building may affect the mind, body and karma of those residing in it. Make sure that the rooms for sleep, study, work, and relaxation are properly defined. There should be at least one sacred room in the house used for meditation and healing.

Vedic Counseling and Mantric Tools

Mantra is the deeper language of Vedic knowledge. It is the most energized form of thought and speech that allows the mind to change its nature and dissolve its past conditioning. To be able to think mantrically allows us to gain mastery over our lives, our thoughts and emotions, and to act with clarity, consistency and focus.

Mantra is dharmic thinking or thinking in harmony with universal law, through which enduring wisdom can be brought into the mind. Mantra is the language of cosmic intelligence, reflecting the vibrations of universal consciousness and the rhythms of nature, not simply ordinary language invented for a particular society. That is why mantra is short, concise, aphoristic and poetic. Mantra brings into our minds the ideal patterns, archetypes and interconnections of life as a whole.

Mantra is the primary language of Vedic counseling. Vedic counseling helps us to develop mantric patterns of both speech and awareness. Each aspect of counseling has its key laws and mantras, such as right intention, right vocation and right relationship, which can be placed in a mantric context. The principles of Vedic counseling are prime mantras or thought patterns for right living, such as non-violence, receptivity, peace and universality. The mantric mind is the mind of the guru and counselor. The mantric mind is our inner guide to life's challenges and our inner doorway to higher awareness.

Mantra is the language of Yoga through which we can move into a deeper state of meditation. The right use of mantra requires that we are able to concentrate and focus our minds with determination and intent. The mantra is a tool for yogic concentration in which we learn to gather in all our distracted thoughts, emotions and sensations into a single purpose. This lack of focus in the mind makes us subject to confusion and causes us to fall under external influences. The distracted and fragmented nature of our thoughts causes wrong judgment, misperception, and creates unnecessary karma.

Each field of Vedic knowledge has its characteristic insights and mantras. The Ayurvedic understanding of the doshas of Vata, Pitta and

Kapha are mantric patterns, as are the planets of Vedic astrology, or the directional influences of Vastu. The eight limbs of Yoga are mantras or key guiding principles of Yoga, leading to samadhi or the complete mantric concentration of the mind and heart.

Mantra begins with the effort to concentrate our own thoughts. Certain special ideas, words, attitudes or affirmations may be employed in order to focus the mind in a beneficial direction. Mantra extends to certain Vedic, yogic and Sanskrit mantras that rely upon the natural mantric resonance of the Sanskrit language, the language of mantra, in order to give more energy and focus to our awareness.

Making Your Thoughts Mantric

To make our thoughts mantric, we must learn to give energy, focus, and clarity to the mind. We must approach our thoughts with a sense of purpose and discipline, holding our awareness within, beyond the distractions of the senses. Otherwise our thoughts will remain scattered, confused and ineffective, whatever we may try to do.

> *We need to develop keywords, key thoughts, and power points within our own minds, and go back to these on a regular basis to sustain our central projects and goals in life.*

For this purpose we must first recognize what our existing mantras may be. Our mantras are our primary thoughts, which we hold to most consistently in our minds and hearts. In this sense each one of us already has his or her own mantras, but we are not always aware as to their nature and consequences. You should first examine: "What are my mantras?"

For most of us our mantras or prime mental focus points, are our dominant thoughts born of desire, fear, envy, worry, or gossip. Such unconscious mantras disempower us, giving responsibility for our lives to others. Most of us will be shocked to really see our prime mental patterns and what they are likely to create for us. That reckoning is a good sign we are beginning to really see how our minds actually work. Most of the time we do not take our thoughts seriously, thinking they are not important and have no real consequences. We easily fall into imagination, speculation, or daydreaming that breeds illusion, desire and wrong judgment. We give our minds away to superficial entertainment or transient stimulation that has little real bearing on who we are and what we would really hope to achieve.

Please take your own thoughts seriously and see what they are creating for your future as well as how they have affected your life in the past. The very act of being consciously aware of our thoughts aids in their transformation. As we substitute yogic mantras, positive thoughts, and spiritual attitudes for our usual mechanical and superficial thoughts our lives will begin to change in a magical way.

To develop this mantric mind, it is important that we cultivate our power of attention in a determined manner. Most of our problems and accidents in life arise from lack of attention or even downright carelessness. If we have a mantra we can use it to replace this inattention that throws our lives into the realm of accident. You can use "Be Attentive" as your first mantra.

Developing Your Own Mantras

Begin to develop your own mantras, which means to concentrate your own thoughts into consistent patterns. What are the key concerns of your life? What do you really wish to achieve? What are your most important prayers, hopes and aspirations?

You can discover powerful mantras in great teachings and traditional spiritual texts, and in the deeper prayers and aspirations of all humanity. Even meditational inquiry, like the question "Who am I?" can be a powerful mantra.

Use mantra and pranayama together to strengthen the mind. Mantras can be silently repeated along with the breath to give them the additional power of prana. In this way we carry the vibration of the mantra into our vital energy and down to the subconscious mind.

Draw in your positive thoughts on inhalation and let go of your negative thoughts on exhalation. Inhale what you wish to become and exhale what you would like to let go of.

Prime Seed Mantras

There are many important yogic mantras, from single syllables to long prayers. Each domain of life (Dharma, Artha, Kama and Moksha) has certain divine principles ruling over it and certain seed mantras to help develop it. Of these the shorter "single syllable" or *bija mantras* are the most powerful and easiest to use and pronounce.

Om	is the main Vedic mantra. It grants all the goals of life but specifically liberation, our spiritual goal. It affirms our deepest attitudes and helps our energy to ascend. Om is Shiva. Om is Purusha. Om is Brahman. Mantric formulas usually begin with Om.
Hreem	is the seed mantra of the heart. It connects us to our inner prana, Shakti and creative force, allowing us to act in a wholehearted manner. It holds the energy of the Divine feminine and World Mother overall. We can use it to energize our dharma, as well as whatever we truly wish to accomplish.
The Goddess Lakshmi	is the main deity of Artha as wealth, prosperity and abundance overall. Her seed mantra Shreem aids in receiving this as we best need it. Yet Lakshmi gives achievement of goals that are rooted in dharma, not just the fulfillment of superficial desires. Shreem also gives health and well-being and is the best overall single seed mantra for all the goals of life.

There are several deities for Kama as Divine Love and the fulfillment of the wishes of the soul. Most important are Krishna among the male deities and Sundari, the Goddess of Divine Beauty, among the female forms. The main seed mantra for Divine love and bliss is the mantra Kleem. This is a mantra of attraction that draws to you what you are really wishing for.

There are many divine powers that help us to reach Moksha, the liberation of the spirit, but Lord Shiva is one of the most important, starting with his mantra Om and extending to his mantra Hoom that burns up all impurities and takes us beyond the ego.

OTHER IMPORTANT SEED MANTRAS

Bija, seed or also called Shakti mantras are important for energizing deeper aspects of mind and prana. They can be very useful in counseling contexts.

AIM	is the seed mantra of knowledge, communication, art, music and literature. It is connected to Sarasvati as the Goddess of Wisdom. It is important for counseling work, helping to focus the mind of both the counselor and the client.
KREEM	is the seed mantra of work, effort and accomplishment. It stimulates us to higher achievements, increasing our power to challenge
SHREEM	is the seed mantra of creative development, evolution, stage by stage growth, ascent and transformation. It aids in giving birth to what we really wish to produce.

One can repeat such seeds mantras as meditation mantras on a regular basis. One can add them to any special personal meditation mantras received.

Divine Names

Divine names form key mantras like Om Namah Shivaya!, which connect us to our highest spiritual aspiration. We can use Divine names towards whatever deity, teacher, divine form or quality that we feel most connected to. All names are ultimately Divine names and all creatures are Divine in essence. Divine names indicate the qualities that we wish to cultivate for our higher development.

Vishnu is the deity of dharma, particularly in the form of Lord Rama. Repeating the name of Rama as Ram, Ram, Ram, helps you develop your own dharma as well as uphold the social and universal dharmas.

Gayatri Mantra and Manifesting your Spiritual Path

Gayatri Mantra to the solar Godhead helps energize our highest purpose and motivation in life, our seeking of the highest light. For this reason, it is the most commonly used Vedic mantra. There are also Gayatri mantras to other aspects of Divinity. Consult a mantra teacher for more details on this longer mantric verse.

Mantras for the Planets

Special mantras for the nine planets may be recommended by a Vedic astrologer as part of their counseling methods. Chanting the mantra to a planet can aid in removing its negative influences and promoting those that are positive. There are name mantras for the planets as well as longer chants for them.

Mantras for the Directions

There are special mantras for the ten directions of space used in Yoga and Vastu. These include name mantras for directional deities. Vastu experts may recommend such mantras to their clients to bring in positive directional influences into their dwellings and remove those that are negative.

Vedantic Affirmations – Tools of universal Self-realization

The great sayings or Mahavakyas of Vedanta are mantric affirmations of our higher nature and inner Self. These are important counseling tools to connect us with our deeper being and its unlimited potentials. They affirm our inner being and higher consciousness beyond ignorance and sorrow. They help us transcend our problems and let them go.

Aham Brahmasmi	I am one with the universal reality or I am God; my true Self is the universal I am.
Ayam Atman Brahman	My true Self is one with the supreme reality, I am the Self of all.
Sarvam Khalvidam Brahma	Everything is sacred or Divine, the entire universe is Brahman.
Tattvam Asi	You are that supreme reality or Divine Self.
Prajnanam Brahma	Inner knowledge is Brahman or the supreme reality and that is your nature.
So'ham	He am I: That pure consciousness is the energy behind the breath, which is the vibration of my own nature.

Vedic Counseling and Meditation

Vedic counseling is designed to lead us to the state of meditation, in which the nature and contents of the mind can be changed in a fundamental manner, not by overt effort but by the inherent power of awareness. All dialogue between the counselor and client should be oriented in the direction of meditation. If we can learn the art of meditation, we can solve all of our problems, which are usually born of the disturbances of the mind.

The Vedic counseling session should proceed slowly and methodically like a guided meditation, with knowledge imparted in a concentrated manner from the counselor to the client in a contemplative state of mind. The counseling session should begin with bringing the client to a state of clarity and composure, in which he or she can take a new and insightful look at their lives. A Vedic counselor should not simply address specific issues, trying to solve these one by one, but teach the client the art of meditation, through which all our human problems can be permanently resolved. *This means that a Vedic counselor must also be a meditation teacher.*

Of course, in the beginning of any counseling work, there may be many other aspects of life and disturbances in the mind that one must first work through before being able to help the a client with the subtleties of meditation. Yet certain aspects of meditation can be taught immediately, like the need to first relax, focus and be receptive in order to engage in any meaningful dialogue.

> *Meditation begins very simply with cultivating an honest observation of oneself and conscious awareness of life as it is.*

This occurs by taking an attitude of a witness, no longer taking things personally or judging others. We should let the reality reveal itself, not try to make it into what we want. This is easier to do with external factors and we can start by observing the world around us in a detached manner. It may be difficult to observe ourselves because we are often hiding things from ourselves, taken in by the opinions of others and the illusions of the world. Yet the more we learn to dispassionately examine what is going on in our own minds moment by moment, the better position we will be in to understand ourselves and find a greater well-being.

Our main dialogue in life is with ourselves - with our stream of thoughts about who we are, what we are doing and what we want. As we become aware of that dialogue, it becomes deeper and we let go of our superficial concerns. Gradually we begin to listen to what is happening within us, rather than getting caught in our impulses. When this occurs, the outer dialogue of personal seeking ends, and the inner dialogue of the search for truth begins, which is the real process of meditation.

While the counseling session works to develop the meditative mind, the client needs to be directed how to bring the state of meditation into his or her life as a whole. This begins with starting a daily meditation practice or at least daily periods of introspection and self-examination. Journaling can aid in this process.

Yet meditation is not just something we should do for only a few minutes during the day, morning or evening, however helpful that may be. We must learn to live a meditative life, which means putting our outer life, relationships and emotions in order and harmony. A meditative life is not simply a life of silence or inaction, much less letting things drift. It is a life of receptive awareness, in which we carefully observe and witness not only what is happening in the external world but, much more importantly, the movements of our own mind.

Most of us are quite good at keeping up with the news or the events of the day, which we look at with much energy, motivation and concern. However we give little attention to what is happening in our own minds, even if it is disturbing. We fail to notice, much less question what our thoughts are creating for us. We allow our minds to dwell in states of distraction, worry, gossip or fantasy without considering how our behavior is being affected. We are not cultivating our own minds, though we may be cultivating many projects in the outer world.

The mind is always breeding something, positive or negative. It has its habits, focus or preoccupation. If we are constantly engaged in negative or distracted thoughts, our mind will be conditioned to remain in a negative and disturbed state. If we are engaged in positive and focused thoughts, our minds will be conditioned to a higher awareness. It is just like the body and food, with bad food damaging and weakening the body and good food providing it strength.

We could say, perhaps bluntly, that "the ordinary mind is a pathology," a breeding ground for disease, unhappiness, and disharmony. This is because we are not in control of the mind in a conscious way. Our mind is normally breeding some problematical emotional state, whether fear, anger, desire, attachment, love or hate, that will likely result in some negative manifestation over time. Our minds are wandering, imagining or daydreaming, constructing speculative, or fantasy realities that are caught up in conflict, drama or agitation. We are not creating a state of peace within ourselves, but one of distraction.

Just like toxins in the body, emotional toxins in the mind will eventually result in diseases at psychological or physical levels. Such conditions may be depression, conflict, anger, anxiety, or other behavioral problems. The mind's contents must spill over into our actions. If we are not in control of our minds, then we will not be in control of our lives either.

Mantra and Meditation

The use of mantra is one of the best foundations for meditation, as we discussed in the previous chapter. Mantra is the main tool for meditation that works in first concentrating the mind.

The Attitude of the Witness

Many forms of meditation follow a process of observation or learning to witness the movements of the mind. Witness based meditation puts us in touch with the Divine Self or Purusha within. We should hold to this state of detached awareness throughout the day as much as we can. Cultivate that witnessing awareness in all that you do.

We should aim at witnessing our problems in life. The witness consciousness over time will allow the solutions to our life problems to arise naturally over time. Sometimes we try too hard to solve our problems by thinking about them, which may in fact make them worse. We must learn to understand the nature of the problem and then the solution to it will arise through meditation.

Vedic Meditation – Self- inquiry

We have noted the importance of Self-inquiry in Vedic counseling. It is fundamental for meditation as well. We must realize that we have problems in life because we really do not know ourselves and are not in control of our lives. We can choose primary questions, like Who am I? and focus on them for a certain period of time, like a week or a month, holding the question in the back of our minds. This is very effective in controlling the wandering mind and removing distracted thoughts.

Devotional Meditation

Meditation should not be just a process of the intellect. There are devotional forms of meditation as well, meditating on the Divine presence within our hearts, either with a particular form or without any form. Devotional meditation can involve meditation on Divine love, beauty or delight. Developing a deeper feeling, sensitivity, and compassion are soothing to the mind and heart.

Meditation Techniques

There are many techniques of meditation, so much so it may seem confusing. These can involve using the breath, a mantra, creating a specific focus for the mind, or contemplating certain spiritual truths, or a defined line of inquiry. They may require specific and ongoing instruction or counseling in their practice. Yet ultimately we must move beyond the technique to the state of meditation itself, which is beyond any thought, action or intention. The silent mind is the ultimate power of all healing and higher truth.

Daily Practice of Meditation

It is good to awaken before dawn and benefit by the meditative energy of the day, which occurs at that time. Yet whatever time we wake up we should begin our day by remembering our higher aspirations and setting a spiritual agenda for the day. We should honor the Divine, our teachers, the great powers of nature, our friends and family, and the stream of life of which we are blessed to be a part. This sets in motion a positive stream of thoughts to uplift us throughout the day.

Clearing the mind before sleep is even more important and helps us remove any mental or emotional toxins that we have accumulated during the day. It allows us to more easily access the peace of the state of deep sleep. At least an hour, preferably two, before sleep, we should give up our activities of the day, shut off the mass media and our computers, forget the world, let our nervous systems rest, and turn within to contact our eternal nature beyond body and mind. We should let go of all worries and allow ourselves to return to our true spiritual home in deep sleep. The world in any case will be there in the morning and we will be in a better condition to deal with it if we are properly rested and renewed within.

In addition, we should take at least one day a week off for spiritual practice, meditation, relaxation and retreat, preferably in a natural setting. Weekends are often the easiest time to do this. We should also take some days or weeks off seasonally to focus on the inner world and let the outer world go. This allows us to attune ourselves to the seasonal forces of nature. We can combine it with a healing retreat or vacation overall. Meditation is easiest done in a natural setting, a forest, lake or mountain.

If we take such breaks from outer reality, the world will certainly not disappear. We must remember that we are only guests in this physical world. Our spiritual home is in the infinite and we need to make sure that we take from this life an essence of love and wisdom. Our wealth or property will not come with us in any case, and some problems in the world will always remain, even if we do our best to help everyone. Returning to our spiritual home in the heart is the best place for creative renewal and is the essence of meditation.

Guiding Your Client into a Meditative State

When your client arrives for counseling, first make them comfortable in a seating posture. Given them some fresh water or a nice herbal tea like tulsi, brahmi or green tea. Make sure the room is well ventilated with fresh air, has some flowers, and perhaps some mild sandalwood incense burning. There should be a pleasant ambiance in the room as a whole. If the counseling session occurs in a meditative atmosphere it is likely to be much more effective.

1 |	Have the client take a deep breath and then relax their breath.
2 |	Have them chant Om, So'ham or another suitable mantra three times.
3 |	Then have them sit quietly and let go of their thoughts for a few minutes.
4 |	Do not engage the client or encourage them to talk further if they are agitated and their minds are disturbed. Bring them first into an atmosphere of peace.
5 |	Direct them to witness their thoughts like a flowing stream and open up to the healing forces of nature through the Sun, the earth and the sky.
6 |	Encourage silent, non-verbal, supportive forms of communication linking to the whole of life, heart to heart communication.
7 |	Eventually have them merge the mind into the heart, returning to the inner core of peace and light within.

Developing the Yogic Quality of Sattva Guna

Vedic counseling begins with the promotion of sattva guna as the primary means of spiritualizing and harmonizing our lives. Sattva guna – our inherent quality of awareness, compassion, clarity and balance – is the key factor in elevating our awareness and bringing us to lasting peace and happiness. It is the main factor in life and nature that allows our spiritual potentials to come forth. *Developing sattva guna is probably the prime principle of Vedic counseling and of Yoga.*

The three gunas of sattva (harmony), rajas (agitation) and tamas (inertia), which we have introduced earlier, are the prime factors of nature, behind the five elements, body and mind. Our lives are a play of the three gunas, inwardly and outwardly. Mastery of life requires being able to develop the higher power of the gunas, which is sattva guna.

All our activities set in motion the energies of sattva, rajas and tamas along with their respective capacities and effects. Unless we understand the gunas properly, we may be setting in motion forces that inhibit the unfoldment of our dharma and bind us to further karma. Everything we do promotes some aspect or quality of the three gunas, creating forces of light or darkness, knowledge or ignorance, unity or fragmentation within us. Normally we create unnecessary tamas and rajas that breed disturbance and resistance. The result is that the higher spiritual qualities within us lack the right field for them to manifest. What is good in us does not come forth, and what is problematical in us we find hard to release.

Nature will bring to us whatever aspects of the three gunas that we set in motion in our lives. Whatever guna we promote will eventually become our own individual nature and form the habitual responses of the subconscious mind. *That is how we speak of sattvic, rajasic or tamasic types of people.* Yet each one of us has all three gunas, which change over the movement of time, starting on a daily basis. We need to learn to promote sattva within us in order to overcome the suffering caused by the other two gunas.

The three gunas also show us the way of development and transformation, or how we can evolve in consciousness, which is one of the main concerns of Vedic counseling. We first must move from tamas to rajas and then second from rajas to sattva. Third and finally, we can move beyond the gunas altogether to our higher Self.

Moving from tamas to rajas	Removing blockage and stagnation with positive action, countering addictions and bad habits with effort and motivation.
Moving from rajas to sattva	Countering agitation and wastage, assertion and aggression, with forgiveness, calm, peace and non-violence.
Developing pure sattva	Developing steadiness in our spiritual path, composure as our state of mind, peace, devotion and compassion as our nature.
Moving beyond the gunas to our true Self that transcends and all dualities.	Returning to the Purusha or seer inherently beyond the gunas. This implies mastery over all three gunas and all of nature, and our own minds.

In our fast moving, stimulation and achievement oriented society, the quality of rajas is promoted the most. We honor outer achievement and recognition as the main goal of life, ignoring more refined sensitivities and capacities. We place our emphasis on the separate self. Its personal achievements breed division, conflict and sorrow which isolate us from the whole of life. Even our counseling models are often rajasic in nature and recommendations, directing us to become more assertive and more outwardly oriented.

- We need to move from rajas to sattva in counseling models. This requires a shift of emphasis from doing to being, from outer achievement to inner realization, from individual effort to following the universal and eternal dharma.

- We need to explore all possible means of developing sattva in our lives on all levels of our being. This should be one of the main guidelines of all counseling recommendations.

Vedic counselors as sattvic counselors	Strengthen sattva as mental clarity and peace in the client as a primary aim.
Vedic guidelines as sattvic intentions and actions	From vegetarian diet to detachment and meditation, sattva is the key factor.
Higher Dharma as sattvic	Our true vocation as raising consciousness, love and wisdom through various activities.
Vedic life-style as a sattvic life-style	We should live every day, starting with our thoughts and breath, to promote more sattva, balance and harmony in all that we do.

Developing Sattva and the Practice of Yoga

Sattva guna is primarily developed through the practice of Yoga and meditation, specifically the system of Raja Yoga and its eight limbs. It rests upon sattvic values as indicated by the Yamas and Niyamas of Raja Yoga, notably non-violence and truthfulness. It requires a sattvic life-style based upon those values, which extends to a yogic diet and a vocation that promotes peace and harmony. Any yogic aspect of counseling must consider the gunas carefully, which means bringing sattva into how we move, breathe, use our senses, mind and heart.

Sattva Guna and Ayurvedic Psychology

In Ayurvedic medical therapy, rajas and tamas comprise the doshas or factors of imbalance at the level of the mind. Increasing sattva guna is the main means of psychological treatment in Yoga and Ayurveda. Ayurveda prescribes Yoga as a sattvic therapy to heal the mind.

Vedic counseling, like most other forms of counseling, is primarily psychological in nature. Understanding psychological imbalances according to the gunas is essential for it. Promoting sattva guna is often the first and primary practice of Vedic counseling. Other psychological systems may promote rajas or tamas by not giving importance to the role of sattva.

Nature and Roots of Sattva Guna	
Consideration of the good of all	Sattva promotes selflessness and letting go of the ego.
Ahimsa *Conflict resolution, reducing friction and disharmony.*	Sattva seeks an end to all conflict, beginning with removing any violence from our own minds and hearts.
Renunciation *Willingness to let go of personal desire in order to achieve something enduring*	Sattva helps us let go of the lower in order to achieve the higher.
Karma Yoga	Emphasis on life as service, rather than personal gain.
Dharma	Emphasis on inner truth and natural law over personal desires.

General Rules of Sattvic living

There are several important rules of sattvic life. We will introduce them here and explore them in detail later in the book.

Need to develop a sattvic intention in life, which upholds dharma	Our intention and motivation should be sattvic. That is, it should aim at developing the greater good of all.
Need to develop a sattvic prana that allows for optimal health and well-being	Our prana and breath should be developed in a sattvic way. This means our actions and exercise should have a calming and harmonizing effect upon body and mind.

Taking in sattvic food	Sattvic physical life-style rests upon sattvic food. Sattvic food is vegetarian food that is naturally grown, whole and rich in prana. It is freshly cooked and prepared with a positive attitude and good feelings.
Taking in sattvic impressions	Sensory impressions are the main food for the mind. Our sensory impressions are the subtle elements that build up the subtle or energy body, which is the mind. Sattvic impressions are natural, gentle, soft and refined. We gain these mainly from the world of nature, particularly relative to the wilderness, plants and the sky.
Developing sattvic associations	Our state of being and level of awareness is closely connected to our associations in life. This includes friends, family, and work associates, but more importantly those whom we emulate at a higher level or honor in our hearts, the role models that we follow. We should all have higher human beings that we look up to and seek to follow. These are our gurus and guides. We should try to associate upward in life, trying to align our action and character.

In the following chapters, we will discuss these sattvic therapies in detail.

Part IV

Specific Approaches of Vedic Counseling - Ayurveda & Yoga

Psychological Nature According to the Three Gunas

Vedic counseling helps us understand our psychology and how to change it in a lasting manner. In the Vedic system, our psychological nature is usually judged according to the gunas, the prime attributes or qualities of nature (Prakriti) as sattva, rajas and tamas. The gunas indicate the mental traits respectively of clarity, distraction and dullness. The three doshas of Vata, Pitta and Kapha have a secondary importance, but have influences that must be recognized.

These three qualities reflect the level of development of the soul. They are not simply intellectual proclivities or emotional types. They show the sensitivity of the mind, its capacity to perceive truth and act according to it.

Psychological Effects Of Sattva Guna

The mind itself is called sattva (clarity) because its basic clear quality allows perception to occur. The mind is naturally clear and pure, but becomes darkened by negative thoughts and emotions, and by attachment to the external world.

Sattva is the divine or godly nature. When pure, it produces enlightenment and Self-realization. It brings about internalization of the mind, the awakening of consciousness and the unification of the head and the heart. It holds the inherent power of healing for body and mind.

Psychological Effects Of Rajoguna

Rajas is distraction or turbulence in the mind that causes us to look outward and seek fulfillment in the external world as our highest goal. It is the quality of the mind agitated by desire, which when frustrated, creates anger.

Rajas consists of disturbed thoughts and imaginings. It includes willfulness, manipulativeness and ego. It involves the seeking of power, stimulation and entertainment. In excess, it creates a violent (asuric) nature.

Pschological Effects Of Tamoguna

Tamas is dullness, darkness and an inability to perceive the truth. It is the mind clouded by ignorance, inertia, dullness and fear. Tamas creates sloth, sleep and inattention. It involves lack of mental activity or focus, insensitivity, and domination of the mind by external or subconscious forces. Tamas creates a servile or animal nature and makes us resistant to positive change.

The Mind

The Three Gunas or Qualities

Gunas	
Sattva	Harmony, balance, order, stability, clarity, purity
Rajas	Dynamic, energetic, changeable, agitating, disturbing
Tamas	Inert, heavy, negative, lethargic, dull, resisting

Mental Constitution Chart

The gunas show our mental and spiritual state through which we can measure our propensity for psychological problems, as well as how we take care of ourselves. The following test is a good index of these qualities and how they work within our life and character.

The answers on the left indicate sattva, the middle rajas and the right tamas. After answering the questionnaire for yourself, you should have someone who knows you very well fill it out for you also.

For most of us, the majority of our answers will likely fall in the middle or rajasic area, which is the main condition in our culture today. We may have various psychological problems, but are able to deal with them and keep them in check. A sattvic nature shows a spiritual disposition. A highly sattvic nature is rare and shows a saint or a sage. A tamasic person has danger of severe psychological problems, but would be unlikely to fill out such a chart or even read such a book. The areas in ourselves that we can improve upon, from tamas to rajas or from rajas to sattva, will help us in our peace of mind and spiritual growth.

Three Gunas Constitution Chart

Ahara/ Intake			
Food	☐ Vegetarian	☐ Some meat	☐ Heavy meat diet
Water and beverages	☐ Pure water, teas and juices	☐ Mixed	☐ Alcohol
Air	☐ Good quality	☐ Medium	☐ Poor quality/ polluted
Sensory Impressions	☐ Calm, pure	☐ Agitated	☐ Dark, violent
Emotions	☐ Peaceful	☐ Disturbing	☐ Dark
Information	☐ Spiritual	☐ Mixed	☐ Material
Ideas	☐ Spiritual	☐ Worldly	☐ Few or none
Associations	☐ Spiritual	☐ Egoistic	☐ Deluded, confused
Vihara/Activity			
Sleep	☐ Good	☐ Disturbed	☐ Poor
Eating Habits	☐ Regular	☐ Irregular	☐ Excessive
Sexual Desire	☐ Low	☐ Medium	☐ Excessive
Exercise	☐ Good	☐ Medium	☐ Low or none
Speech	☐ Calm and peaceful	☐ Agitated	☐ Dull
Work	☐ Selfless	☐ For personal goals	☐ Lazy
Negative Emotions			
Anger	☐ Rarely	☐ Sometimes	☐ Frequently

Fear	☐ Rarely	☐ Sometimes	☐ Frequently
Desire	☐ Little	☐ Some	☐ Much
Pride	☐ Modest	☐ Some ego	☐ Vain
Depression	☐ Never	☐ Sometimes	☐ Frequently
Attachment	☐ Little	☐ Some	☐ Much
Greed	☐ Little	☐ Some	☐ A lot
Yoga Practices Of Yamas and Niyamas			
Non-violence	☐ Always	☐ Mainly	☐ Rarely
Truthfulness	☐ Usually	☐ Partly	☐ Never
Right use of Sex	☐ Always	☐ Mostly	☐ Rarely
Non-stealing	☐ Always	☐ Sometimes	☐ Rare
Non-coveting	☐ Always	☐ Sometimes	☐ Never
Self-discipline	☐ High	☐ Medium	☐ Low
Self-study	☐ High	☐ Medium	☐ Low
Surrender to God	☐ High	☐ Medium	☐ Low
Cleanliness	☐ High	☐ Medium	☐ Low
Contentment	☐ High	☐ Medium	☐ Low
Main Yoga Practices			
Asana	☐ Good	☐ Medium	☐ Low
Pranayama	☐ Good	☐ Medium	☐ Low
Pratyahara	☐ Good	☐ Medium	☐ Low
Concentration	☐ Good	☐ Medium	☐ Low
Meditation	☐ Good	☐ Medium	☐ Low
Samadhi	☐ Frequent	☐ Occasional	☐ Never
Yogic Qualities			
Devotion	☐ High	☐ Medium	☐ Low
Compassion	☐ High	☐ Medium	☐ Low

Self-Knowledge	☐ High	☐ Medium	☐ Low
Service	☐ High	☐ Medium	☐ Low
Yoga Practice	☐ High	☐ Medium	☐ Low
Internal Peace	☐ High	☐ Medium	☐ Low
Mental Qualities			
Discrimination	☐ High	☐ Medium	☐ Low
Detachment	☐ High	☐ Medium	☐ Low
Memory	☐ Good	☐ Moderate	☐ Poor
Will Power	☐ Strong	☐ Variable	☐ Weak
Ayurvedic Considerations			
Dosha Accumulation	☐ Low	☐ Medium	☐ High
Ama Accumulation	☐ Low	☐ Medium	☐ High
Agni {Digestive Fire}	☐ Balanced	☐ Erratic	☐ Low
Dhatus {Tissues}	☐ Good quality	☐ Medium	☐ Poor quality
Malas {Waste-materials}	☐ Low	☐ Medium	☐ High
Channel systems	☐ Clear	☐ Disturbed	☐ Blocked
	Sattva	**Rajas**	**Tamas**
Total			

This chart, like others of its kind, is a working model that we can use to better know and improve ourselves. It is not for critically judging anyone. Our current culture has a lot of rajas and tamas, so any sattva in a person is to be appreciated. The main goal is to increase the level of sattva in our lives, regardless of the state we may find ourselves in to begin with.

Sattvic types have a Deva or divine constitution. They have higher or godly traits, virtues and clarity. We should learn to cultivate those spiritual traits in others. Generally spiritual names are given to people in order to help promote their sattvic qualities.

Rajasic types have an Asura or egoistic and rash temperament. They have aggressive traits that easily become hostile. We should learn to restrain the rajasic traits within ourselves. This requires self-discipline.

Tamasic types have an animal nature (in the negative sense of lack of discrimination). They respond only relative to their bodily needs and urges and are not sensitive to others. They may have deep seated attachments and blockages. We should strive to remove the tamasic traits in ourselves. This requires effort.

Seven Guna Types

1	Pure Sattva
2	Pure Rajas
3	Pure Tamas
4	Sattva-Rajas
5	Sattva-Tamas
6	Rajas-Tamas
7	Sattva-Rajas-Tamas

Totally pure sattva (shuddha sattva) affords enlightenment and Self-realization. A pure rajas type can be very successful in the outer world but lacks inner awareness and sensitivity. We see this quality of rajas in people who have power, money or social recognition that they take pride in but are inconsiderate of others. A pure tamas type is caught in darkness and inertia that can lead to incapacity and addictions.

Each individual should examine these mental traits and see which most fit their nature and behavior. Those factors that are negative, like disease-causing habits, should be reduced by the appropriate remedial measures like: meditation, prayer, mantra, rituals, self-examination, and surrender to the Divine.

Our culture today is very rajasic—highly distracted, disturbed, hyperactive and over stimulated. Some rajasic traits within us may be owing to outer circumstances rather than being indicative of our own inner disposition. Yet excess rajas leads to tamas, just as excess activity leads to exhaustion. After our excessive activity, we often fall into states of low energy, inertia and depression. For this reason, tamas often prevails at the end of our hectic lives.

The Three Doshas: Our Prime Biological Energetics

Ayurveda plays an important role in Vedic counseling for both body and mind. All Vedic counselors should possess a working knowledge of the prime factors of Ayurveda, notably the three doshas, and be able to understand their clients according to these. They need not be Ayurvedic clinicians who can treat specific diseases, but should understand the general forces and constitutional energetics of the doshas, as part of any Vedic life-style orientation.

Similarly, Ayurvedic practitioners need good counseling skills, which are not always taught as part of Ayurvedic programs. Ayurveda does not merely rest upon the giving of medications or the performance of therapies. Its foundation lies in promoting a healthy life-style for the patient that requires educating the patient.

For Ayurvedic practice, counseling skills are as important as clinical skills. Developing the proper rapport with the patient is central to the success of the treatment and its long term implementation. As Ayurveda is not just a physical medicine, but is rooted in Yogic and Vedic thought, all Ayurvedic practitioners should know the broader field of Vedic counseling, particularly to psychological issues and life-style guidance.

Ayurveda follows the same broader principles and greater cosmic forces as all of Vedic thought. Our health and well-being is not just a matter of taking the right medications but of balancing the forces of nature within us, which requires an organic approach to life and healing. To do this we must first understand how nature works within us and learn to honor the wisdom behind its processes. This is the foundation of Ayurvedic medicine.

The Three Doshas

Ayurveda rests upon an understanding of the three doshas or biological humors of Vata, Pitta and Kapha, which reflect the primary powers of the air, fire and water elements at a biological level and the corresponding cosmic powers of energy, light and matter.

Our biological existence consists of a dance of the three doshas. Life is a multicolored tapestry of their movement in various plays of balance and imbalance, coming together and going apart. These three powers color and determine our conditions of growth and aging, health and disease. *Dosha* means a fault or a blemish and indicates the factors that bring about disease and decay.

The doshas are the factors that produce the physical body and are responsible for its substance and its function. Our tissues starting with the plasma or our basic fluid reserve are mainly Kapha or watery in nature. The digestive system, which rests upon the ability to transform food into bodily tissues, is mainly Pitta or fiery in nature. The nervous system and its movement of quick electrical impulses is mainly Vata or like air in action.

One of the three doshas predominates in each individual and determines individual constitution or mind-body type. In this regard, Ayurveda classifies individuals as Vata types, Pitta types or Kapha types relative to their predominant dosha. This is reflected in bodily structure, movement and energy extending to emotional responses, perceptual abilities and mental nature.

Ayurveda treatment occurs on two levels relative to the doshas. The first is the prescription of general life-style therapies relative to the doshas, including daily and seasonal health regimens for optimal well-being. The second consists of specific prescriptions relative to particular diseases, whether chronic or acute. Counseling is more important to the first level.

Doshas

Vata, Pitta, Kapha

VATA	***The energy of action, transportation, and movement.***
Composition	Ether + Air
Qualities	Light, dry, cold, rough, subtle and mobile

PITTA	***The energy of transformation, conversion, and metabolism.***
Composition	Fire + Water
Qualities	Light, hot, sharp, oily, mobile, liquid

KAPHA	***The energy of construction, lubrication, and nourishment.***
Composition	Water + Earth
Qualities	Heavy, cold, moist, dull, soft, sticky and static

Vata Dosha

Vata is the motivating power behind the other two doshas, which are lame or incapable of movement without it. Vata is primarily ether in substance and air in motion. It exists as the air that we hold in the empty spaces of the body, like in the hollow organs, joints, and bone cavities, particularly the hips and lower back. On an inner level, Vata is both the life-force and the energy of thought that moves in the space of the mind.

Vata's sense organs are the ears and skin and its motor organs are speech and the hands, which relate to the ether and air elements and sensory potentials. On an inner level, Vata governs sensory, emotional and mental harmony, and promotes mental adaptability and comprehension. Vata endows us with positive traits of creativity, enthusiasm, speed, agility and responsiveness that allow us to achieve our goals in life. Its sense organs are the skin and ears, its motor organs are speech and hands, which relate to the air and ether elements and the sense qualities of touch and sound.

Vata's primary physical site of accumulation is in the colon. Vata is a positive factor in the energy produced through the digestion of food. As a toxin or disease-causing factor, it is the excess gas resulting from faulty digestion. Disturbed Vata causes mental, nervous and digestive disorders, including low energy and weakening of all bodily tissues.

Yet Vata is not separate from the other doshas. Like the wind that moves with the clouds in the sky, Vata contains within itself subtle particles of water and the potential of fire in the form of electric force. After all, it is changes in temperature (fire) and pressure (water) that make the wind blow. The clouds of Vata generate the lightning or fire that gives rise to pitta and the watery particles or rain that give rise to Kapha. Vata is the origin of the other two doshas. Proper balance of Vata depends upon the right amount of Pitta and Kapha held within it, just as the amount of heat and water in the wind determines how it blows.

The key to managing all the doshas is to care for Vata. The cosmic Vata, or *Vayu,* energizes and upholds dharma or cosmic law. Similarly, the proper control of Vata brings dharma or natural order to all the workings of the body and mind.

Pitta Dosha

Pitta means "the power of digestion or cooking" — that which causes things to ripen and mature. As fire cannot exist directly in the body, Pitta exists in the body in the medium of oily and acidic secretions and so is said to contain an aspect of water as well. Pitta is responsible for all forms of digestion and transformation in the body, from the cellular level to the workings of the gastrointestinal tract. Pitta governs digestion on mental and spiritual levels as well — our capacity to digest impressions, emotions and ideas in order to arrive at a perception of truth. Pitta endows us with positive traits of intelligence, courage and vitality. Without it we lack the decisiveness or motivation to accomplish our goals.

Pitta is located in the small intestine and stomach among the organs, the sweat and sebaceous glands, and the blood and lymph among the tissues. Its sense organ is the eyes and its motor organ is the feet, which relate to the element and sense quality of sight. Its main site of accumulation is in the small intestine, where it builds up as acidity. Pitta is produced as the positive energy or heat of the blood. As a disease factor, it manifests through excess or toxic blood that gives rises to inflammation and infection.

Pitta depends upon Vata for its enervation and movement and on Kapha for its support, just as fire requires both oxygen (air) and fuel in order to burn properly. It holds some degree of Vata or nervous energy within it and grounds itself with the appropriate Kapha or water. Pitta is closely related to the Agni or digestive fire. It is responsible for the heat that sustains our bodily existence.

Kapha Dosha

Kapha, which also indicates mucus or phlegm, means "what makes things stick together" and refers to the power of cohesion. Kapha serves as the bodily container for Pitta and Vata, or energy and heat. Kapha itself, as water, is held in the medium of earth, the skin and mucous linings, affording it a secondary earth element as well.

Kapha is primarily located in the chest, throat and head in the upper body, the sites of mucus production. It also predominates in the pancreas, sides, stomach, and in the middle body where fat accumulates. It is also found in lymph and fat tissues that are generally watery in nature. Its sense organs are taste and smell, the nose and tongue. Its motor organs are the urinogenital and excretory organs, which relate to the water and earth elements and the sense qualities of taste and smell. Kapha endows us with emotion and feeling. This gives love and caring, devotion and faith, which serve to keep us in harmony internally and unite us with others. Kapha allows us to retain what we have achieved through our efforts.

Kapha's primary physical site of accumulation is the stomach, where mucus is produced, which then overflows into the lungs and lymphatic system. Kapha is produced through the plasma, which is the main Kapha tissue in the body, providing hydration and nourishment to all the tissues. As a disease factor, Kapha manifests through excess plasma that becomes mucus. This causes excess weight, edema, lung diseases, swollen glands and other Kapha disorders.

Kapha depends upon Vata for its stimulation and movement. It requires pitta for its warmth. The body, though primarily composed of water (Kapha), is a special form of water in which heat (Pitta) and vital energy (Vata) are contained. Water that is cold or does not move cannot sustain life.

The Doshas as Constitutional Factors

The Doshas create three different primary individual constitutions or mind-body types. No type is necessarily better or worse than the others. Each has its benefits as well as its weaknesses. Kapha types possess the strongest build but can lack in motivation and the adaptation needed to use their strength properly. Vata types have the weakest build but the greatest capacity for change and adaptation to protect their bodies. Pitta types have moderate physical strength but greater mental and emotional force.

Note that doshic types are only one aspect of personality types. Doshic types reflect disease tendencies and not the full range of your personal inclinations, temperament or spiritual potential in life. This depends upon your karmas and samskaras (mental tendencies)

Below is included a simple test to determine the doshas in your own nature. No person is of one type only, so expect some combination of traits. The predominant trait will determine your doshic type. Dual types also exist, where two doshas may exist in relative equal amounts.

Ayurvedic Constitution Chart

	Vata (Air)	Pitta (Fire)	Kapha (Water)
Height	☐ tall or very short	☐ medium	☐ usually short but can be tall and large
Frame	☐ thin, bony, good muscles	☐ moderate, developed	☐ large, well-formed

	Vata (Air)	Pitta (Fire)	Kapha (Water)
Weight	☐ low, hard to hold weight	☐ moderate	☐ heavy, hard to lose weight
Skin luster	☐ dull or dusky	☐ ruddy, lustrous	☐ white or pale
Skin texture	☐ dry, rough, thin	☐ warm, oily	☐ cold, damp, thick
Eyes	☐ small, nervous	☐ piercing, easily inflamed	☐ large, white
Hair	☐ dry, thin	☐ thin, oily	☐ thick, oily, wavy, lustrous
Teeth	☐ crooked, poorly formed	☐ moderate, bleeding gums	☐ large, well formed
Sweating	☐ scanty	☐ profuse but not enduring	☐ low to start but profuse
Stool	☐ hard or dry	☐ soft, loose	☐ normal
Urination	☐ scanty	☐ profuse, yellow	☐ moderate, clear
Sensitivities	☐ cold, dryness, wind	☐ heat, sunlight, fire	☐ cold, damp
Immune function	☐ low, variable	☐ moderate, sensitive to heat	☐ high
Disease tendency	☐ pain	☐ fever, inflammation	☐ congestion, edema
Disease type	☐ nervous	☐ blood, liver	☐ mucous, lungs
Activity	☐ high, restless	☐ moderate	☐ low, moves slowly

	Vata (Air)	Pitta (Fire)	Kapha (Water)
Endurance	☐ poor, easily, exhausted	☐ moderate but focused	☐ high
Sleep	☐ poor, disturbed	☐ variable	☐ excess
Dreams	☐ frequent, disturbed	☐ moderate, colorful	☐ infrequent, romantic
Memory	☐ quick but absent-minded	☐ sharp, clear	☐ slow but steady
Speech	☐ fast, frequent	☐ sharp, cutting	☐ slow, melodious
Temperament	☐ nervous, changeable	☐ motivated	☐ content, conservative
Positive emotions	☐ adaptability	☐ courage	☐ courage
Negative emotions	☐ fear	☐ anger	☐ attachment
Faith	☐ variable, erratic	☐ strong, determined	☐ steady, slow to change
	Vata	**Pitta**	**Kapha**
Total			

Ayurvedic recommendations are generally prescribed according to dosha. When dual doshic types exist treatment usually aims at the dosha that is most high in the person at any given time, or it follows seasonal recommendations; anti-Kapha approaches during Kapha time (February to June), anti-Pitta during Pitta time (June-October) and anti-Vata during Vata time (October-June)

The doshas are also the main factors behind the disease process, which occurs when the doshas accumulate and become excessive. Generally we treat the dosha behind the disease, not simply the disease itself. The dosha behind the disease is usually the same as the birth constitutional dosha but can be different, particularly for short term problems.

Prana, Tejas and Ojas – The Master Forms of the Doshas

The doshas are primarily disease-causing factors. Yet each dosha is also a factor of positive health and longevity. In ordinary Ayurvedic treatment, we aim at reducing excess doshas as disease-causing factors. In deeper Ayurvedic treatment, we aim at increasing the master forms of the doshas as factors of positive health and well-being.

Dosha	Master Form	Energy
Vata	*Prana*	Breath of vitality, creativity and adaptability, healing power
Pitta	*Tejas*	Fire of health, radiance and self-confidence, courage
Kapha	*Ojas*	Power of immunity, endurance and patience

Most Vedic counseling occurs at the level of wellness recommendations and life-style consultancy, rather than treating serious or acute diseases (for which, a clinician is required). For this purpose, the counselor should also be aware of the means of strengthening Prana, Tejas and Ojas as master forms of the doshas that help promote positive health. Prana, Tejas and Ojas also relate to higher Yoga practices.

Prana	Prana is strengthened through pranayama that involves slow and deep breathing, by developing inner powers of listening, by drawing in the prana of nature including through the Sun, by expanding awareness, meditation on the void, and creating a sacred space of higher knowledge.

TEJAS	Tejas is increases by the practice of mantra, by increasing the power of concentration, by developing inner powers of seeing, by cultivating such qualities as fearlessness, daring and will power, and by meditating on Agni or the Divine flame within the heart.
OJAS	Ojas is increased by a rich nutritive vegetarian diet, by Ojas-increasing herbs like ashwagandha, shatavari and amla, by adequate rest and relaxation, by cultivating such devotional qualities as faith, devotion, compassion and endurance, by contacting the inner Soma or nectar of bliss.

Ayurvedic Psychology: Gunas and Doshas

The three doshas are a biological classification that is horizontal in application, with no necessary spiritual implications. A Vata type may be a wise man or a fool; the same is the case with the other two types. The gunas are a spiritual classification that is vertical in nature. It has no necessary physical implications. A wise man or a fool may be Vata, Pitta or Kapha in bodily energies.

Putting these two classifications together – like combining horizontal and vertical lines – we can arrive at a precise indication of where a person is at in life. Please do both the dosha and guna tests to see how these two factors combine in your nature. Learn not only if you are Vata, Pitta or Kapha, but also to see if the dosha is at a level of sattva, rajas or tamas.

The Doshas as Psychological Factors

Let us examine in detail the psychological consequences of the three doshas. The doshas promote various psychological and emotional states within us. These can either cause physical imbalances or be caused by them. We need to determine these psychological effects of the doshas in order to deal with them at an outer level as well.

Psychological Profiles Of The Doshas

	Vata (Air)	Pitta (Fire)	Kapha (Water)
Temperament	☐ nervous, changeable	☐ motivated, ☐ determined	☐ content, conservative
Positive emotions	☐ adaptability	☐ courage	☐ love
Negative emotions	☐ fear	☐ anger	☐ attachment

	Vata (Air)	Pitta (Fire)	Kapha (Water)
Sense of ego	☐ weak, erratic, prone to extremes	☐ strong, fixed, ☐ proud	☐ based on family, possessions
Sensitivity	☐ hypersensitive, easily hurt	☐ insensitive, critical	☐ insensitive, self-content
Psychological disease tendency	☐ easily imbalanced, prone to psychological problems	☐ disturbed when obstructed	☐ dependent, childish
Psychological extremes	☐ hysteria, suicidal	☐ psychopath, sociopath	☐ dependent, childish
Emotional tolerance	☐ easily disturbed, reacts quickly	☐ good resistance, holds grudges	☐ slow to disturb, unwilling to change
Ability to handle stress	☐ very little, breaks down easily	☐ moderate, gets angry	☐ handles well, ignores
Anger	☐ erratic	☐ quick, steady	☐ slow to anger
Attachment	☐ changing, detached	☐ fixed, focused	☐ deep-seated, unable to let go
Depression	☐ severe, up and down	☐ based on sense of failure	☐ steady but low grade
Anxiety	☐ easily falls into	☐ rare	☐ low grade only
Compulsions	☐ trivia, novelty, freedom	☐ achievement, victory	☐ possession, ownership

	Vata (Air)	Pitta (Fire)	Kapha (Water)
Addictions	☐ entertainment, sensations	☐ alcohol, power	☐ food, possessions
Rationality	☐ prone to imagination	☐ strong but can be biased	☐ weak, slow, steady
Attention	☐ variable, changing	☐ steady, can be obsessive	☐ slow
Activity level	☐ high, hyper, easily exhausted	☐ steady, focused	☐ slow, prone to inaction
Effort	☐ quick, unsustained	☐ steady, determined	☐ slow, but can endure
Memory	☐ quick but absent-minded	☐ sharp, clear	☐ slow but steady
Speech	☐ fast, frequent	☐ sharp, cutting	☐ slow, melodious
Sleep	☐ poor, disturbed	☐ variable	☐ excess
Dreams	☐ frequent, disturbed	☐ moderate, colorful	☐ infrequent, romantic
Life-style	☐ irregular, erratic	☐ organized, inflexible	☐ routine, lazy, resists change
Faith	☐ variable, erratic	☐ strong, determined	☐ steady, slow to change
Relationships	☐ changeable, unreliable	☐ fixated, domineering	☐ steady, clinging
Social temperament	☐ rebel, innovator	☐ leader, fanatic	☐ conservative, provider

	Vata (Air)	Pitta (Fire)	Kapha (Water)
Response to therapy	☐ needs to be calmed	☐ needs proper direction	☐ needs to be motivated
Reaction to medications	☐ unpredictable, quick to side-effects	☐ can get overheated by	☐ easily becomes dependent on
	Vata	**Pitta**	**Kapha**
Total			

Overview of Doshic Types

Let us now take a quick overview of the psychological tendencies of each doshic type.

Vata Psychology

Individuals with Vata (air) physical types will usually have Vata (air) mental types, with emotional tendencies towards fear, anxiety, insecurity and ungroundedness. They will be mentally changeable, excitable and indecisive with fluctuating and unpredictable moods and interests. Their minds and senses are sensitive and vulnerable, but unsteady.

Vatas have good but erratic mental powers. They are quick to perceive and to react, but not always consistent in their judgments and opinions. They can be very comprehensive in their views or very superficial. They will have many ideas and speculations but lack in practical application, being easily influenced by threats or promises. Their intellect is often well-developed with the ability to grasp much information. They are able to develop the abstract and philosophical part of the mind once they gain control of their wandering thoughts.

Vata minds are good at both grasping and forgetting. They are quick at both attachment and detachment, fast at getting emotional and expressing emotions, as well as at forgetting them. They do not have much courage or daring and tend towards cowardice. Yet they seldom become vindictive and usually blame themselves.

Generally, Vatas are not good at forming long lasting relationships. They will be solitary or have many friendships of a transient nature. However, they are good at forming friendships with people outside their social sphere or age group and may have many acquaintances. They do not make good leaders, but they will not be good followers either. They will not be very materialistic and are not so concerned with accumulating possessions or money. They spend money quickly and easily, but also make it quickly and easily.

Pitta Psychology

Those with Pitta physical natures will tend towards fiery emotions like irritability, anger and hatred. Their minds will be sharp, penetrating and aggressive. They will be logical, critical, perceptive and intelligent. They are quick to get emotional, though they usually do not consider themselves to be emotional (in this regard they are seldom sentimental) and have no trouble expressing anger. They have difficulty, however, in controlling anger.

Pittas are determined, articulate, convincing and usually get their point across, dominating others with the force of their ideas. They often become self-righteous, sometimes fanatical. They usually possess strong wills, are dignified and make good leaders. They are ambitious, have great goals in life and work hard to achieve them.

While very helpful and kind to friends and followers, Pitta types can be cruel and unforgiving to opponents. They are bold, adventurous, daring and reckless and like danger and challenges. They are inventive, ingenious and possess good mechanical skills. They enjoy the use and expression of energy and technology. Their memory is sharp and logical. They have much clarity but may lack in compassion. They are more concerned with the accumulation of power than with gaining material resources, but will gather material resources to reach their goals.

Kapha Psychology

Those with Kapha constitution tend towards watery emotions like love and desire, romance and sentimentality or, on the negative side, toward greed and lust. They are kind, considerate and loyal, but not always capable of change and adaptation. They can be slow to respond, conservative, shy and obedient. Or they can be obstinate, fixed in their views and unwilling to make efforts.

Kaphas usually have many friends and are very close to their family, community, culture, religion and country. They can be closed minded outside their sphere of habitual activity, however, and tend to be suspicious of strangers. They travel less and are happier at home. They easily get attached and find it hard to let go of the past. While they can display affections easily, they are slow to express negative emotions, particularly anger. They prefer their habitual routines and can get caught in a routine.

Mentally, Kapha types are steady with good forethought, but need time to consider things properly. They find it difficult to grasp abstract ideas and learn better through something practical. They are not always sensitive or perceptive, but are seldom negative, rude or critical. They may throw their weight around, however, and like to expropriate things for themselves. They accumulate possessions and value material objects and resources.

Variations of Mental and Physical Types

It is not uncommon to find exceptions to this correspondence of doshic physical and psychological types. Nature has many different ways of making human beings and every possible variety must be manifested. Moreover, the energetics between the outer and inner aspects of our nature are not always simple. If we apply Ayurveda rigidly in this regard, our approach may be psychologically naive.

A Kapha (heavy) physical type may at times have a Vata (light) mind, as, for instance, an obese but very talkative schoolteacher. Hence, we must not treat psychological conditions simplistically according to the physical

Dosha. The physical body may not simply reflect the mental nature, but may try to balance or compensate for it.

As mental nature is subtler than physical nature, more variations in it are possible. As mental nature is more changeable than physical nature, it can easily take on temporary disturbances of a type different than the physical constitution. Mental disturbances therefore, are more likely to be different than the physical constitution, whereas physical diseases may be more similar. The mind is very easily disturbed by the disease process and not always in a way that is of the same quality as the disease. Generally, all diseases make us afraid, bringing up the basic fear of death, and aggravate Vata by creating anxiety in the mind.

When a difference between physical and mental nature exists, we must be careful not to aggravate one in treating the other. Special herbs for the mind may have to be given as well as those for the body. We must learn to look at the mind directly, not just in the stereotypical emotional pattern that goes with the physical constitution. Vedic astrology often provides a better understanding of the details and variations in the psychology of a person.

Sattvic Types

Sattvic types have the greatest freedom from disease. Their nature is harmonious and adaptable. They strive towards balance and have peace of mind, which cuts the psychological root of disease. They are considerate of others and take care of themselves. They are good custodians of their physical bodies. They see all life as a learning experience and try to see the good in all things, including disease.

Rajasic Types

Rajasic types possess good energy but tend to burn themselves out through excessive activity. They attempt too much, expect too much and overextend themselves. Disease symptoms are acute and recovery is possible with the right remedial measures. They are impatient and inconsistent in dealing with disease and do not wish to take time or responsibility to get well. They will blame others for their condition and expect others to cure them.

Tamasic Types

Tamasic types have more chronic diseases including suppressed emotional conditions like cancer. Their energy and emotion tends to be stagnant and they are caught in a pattern of negativity and self-destruction. Their own mental darkness is the main block to improving their condition. Their diseases tend to be deep seated, obstinate and difficult to treat. They do not seek proper treatment and usually have poor hygiene and devitalized diet. They will accept their disease as fate and will not take advantage of the methods that may cure them.

The Three Mental Types and the Three Doshas

The main method of working with the doshas and the gunas is to move from their tamasic and rajasic sides to their sattvic (spiritual) side. It is usually not possible to transcend one's predominant dosha, but one can move to its higher level of functioning. For example, a Kapha (water) type can move from greed (a tamasic or rajasic emotion) to devotion (a sattvic emotion), thus transforming an emotional disease tendency into the power of health and enlightenment. Vedic counselors should consider this strategy carefully in their practice.

Combining the three qualities and the three doshas, the following picture of mental development in human beings emerges: Each dosha is divided according to the three qualities. In this way, we see that no dosha is necessarily better than the other in terms of mental nature; the qualities vary but higher and lower aspects exist in each type. Seven different mental types can be ascertained for each dosha (like the seven different Doshic types).

Vata Mental Nature

Sattvic {Harmonious}	Energetic, adaptable, flexible, quick in comprehension, good in communication, strong sense of human unity, strong healing energy, good enthusiasm, positive spirit, able to initiate things, good capacity for positive change and movement
Rajasic {Disturbed}	Indecisive, unreliable, hyperactive, agitated, volatile, restless, disturbed, distracted, nervous, anxious, overly talkative, superficial, noisy, disruptive, false enthusiasm, excitable
Tamasic {Darkened}	Fearful, servile, dishonest, secretive, depressed, self destructive, drug addict, prone to sexual perversions, mentally disturbed, suicidal

Pitta Mental Nature

Sattvic {Harmonious}	Intelligent, clear, perceptive, enlightened, discriminating, good will, independent, warm, friendly, courageous, good guide and leader
Rajasic {Disturbed}	Willful, impulsive, ambitious, aggressive, controlling, critical, dominating, manipulating, angry, wrathful, reckless, proud, vain
Tamasic {Darkened}	Hateful, vile, vindictive, violent, destructive, psychopath, criminal, drug dealer, underworld figure

Kapha Mental Nature

Sattvic {Harmonious}	Calm, peaceful, content, stable, consistent, loyal, loving, compassionate, forgiving, patient, devoted, receptive, nurturing, supportive, strong faith

Rajasic {Disturbed}	Controlling, attached, greedy, lustful, materialistic, sentimental, needing security, seeking of comfort and luxury
Tamasic {Darkened}	Dull, gross, lethargic, depressed, apathetic, slothful, coarse, slow comprehension, insensitive, a thief

Ayurvedic Examination of the Mind

From the moment we are born, our mind grapples with an overpowering ego or sense of bodily identity. We are programmed to survive and the ego is a lifelong slave to that biological need. Everything in our being demands that we satisfy the urges of our bodies and minds. Yet at the same time, we live with the gift of higher consciousness. We have a sense of awareness that lifts us out of our animalistic nature. It shows us a view of ourselves and the world beyond the ego. In this frame of mind, we exist in a world of unity. In the former, we live in diversity and separation.

The purpose of human life is to rise above the Subject-Object split and its resultant duality and conflict. In Vedic terms, we need to penetrate the veil of Maya. This is the dichotomy of the mind. It exists along a continuum where it is either a patron of mundane worldly desires or a champion of higher consciousness. Fortunately, Vedantic wisdom guides us through understanding this duplicity of the mind. Its philosophy dives deeply into the minute subtleties of its nature so that we can learn how to render it useful to our Spiritual evolution.

The Mind-Body-Spirit Complex in Healing

The human condition is one that struggles to reconcile the massive pull of the ego with the sweet and subtle light of greater Consciousness. We live through a daily tug-of-war between the dynamic forces of our mind, body and spirit. We have three competing but coexisting pillars of existence: mind (sattva), soul (Atman) and body (sharira). Each one of these aspects of our reality is intricately connected to the others. For instance, in physical disease there is a mirror component of mental and spiritual imbalance. Likewise, in the case of mental disturbance, there is a corresponding disruption in the physical and spiritual landscapes. But of the three elements, the mind is the key. It acts as a doorway that opens lines of communication to the other two players. The mind is the intermediary factor, or 'middle man,' that can send messages between the body and the soul. It is also the entry point Vedanta uses to access the Soul. It is the key to the door that opens to the Absolute.

The mind does not do this easily. It is a "wild card," subject to unpredictable impulses. It needs to be tamed and trained in order to properly serve a higher purpose. It takes determined discipline and practice for the mind to be brought to its true destiny as a channel for Spirit.

The role of the mind is critical because it is only through the mind that the Spirit can be realized. When the mind is poised in the light of the *Atman*, it is seasoned with harmony, peace and love. A mind that is fully directed inward is a mind that has reached *yoga*, or self-realization. Conversely, a mind that is focused outward and fixated on external preoccupations is in a state of *bhoga*, or insatiable desire. *Bhoga* inevitably leads to *roga*, or disease.

Fortunately, Ayurveda has the tools to transform the mind and use its potential to unite with Spirit to cure disease. It recognizes and takes advantage of the positive feedback loop that exists between the mind, spirit and body. The more connection with Spirit the mind cultivates, the more positive states of energy occur within the body. When the mind dwells in Spiritual concentration, the body is in a state of effortless health. In other words, freeing the mind allows for the Spirit to descend into the body and mind and do its healing work. There, it plants the seeds of perfect, lasting health.

Overall, it is helpful to envision the relationship between mind, body and Spirit as a triangle. The mind and body are located at the two bottom corners of the triangle and the force of Spirit lies at the pinnacle. Although the mind is the access point to the Spirit, the Spirit maintains ruling authority over it and the body. It is the ruling force that has the power to unlock a limitless healing capacity. Therefore, spiritual realization through the proper training of the mind, is the ultimate destination of Ayurvedic psychological medicine, just as it is of Yoga.

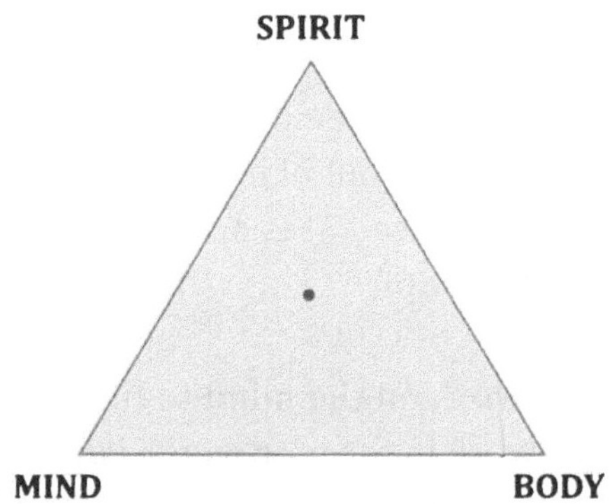

Diseases only have two locations: physical and mental. In the spiritual realm there can be no disease because it is inherently beyond time and space, body and mind. Attempting to access lasting health and happiness within the limited spheres of both body and mind is literally a dead end, as both are limited by time. Without the third dimension of the eternal Spirit, we become lost in a battle with the ego, time and circumstances.

Let's look at some examples of how this works in our everyday lives. Say for instance, you make the decision that you must lose weight in order to improve your health. Your mind will be eagerly trying to impose this goal upon your body. You will be using sheer will to demand yourself to resist that cookie, as it were. Slowly though, your will power will begin to dwindle and you will think about taking a bite anyway. This process is an example of a superficial decision made at the level of the ego. It is ineffective because it requires the mind to continuously fight with itself. It is constantly struggling to auto-correct, which breeds friction. At some point, the mind is bound to buckle-up and decide that it is done with the effort of enforcing the rules (which it will conveniently forget were its own). At the end of the day it would rather just rebel!

The alternative to this self-defeating process of mental struggle is aligning the mind with Spirit. When this happens, the perception of the cookie totally changes and there is no resistance in the first place. Suddenly the tasty item is not so appealing anymore. There is a realization that eating the refined flour and sugar the cookie is made of is not in your highest good and will cause long term harm. When this insight dawns, the mind naturally turns away from the cookie without any effort. This is the game changer. What we see here, is that the preferences of the mind are transformed, but not out of force. The mind is not suppressing either itself or the body. Instead, it is acting effortlessly in response to the higher directive of the Spirit. This is the way to make real, lasting changes happen.

Clearly, trying to work on the mind to fix the body, or the body to fix the mind, does not work in the long run. It isn't enough. When we try, we take part in an exhausting yo-yo game between the incessant, back and forth efforts of the body and mind. They flip flop, trying desperately to keep each other in check. For instance, when the mind is managed, the body becomes aggravated; and when the body is managed, the mind becomes irritated. If we please the body with something that superficially feels good, the mind may suffer on a deeper level, and the opposite is true as well. Why is this so? Why can't the body just be satisfied when the mind forces it to sit still all day long at the computer? Or, why can't the mind just be awake and alert when the body indulges in three slices of tasty stuffed crust pizza? The constraint of one induces the rebellion of the other. The urges to satisfy the desires of the mind and body are never ending. They are both at the mercy of the ego and on the level of illusion *(Maya*).

Working to try to heal either at this level is ineffective. It is like scrambling to stop water from flowing out of a fountain by blocking it in all places except the fountainhead itself. The fountainhead is the original source of the problem so it must be directly blocked if the water is to be stopped. Trying to quell the desires of the mind and body is a chaotic game that is blind to the source of its own dissatisfaction - separation from the higher Self. Therefore, the purpose of Vedantic counseling is to promote spiritual evolution in order to transcend the *Maya* (the illusion of diversity) and move toward *Mahat* (cosmic intelligence), where the source of the problem can finally be addressed. In that unbounded space of cosmic intelligence, the mind and body are spontaneously drawn towards what is good and true for them. Their desires are minimized and healing can effortlessly unfold.

The Three Bodies in Healing

Energetically speaking, the body of a human being has several layers. Ayurveda holds that we have three energetic bodies or *shariras,* which can be visualized as concentric circles around a single person. These three bodies are: our outermost physical or gross body (*sthula sharira*), our subtle body (*sukshma sharira*), and our innermost causal body *(karana sharira).* If we can understand how our energetic bodies operate, we can get a better idea about how to heal ourselves and our clients. It is our job to take care of each of these levels of our being and then to lead our patients to do the same.

The outermost body in the series of concentric circles is the gross body or *sthula sharira.* This is the skin and bones level of our being. If we want to take care of this body, we have to eat the right kind of foods, have proper exercise, breathe clean air, and spend adequate time outside in nature. This is intuitively known by us all. We know that if we want to have healthy physical bodies we can't neglect them, and we have to give them the right raw materials to work with. But the level of the middle body is slightly more elusive to care for in modern day culture.

The middle body is the subtle body or *sukshma sharira.* It consists of the activities of the mind and emotions. It processes all incoming information in the form of experience. It assimilates all that is watched, read, thought or felt. We can attend to this energetic level by journaling about our internal thought patterns and feelings. And, although it is not the cultural norm, we can practice "consuming" only good sensory information. Examples of this are: reading spiritual books, listening to beautiful, peaceful music, or watching uplifting movies with a good, touching, ethical message.

Lastly, the innermost circle is causal body or *karana sharira*. The causal body is the witness or guide behind all thought and action. To nurture the causal body, practices like meditation and mantra are needed to help us cultivate the witness within. Out of all these three bodies, normally we are only aware of the physical. We employ the subtle body mainly in dreams and while experiencing intense emotions or inspiration, but we are not usually conscious of it. We touch upon the causal body in deep sleep, profound perception, or deep silence of the mind (transcendental Consciousness).

These three bodies have a unique role in the understanding of the mind-body-spirit complex and its proclivity towards health or disease. In our attempt to achieve optimal health and to eradicate disease, we may consider one of two ways to work with our energetic bodies. In the first option, we decide to funnel all of our efforts into the level of the physical body (outermost circle or *sthula sharira*). In this process, we gain only transient satisfaction and achieve little success because we cannot move deeper into the interior circles of being where lasting change occurs. In the second case, we decide to concentrate our focus on the innermost, causal body and move from within.

Coming from this body of awareness, our mindfulness increases and we are then able to apply our newfound wisdom to the outer, physical plane of our being. Automatically we begin to make the correct choices of diet and lifestyle. We are no longer forcing our mind or body to comply with the imposing agenda of our ego. In other words, our healing comes effortlessly from the inside out. This is because the river of health flows in one direction – from the causal body, outward. The momentum we gain from moving this way will then give us the strength we need to heal the outer, more superficial layers of our energetic bodies.

Nature of the Mind

The ultimate purpose of Ayurvedic counseling is to guide the patient toward their own spiritual evolution so that they can transcend the illusion of diversity and return to the blissful state of unity. Ayurveda has long recognized that the point at which this transformation can take place is at the level of sattva, which is the original nature of the mind.

On one end, the mind is connected to all our sensory faculties and the external world. On the other end, it is connected to the cosmic intellect or higher intelligence, in the inner world. The mind is the link between the realms of diversity and of unity, outside and inside. The mind is the thinking mechanism. It is needed to access the divine, but also can be pulled by the undivine. This is why Ayurveda places such great emphasis on therapies that purify and mold the mind into a channel for Spirit.

To begin with, the mind is responsible for our perception of the external world. This knowing starts at the level of our senses. Our sensory organs (*jnanendriyas*) receive vibrations from objects. The mind then analyzes and interprets these vibrations. For example, the eyes receive the input of something small and red on our kitchen table. The mind then recognizes this object as an apple. After that, the mind gives it a meaning of "delicious, sweet, crispy fruit." Then, the mind is motivated to direct the organs of action (*karmendriyas*) to operate; "walk over there and pick up the fruit so I can eat it."

The mind is not just a passive organ that receives sensory information; it is also an active organ that directs actions in the body. It is both a sense organ and a motor organ at once. The mind is a source not only of knowledge, but also of the motivation produced from that knowledge. Interestingly, neither the sense organs nor the motor organs can work without the association of mind, but the mind can function independently of both of them. The senses need the mind to interpret their data so that hearing is made into listening, touching into feeling, eating into savoring, seeing into observing, and smelling into fragrance. Without the mind, the function of each sensory organ is limited and not connected to the others. The ears can only hear and the eyes can only see, but with the mind they become alive. For the mind, however, there are no limitations – it needs nothing else to realize its highest potential. The mind can function without the sense organs, as it does in sleep or deep meditation. Therefore, it is beyond the senses. The mind is by its nature then, set up to transcend the human sensory experience to reach eternal bliss, so long as we turn it within.

The Mind Channel

The mind pervades the entire field of perception. It does not have one location only. It penetrates the whole body, leaving not an inch unsaturated without its presence. However, although diffuse in nature, the mind has its root in one particular area of the body. Logically, one might think this would be in the brain. According to Ayurveda though, the home of the mind resides in the heart; in the chest, in between the lungs. And because the mind is the gateway to higher Consciousness, the seat of *Atman* also resides in the heart, not as a physical organ but as the center of one's being.

The mind is enveloped in streams of incoming information that it processes all day long. These thought forms carry energy with them. That energy moves through a subtle channel called the *manovaha srotas* (the channel of the mind). This transport system of mental energy begins in the heart and branches out to the brain, just as our blood is pumped through the heart but the greater portion of it goes to the brain. Though rooted in the heart, the mind expands its activity through the brain. Together the mind's fields of action are the heart and brain. Their combined influence encompass the entire body.

Everything that comes through this mind channel must be digested, metabolized and absorbed, so to speak. For instance, say we have a feeling of shame we have never dealt with. That emotion of shame is left unprocessed in the channel of the mind. As unmetabolized material, it ferments and creates something called *ama*, or toxicity. Mental *ama* is like a sludge that keeps us in a dull or *tamasic* state of mind, clouding our mental and emotional clarity. To maintain a vibrant, healthy mind-channel (*mano-vaha srota)* we need to make sure we acknowledge and then transform any unpleasant emotions so their negative energy flows away.

We all have a life-force energy referred to in Ayurveda as prana. It is a stimulating force that circulates throughout the entire body. In essence, prana is the energy of pure consciousness. Like the channel for the mind, prana also emerges from the heart but travels along a different highway. The energy of our Consciousness moves on tiny, little energetic tracks called *pranavaha nadis* or channels of prana. These are more minute and subtle than even the channel of the mind. In fact, they feed and give power to the greater mind channel.

The channels of prana are responsible for our mind's well-being. If blocked, psychological disease will result. Similar to the mind-channel, unprocessed grief or traumas become blockages to a smooth flow of energy within these pranic channels. We must put down these burdens so that our consciousness can flow unobstructed. We need to keep these subtle channels of consciousness free to circulate and bathe our being with the pure light of awareness.

Functions of the Mind

When the mind receives vibrations from the sense organs it acts as a coordinating center. It makes decisions based on the incoming information so as to decide what action to command the body to take. It is the master control center that maintains homeostasis and thus balances the overuse or underuse of the senses. The mind is incessantly intercepting signals and demands from the body as well as from its own thought patterns. In spite of all the many thoughts that fly relentlessly through the mind though, only a few end up manifesting as actions in the real world. This is because the mind actively sorts through the bombardment of incoming information and selects only what it considers to be relevant at the moment. It has to choose which ideas deserve real attention, and which can be left behind. In order to make this judgment call, the mind has five different, successive strategies it uses.

The first of these is the action of "thought-based filtering." In this beginning step, the mind is sifting through the massive onslaught of material it receives. It does a broad sweep of all incoming information and picks only a few thoughts, which seem to superficially pose a useful potential.

Then, the mind goes through a second step in which the chosen thoughts are put through a process of deeper scrutiny. The mind weighs their pros and cons to assess the selected ideas for their validity. This second step of analysis is inquiry or "examination." After the test of examination, one idea emerges victorious and becomes the basis of the mind's subsequent activity.

The action of selecting that top idea and eliminating all the others is "judgment". At this point the winning thought has been crowned as a worthy investment. Since the mind knows it will take energy to bring this thought into action, it has carefully chosen the one it thinks will be most worthwhile. Now, to make sure its champion idea does not go to waste, the mind sets goals that will ensure the thought becomes a reality. This is called "contemplation." Then, after all this, during the final stage of the forming of intention, the last thing the mind has to do is use its cognitive power. It initiates "executive order" thinking to set up a detailed plan of action to realize its goals.

The amazing thing is that our minds go through each one of these laborious steps in only a matter of moments! Every time we make a decision, no matter how big or small, our mind uses these five functions to manifest it into reality. Now we can see just how much work the mind is doing all the time. With all of its demanding duties, the mind can have a hard time learning how to slow down the oscillations of thought and hone in to a one-pointed focus. The capacity of the mind to arrest the bombardment of thought and focus in on only one thing (like the breath for instance) is at once its greatest challenge and most redeeming virtue. Hence, the practice of meditation can be a strenuous, albeit worthwhile, discipline for the mind.

The Four Aspects of Mental Activity

According to Vedanta, there are four functional components of the mind that collaborate to bring about the fully operable organ known as the mind. These four aspects of the mind are called: *manas*, *ahamkara*, *buddhi* and *chitta*, referring respectively to the outer mind, ego, inner intelligence, and the mental field as a whole.

To begin with, *manas* or outer aspect of the mind takes care of the most basic, mechanistic functions. It is the fundamental part of the mind that is connected to the senses. It is the carrier of all thought. Because it is continually bombarded by a plethora of raw sensory information, it is inherently *rajasic* in nature – always busy and constantly moving.

Ahamkara, or ego, on the other hand, is not merely a receptacle, or even an interpreter for what is seen, heard, tasted, touched or smelled. Instead, it is the aspect of the mind that attaches an identity to all that it perceives. It contains the sense of self. It binds the mind to the perception of I-ness. *Ahamkara* creates a division between inner and outer worlds and between self and others. It erects the illusion of separation and shrouds unity. It is also *rajasic* in nature; as it eagerly wants and desires for its own gain. Yet it easily leads to tamas by its identification with the gross body and external world. But inasmuch as this component of the mind appears to be the doer of all evil, it does have redeeming virtues. First of all, it is the aspect of the mind that motivates us to survive. Clearly, this is a necessary function, or most of us wouldn't be around today! Secondly, if *ahamkara* is experienced rightly, and connected to *Atman* (inner consciousness), it can become a great tool for spiritual advancement. At this level of operation, it has the ability to transcend animalistic desires to survive and reproduce, and become a reflection of God. This advanced functioning of *ahamkara* is the opposite of what it normally would be. It allows us to conceive of the oneness that exists within the many, and there is no greater gift than that. Again, we can see here how the mind is able to act as the access point for Spirit.

Next is the part of the mind called *buddhi* or cognitive intelligence. *Buddhi* is the discriminator, which allows decisions and determinations to be made. It is the force that when functioning properly, enables us to self-correct even in the face of the temptation to indulge the senses in something that might ultimately be harmful to us. Human beings are the only creatures on earth whose *buddhi* can be fully activated. *Buddhi* is the bridge between heaven and earth, division and unity, *Maya* and *Purusha. Buddhi* helps us transcend the outer world of desire and become one with *Sat Chit Ananda,* or eternal Being-Consciousness-Bliss. *Buddhi* represents the individualized *Mahat,* or cosmic intellect, that connects us to the inner Self. Because of this, *buddhi* is naturally *sattvic* in nature. Emotionally, a person operating from the level of *buddhi* is calm, content and happy.

Finally, the last function of the mind is memory or *chitta. Chitta* stores all memories from our current and past lives. It is the cumulative product of lifetimes of conditioned consciousness. *Chitta* represents the net effect that both nature and nurture have through time on the temperament of our minds. Given our genetic makeup and environmental exposure, our minds develop fundamental ways of being and manners of behavior – that is our *chitta*. Essentially, we can see *chitta* as the individual disposition of each one of our minds. In other words, *chitta* manifests as the unique psychological temperament we are all born with. Because of this, *chitta* can be innately *sattvic, rajasic* or *tamasic,* depending on the person's frame of mind.

Together these four aspects collaborate to form the whole, dynamic, complex and multi-faceted unit that we call the mind. To review, the *manas* aspect carries the vibrations from the world around us. *Ahamkara* gives those vibrations (including ourselves) an identity separate from others. The facet of *buddhi* makes the decisions, and *chitta* holds on to the memories of our collective life experiences. If we use the analogy of a computer system, we can start to understand how each component of the mind is related with the other. *Manas* works as the connection cord between the CPU and keyboard, processing all incoming information. The CPU itself acts as *buddhi,* the file name as *ahamkara,* and the saving of the file as *chitta.* Knowing these principals of the mind, we can see that it is at once a mundane and spiritual organ. It has the capacity to both process commonplace sensory information and connect to higher

Consciousness. It is the bridge that connects both worlds.

The Three Etiological Factors of Disease

According to Ayurveda, there are three main reasons why we fall ill. In the discussion of Ayurvedic psychology and the role of the Vedic counselor, the second of these three successive causes is the most relevant. It is referred to as *Prajnaparadha,* meaning "failure of wisdom," "mistake of the intellect," or "crime against wisdom."

The significance behind this etiological factor for disease is potent. It recognizes that we ourselves are at the crux of our own illness, as both the cause and effect. When we habitually choose to do things that our inner wisdom tells us not to, we are setting ourselves up for disease. The concept of *Prajnaparadha* leaves us with a powerful message to take responsibility for ourselves by listening and acting on our own higher knowing. When we do not do this we are by default, enacting *Prajnaparadha*.

We may choose to go against our better knowing if there is a dysfunction in our deeper intelligence or *buddhi. Buddhi* is our higher discrimination and right judgment. If it goes wrong, we start to make choices that are not good for us. Our vision becomes clouded with the qualities of *rajas* and *tamas,* agitation and darkness. Our choices become harmful and can result in three different types of transgressions known as: degradation of the intellect, degradation of courage, and degradation of memory.

In the case of the first transgression, the intellect misjudges what is actually harmful to be beneficial. Discrimination is directly opposite of its correct orientation. This can have devastating consequences and is the cause of much suffering in the world. Nazi Germany for example, saw the German peoples as superior to the rest of humanity. In WWII, they actually believed that ethnic cleansing was a good thing for the world. Their moral discrimination was clearly completely reverse from the truth. They were poisoned by the transgression of the wrong judgment of intellect.

The second affliction, the lack of firmness or courage, occurs when the mind and sense organs of a person are so strongly propelled towards detrimental behavior that they have no control over their actions. We can clearly see this in cases of physical and mental additions. It is difficult for people who have this mistake of intellect to be able to follow a counselor's guidance regarding dietary and lifestyle changes. They will not have the patience or discipline to stick to what is right for them. They have lost their inner courage to say "no" to what harms them.

The last of these three transgressions is translated as the degradation of memory. This concept is based upon the idea that memory functions as a teacher. In the past, if the intellect had determined something to be useful, helpful and *sattvic*, then it should normally inform the mind to repeat such an action again. In the case of degradation of memory however, memories about proper and improper actions are diluted. For instance, even though you may have felt awful after you ate a bucket of ice cream last week, you nevertheless buy it once more and come home to eat it all over again! It is as if you already forgot what had happened last week. Your cellular memory should be reminding you to stop and put the bucket down, but it is not. In this case your intellect is no longer maintaining the right information about your past experiences.

The challenge of the counselor is to determine how to strengthen the patient's decision-making ability, so that they are able to stick to what is good for them. This is possible in part by working with the patient to cultivate a better cellular experience. For example, encourage them to take a yoga class every week and their body will begin to crave what is good for it. Whereas before they may have been completely inactive, now they will never want to miss a Yoga class! Reprogramming of the mind and body begins by cultivating positive cellular memories.

To know how to effectively intervene and strengthen your patient's intelligence, you will have to grasp the ins and outs of their daily experiences. You will need to understand who your patient really is. What are they thinking? What is their mindset? How do they live their lives? Why are they prone to certain habits and addictions? What makes them do what they do? Asking these questions to the client will inform you about how to introduce the activities necessary to strengthen their minds. For the patient, clarifying their intellect may not come quickly but with the trust and guidance of their faithful counselor, the journey becomes much easier.

Psychological Constitution – Manas Prakriti

To be an effective Vedic counselor, you must deeply examine the nature of your patient's mind. Each individual patient will need his/her counselor to adapt their course of therapy to their innate psychological character and their developed strength of mind. If the counselor is not aware of these it is unlikely treatment will be successful. The basic make-up of a person's mind is classified in Ayurveda by three main types of *manas Prakriti*, or mental constitutions. These delineations are based on the three gunas and are referred to as: *sattvic, rajasic* and *tamasic* character types.

Sattvic Types

One who possesses a *sattvic* character will have good intellect and will power. They are naturally drawn towards cleanliness, harmony, peace and knowledge. Their faith in the divine is strong and they are devoted to their work. Among the *sattvic* types, there are seven subtypes. These subtypes specify the unique inclinations of the people who fall into this particular psychological temperament. See the table below, for more details on each type.

Sattvic Sub-Type	Characteristics
Arsha	Highly religious sage, a person of great insight.
Brahma	Powerful authority and guide, beyond passion and anger.
Mahendra	Courageous and knowledgeable leader.

Sattvic Sub-Type	Characteristics
Varuna	Loveable and attractive. Good discrimination. Knows when to appropriately display emotion.
Yamya	Good leader with self-control. Acts in wise timing and is free from ignorance and envy.
Kubera	Rules over great wealth in a benign manner. Pure of heart. Displays patience and courage.
Gandharva	Plays with wealth and passion. Takes joy in art, flowers, perfumes, poetry and luxury.

Overall, these seven subtypes remind us that *sattvic* can take on many different forms. *Sattvic* persons can have interests in music, the outdoors, green living, art, or any number of other things. They do not have to be someone who is overtly pious or even someone who is a spiritual seeker. The unifying quality among them is their inherent moral strength and the purity of their minds. Because of these attributes, they are naturally *sattvic* and live in harmony with life.

Rajasic Types

Those with a *rajasic* character, on the other hand, are ruled by their ego. They are always striving for higher positions and more possessions for their personal benefit. They are dramatic, excessively ambitious, and can be overpowering and hot-tempered. The variation among the *rajasic* mentality is broken up into six different delineations of personality: *asura, rakshasa, paishachika, sarpa, preta* and *shakuna.* These terms are symbolic and relate to arrogance, anger, crudeness, action like a serpent, a ghost or a vulture. All of them are prone to emotions fueled and dictated by heat: envy, jealousy, greed, ambition, and superiority. Often their physical nature also corresponds to this and gives them a hot, sharp appetite for food and drink.

Rajasic Subtypes	Characteristics
Asura	Cunning, proud and vain. Likes to disguise his real nature. Internally full of both envy and insecurity. Seeks to belittle others in order to praise himself.
Rakshasa	Cruel, angry, judgmental. Indulges in too much sleeping, eating and drinking.
Paishchika	Uncleanly and is distracted by the opposite sex. Lacks healthy diet or daily routine.
Sarpa	Defensive, fearful and cowardly, but harmful.
Preta	Greedy, envious and unmindful of his excessive appetite.
Shakuna	Ruled by his passion. Unpredictable in behavior and ruthless in drive.

Tamasic Types

The third and final description of mental types is that of the *tamasic* person. This kind of mental formatting lends itself to laziness and ignorance of both mind and body. The mind of a *tamasic* person is ruled by a preoccupation with the basic animal desires of sleeping, drinking, eating and sex. This person lacks motivation because he is too afraid to initiate anything on his own and he is generally unhealthy and uncleanly. There are three subtypes of *tamasic behavior*: *pashava, matsya and vanaspatya,* meaning like an "animal, fish or tree", which metaphorically reflect various states of inertia.

The commonality among these types lies in the fact that they do not exercise their minds adequately and cannot moderate their desire for gratification. It is interesting to note, however, that this is different than the immoderation we see in the *rajasic* person. In the case of *tamas,* the appetite for food and drink comes more from boredom and lazy indulgence than it does from a fiery, aggressive hunger, as seen in the *rajasic* person.

Tamasic Subtypes	Characteristics
Pashava	Diminished intelligence. Lives only for animalistic urges – especially sex and sleep.
Matsya	Cowardly and unsteady. Immoderately consumes water and other beverages.
Vanaspatya	Little curiosity about the world. Lack of movement. Exercises minimal intelligence.

Three Tiers of Mental Strength

Overlaying the concept of mental constitution is a tiered structure of stratification, which plots various degrees of strength or weakness that exist within each type. These strata of mental stamina are collectively referred to as *manas sattva* or mental strength. There are three types or ranks: superior, medium and inferior, which are loosely associated with the three doshas: *Vata, Pitta* and *Kapha*.

Each biological constitution tends toward a certain level of psychological strength. Someone who is dominantly Kapha in physique is more likely to be endowed with the virtue of mental strength, owing to their potential for patience and endurance. A Pitta individual maintains a mental condition within the medium range, owing to their critical nature, and a Vata person usually struggles with inferior mental strength, due to their excessive fear and anxiety. Yet these are only general capacities and potentials.

These tiers of mental endurance are not fixed or permanent in any way. They are not inexorably tied to any one particular doshic make-up. Kapha types can easily become attached and lose their advantage. Vata and Pitta types can develop self-control and improve their mindsets. It is possible to enhance psychological strength through behavioral therapy and behavioral rejuvenation methods. With the right outlook, experiences, and practiced resilience, any person with any constitution, can develop their mind to a higher level.

Clinically, if a person of high mental strength is told that she must drink only hot water and lemon for three days, she would be willing and able to do it without hesitation or fear. Because of her superior mental strength, the counselor can have total confidence in her compliance with any number of recommended therapies. There would be no need to facilitate her treatment greatly because she would have the ability to competently implement it herself.

If the same treatment was needed for someone with a medium strength of mind, they could succeed but only with the addition of some outside support. A person with this level of mental fortitude may need a "buddy system" so that someone else can help keep them accountable. They might need more encouragement and positive reinforcement to execute tasks that require more motivation and discipline.

Finally, the person of the inferior quality of mind needs their hand to be held every step of the way. In this case, the counselor may need to invest more time with this patient, or even change their treatment plan may so that it is more comfortable and less intimidating.

Overall, being able to assess the patient's current status of mental strength helps the counselor to correctly select the best treatment for that individual. Since the aim is always for the patient to succeed, undoubtedly, the optimal prescription would be one within the constraints of the individual's mental stamina.

Clinical Application

For healing of the mind to take place, the counselor must first learn to listen and allow the patient to be fully heard. A gentle unwinding can then occur in the heart of the patient as they allow their story to unravel. It is from this place of receptivity that a healing relationship and deep understanding between counselor and patient can be developed. From this platform, the counselor will be able to see which treatments are most appropriate and how to most effectively introduce them for the intimate idiosyncrasies of their client.

In Ayurveda, the first job of the counselor is to assess both the mental and physical constitutions of their patient. Knowing these two aspects together provides a complete picture of the physical and psychological foundation and tendencies behind the patient's complaints. When this is understood the counselor can properly ascertain the pathogenesis, treatment and prognosis for the particular affliction. For instance, someone with a Pitta physical constitution and a sattvic mental nature will have the energy to change the world. On the other hand, if someone comes in with the same Pitta constitution, but they have a *tamasic* mental state, then they may have the potential for violence or even homicide. Clearly, it behooves the counselor to be cognizant of the dynamic interaction between the physiological and psychological proclivities of their patient through the doshas and guans. This way the counselor can adopt the best approach and select the most effective treatments for their patient's unique combination of biological and mental dispositions.

Deeper Healing

In Ayurveda there is a saying that, "health is the byproduct of enlightenment" and "disease is the best thing that can happen to you." What this means is that health comes naturally when the state of mind is divinely oriented, and that disease is often the catalyst for that change in orientation towards a spiritual nature. This is because disease gives us a "wake up call" from the zombie-like slumber of everyday mindlessness. It demands attention be paid to its grievances. The futility of a non-spiritual way of life may be recognized in the face of end stage breast cancer, coronary bypass, or a major organ transplant. That vulnerability in the confidence of the mind is the gateway to spiritual resurrection. And finally, in the wake of spiritual reconnection, health is a welcomed, and perhaps even unintended, side effect.

On the same note, Ayurveda says that "the real treatment begins after the symptoms are successfully eliminated." When a patient returns to the Ayurvedic practitioner and reports that all is normal and well, it is only then that the deeper discussion about the roots of the disease can take place. At this stage, the counselor can gently reflect to their patient the reasons why the disease was initially created. They can educate their patients on the weak points of their bodies, explain to them how they respond to various environmental triggers, and guide them on a path that will prevent future disharmonies from arising. The role of the Vedic counselor is thus to empower the patient by teaching them the way of living and thinking that is right for them. They can do this by giving their patients the tools they need to purify their minds so that they can realize their highest potential.

Ayurvedic Treatment of the Mind

Ayurveda is a science of life. It addresses what goes on in people's lives and how they respond to any given situation. It aims to truly understand the patient in all regards – spiritual, psychological, emotional and mental. It is a holistic system that sees each individual as a whole, entirely unique human being. Naturally then, it offers each person a treatment plan tailored to their particular set of psychological, physiological and spiritual needs. Ayurveda's approach is comprehensive. It offers everything from botanical medicine and therapeutic bodywork to gemstones and mantras, as tools to attain lasting health and well-being.

Ayurveda has three main avenues of treatment it employs to address overall health and restore well-being. Each pathway to healing employs targeted therapies that are aimed at addressing either the mind, body, or spirit. It is interesting to take note that two thirds of these healing modalities are dedicated to caring for the internal, intangible, energetic landscape of a person. The main emphasis in Ayurveda, therefore, is on fine-tuning subtle internal processes that are a part of every human being. Unfortunately, however, this side of Ayurveda is rarely seen in the West. The practice of Ayurveda outside of Asia is commonly reduced to the grosser, tactile, physical level of existence. Seeing Ayurveda through this lens still has much value, but it ultimately leaves the viewer with a limited and blunted perspective of the medicine. Generally, because the west has adopted a physiologically based model of Ayurveda, they've inadvertently ignored the spiritual and psychological treatments it offers.

Perhaps the focus on the purely physical level of Ayurvedic treatment is a reflection of the values of western culture. In the west, physical healing is often given greater consideration than the less tangible components of our existence like psychological and spiritual well-being. Depression and loneliness are still stigmatized, but physical diseases like diabetes or obesity are easily acceptable reasons to visit the doctor. In any case, given that the west's attention is exclusively fastened onto the physical component, there is an unintentional neglect of the psycho-spiritual aspects of healing. We must remember that Ayurveda is truly a holistic medicine, in that it traditionally gives attention not only to the body, but to the mind and spirit as well. It sees each of these facets as dynamically interactive and as having their own unique impact on the healing process.

Each avenue of treatment Ayurveda uses offers distinct strengths and virtues. It is up to the Ayurvedic practitioner to determine which therapy or combination of therapies, is best suited for their client. Every person cannot be given every single treatment. The most potent and appropriate medicine needs to be prioritized for each client's unique situation. Choosing the correct therapies is an art and a science. The ability to prescribe a treatment plan that really works comes from the practitioner's deep understanding of the nature of their client. The counselor needs to have taken a thorough history, used keen sensory observation, activated their intuition and knowledge, and listened deeply and compassionately to their patient's story. This will give them an accurate assessment of their client's physical and mental nature, as well as their general mental stamina. From that platform, the counselor will be able to pick which treatment modality or combination thereof, is most beneficial for their client.

Treatment Branch	Clinical Approach
Yukti-vyapashraya	Objective, rational, balancing doshas
Sattvavajaya	Psychological, increasing sattva guna
Daiva-vyapashraya	Spiritual / Divine, reducing negative karmas

Objectively Planned Therapy - Yukti-vyapashraya

It is *yukti-vyapashraya,* or objectively planned therapy, that encompasses what most people think of as Ayurveda. Objectively planned therapy works under the objective tenets of the three gunas, three doshas and five elements in order to delineate the prognosis and treatment of disease. It addresses problems of physical origin and pathology and employs tangible, material resources in its protocols. This therapy is the outlier among the others because it is based purely in the gross, physical realm of existence. The other two modalities focus on the unseen, subtle energetic components of the human experience. Objectively planned therapy however, works primarily through the body to obtain results. Its modalities consist of dietary changes, botanical intervention, alterations in lifestyle, or the traditional detoxification and purification system of Pancha karma.

This system of treatment is grounded in the physical reality of someone's day to day life. It employs the body as a channel to reach the mind. Since body and mind are merely different points on the same continuum of existence, objectively planned therapy changes the input into the body in order to reconfigure the output of the mind. *Yukti-vyapashraya* outlines options for tools like changes in diet, exercise and herbal regimens that will affect the subtle channels of the mind. In every case, the aim is always to support the mind via the body, in reaching or maintaining a state of sattva. Finding the way to peace, harmony and connection with the divine will nevertheless look different for every person. Each client will still need their own, hand-picked therapies designed for their constitutional make-up and the root cause of the imbalance they are facing.

To begin with Ayurveda's objective therapy uses food as medicine. In today's world the concept of food being a substance that heals or even cures a disease, is a foreign idea. Most allopathic medical providers receive extraordinarily minimal training on nutrition while in school. The bulk of their focus is on studying drug-based interventions. This is simply the conventional model of medicine as it stands today. Society at large doesn't value the impact of nutrition. It has yet to recognize food's role as a potent drug in and of itself. Like almost any drug, food has the power to either heal or harm, depending on its quality, quantity, and also the person who is using it. It is a process of unlearning to begin to see food as more than just fuel to "fill up the tank" so that we can get on with life and pay attention to more important things. Seeing the food on our plate as either medicine or poison, depending on the quality and content, is a striking change in perspective. Ayurveda bolsters this awareness with specific guidelines for the right nutritional choices in cultivating a *sattvic* mind.

Nutritional Therapy

Most simply, Ayurveda says to eat food that is from the earth. Refined flours, sugars and proceeded foods with additives and preservatives are manmade foods, not "God-made" foods. Foods that are in their fresh and whole form, without any adulteration, are products of nature or God. These are the foods that can work in our bodies as medicines. They hold within them what Ayurveda refers to as the six tastes (six *rasas)*: sweet, sour, salty, pungent, bitter and astringent. Naturally all these tastes predominate within different food sources. For instance, white rice and milk are dominantly sweet, black pepper is mostly pungent, beans are primarily astringent, celery is salty, and yogurt can be very sour. In order to ensure that we're getting the best possible range of nutrition, Ayurveda encourages us to have a little of each of these tastes on our plate. In this way, your meal is well balanced and not dominating in one or two particular qualities.

Typically in America, we are accustomed to a diet that overwhelmingly consists of sweet and salty flavors. This leaves out bitter, sour, astringent and pungent tastes, which assist in digestion and absorption. Having imbalanced flavors consistently can lead to clogging of the channels, including the subtle channels of the mind. Therefore, it is most important to eat food that is whole in nature and well-balanced in flavor, if we want to ensure our minds are getting the best raw materials possible.

The food we eat should feed all of our sense organs. It should sound, taste, feel, smell and look pleasing to the senses. We can also consider sharing it, or 'breaking bread' in the company of loved ones. They will bring light and good energy to the qualities of the meal. When we do these things, eating can become a ceremony of awareness and gratitude. It automatically becomes medicine because we are eating in mindfulness. Plus, we also will digest our food better because we are actually taking a moment to smell it and chew it! The action of smelling food stimulates gastric secretions, and chewing well activates enzymes that break down hard to digest molecules. When our digestion, absorption and assimilation improve, the substance of our vitality, or *Ojas,* grows. With good standing *Ojas*, the mind is nourished and becomes strong, happy, calm and energetic.

Herbal Therapy

The next line of treatment within *yukti-vyapashraya,* or objective therapy, is botanical intervention. Today, herbs have become very popular but are often used carelessly. They are taken irrespective of the constitution of the consumer and their current state of health. In Ayurveda, we consider the whole picture. We look at all qualities of the herb, the person taking it, the context of their life, and the time of year. Herbs are powerful medicines, so it is important to accurately select the botanicals that will be most appropriate.

If your client is dominated by a *tamasic* state of mind, he may need to remove mental toxins, or *ama*. The accumulations in the channels of his mind need to be flushed out. This way, his mind can become more active. The herbs that would be best suited for him would have a pungent taste like vacha, *(Acorus calamus).* Taking this herb, his mind will awaken from its tamasic slumber. Conversely, there could be a situation in which sweet and nourishing herbs are necessary. Instead of clearing, these herbs will build. Someone who experiences intense anxiety may need nervine herbs like jatamamsi *(Nardostachys grandiflora)* or shankapushpi *(Evolus alsinoides).* They will help remove the *rajasic* activity of the mind and pull it towards a sense of mental calmness and contentment (sattva*)*.

The herbs that work specifically on the channel of the mind are called *medhya* or "wisdom-promoting" herbs in Ayurveda. Generally, these herbs promote sattva, the basic clarity of the mind, and reduce rajas and tamas, the factors of agitation and inertia in the mind. They rejuvenate the mind and the nervous system and restore psychological well-being. There are three main ways these herbs can be administered:

orally (through tablets, powders, teas or syrups), nasally (by applying medicated oil into the nasal passage), and externally (by placing herbal infused oil onto the skin). In any case, the body must metabolize the incoming herbal medicines and unlock their healing potential. No matter how they are administered, the aim of all of the herbs is to transform the mind to a state of sattva.

Being able to bring the mind to a state of calm and harmony does not always come easily in today's modern world. Just by virtue of being a part of modern civilization we are overloaded with sensory information every day. Often, in an effort to manage the bombardment of stimuli, we end up multi-tasking or using drugs and alcohol to cope with our pervasive feeling of stress. Sometimes our bodies forget how to turn off the signals of stress. When this happens the mind becomes a slave to the fight or flight, and sympathetic nervous system response.

At this point, it is valuable to intercede with what are called adaptogenic herbs. These kinds of herbs help us adapt to whatever our provoking environmental stimuli may be. In the case of an all out war, they will summon the physiological forces needed to fight the battle. In the case of your approaching bedtime after a long day of work, they will induce a calming and soothing chemistry in the body. In this way, these herbs adjust the response of the body based on the needs of your life. Ayurveda's pharmacopeia has several adaptogenic herbs, the most notable and widely recognized being Ashwagandha (*Withania sominifera).* See the upcoming table for a list of other adaptogenic herbs used in Ayurvedic medicine. These herbs are nature's remedies for the plight of the modern world. With their help, the mind can becomes more flexible and resilient to today's *rajasic* culture.

In Ayurvedic medicine adaptogenic herbs may be considered to be physical *rasayanas* or rejuvenators, because they restore the resilience of the body as a whole. In treating the mind, these generally tonifying herbs are used to augment the effects of *medhya rasayanas* (or the nervines we have been discussing).

Ayurveda uses a variety of traditional nervines to act as natural reinforcements for the psyche. More now than ever, nervines of all sorts are needed to help the nervous system cope with the variety of assaults that offend it daily. Nervines have powerful beneficial effects on the nervous system in one way or another. These special herbs have the ability to relax, tonify or stimulate the nervous system. Nervines that are relaxing soothe the central nervous system, while those that are stimulating augment the activity in the brain. Tonifying nervines actually restore, rebuild and rejuvenate nervous tissue. They "feed" the nervous system thereby promoting its strength and integrity. Additionally, there are herbs which are generally tonifying to the body at large, but which don't exclusively target the nervous system. These support the overall nourishment of each of the seven tissues of the body. Particularly, they have a strengthening effect on the nervous tissue and often the reproductive and muscle tissues as well.

Many times when we are greatly stressed we feel our heart pump quickly and we know our blood pressure must be soaring. Our bodies are gearing up for a great battle. Most times however, there is no real battle. The mind interprets that we need to be prepared for war because of our state of chronic stress. In this situation, we may need herbs to sooth the rhythm of the heart and manage dangerous hikes in blood pressure. This is why the following table of Ayurvedic herbs used for the mind includes some botanicals that work to protect and nourish the heart. Terms like 'cardioprotective' or 'hypotensive' indicate that there is a beneficial effect on the cardiovascular system. These kinds of herbs address either the physical or emotional components of the heart. Working with the heart is yet another channel through which the mind can be quieted and calmed.

The table below depicts the top fifteen herbs Ayurvedic medicine used to buffer against the challenges the psyche faces on a daily basis.

Common Name	Scientific Name	Indications for the Mind	Medicinal Properties*
Ashwa-gandha	*Withania sominifera*	**Improves**: strength and resilience, Ojas **Relieves**: insomnia, neurosis, anxiety, hyperactivity, stress, exhaustion	*Adaptogen, Tonic, Rejuvenative, Nervine, Mild Sedative, Analgesic, (Physical rasayana)*
Jatamamsi **Also known as Muskroot*	*Nardostachys grandiflora*	**Improves**: intellect and mental clarity **Relieves**: hysteria, nervousness, epilepsy, insomnia, dull headaches	*Nervine, Sedative, Anti-spasmodic*
Brahmi	*Bacopa monniera*	**Improves**: memory, concentration, and learning **Relieves**: epilepsy, mania, hysteria, stress, exhaustion, depression	*Sedative, Nervine, Cardiotonic, Alterative*
Gotu kola **Also known as Indian Pennywort*	*Centella asiatica*	**Improves**: concentration and memory **Relieves**: stress, insomnia, emotional disturbance, epilepsy, behavioral disorders,	*Nervine, Mental Tonic, Alterative*
Shanka-pushpi **Also known as dwarf morning glory or aloeweed*	*Evolus alsinoides*	**Improves**: coherence of the nervous system **Relieves**: insomnia, anxiety, epilepsy and convulsions, stress, pain	*Nervine, Sedative, Tonic, Rejuvenative*

Common Name	Scientific Name	Indications for the Mind	Medicinal Properties*
Indian Valerian **Also known as Tagar*	*Valeriana wallichi*	**Improves**: concentration, balance of sadhaka pitta (power of judgment) **Relieves**: tension, anxiety, hyperactivity, insomnia, panic attacks, mania, withdrawal symptoms from addiction, headache, dizziness, epilepsy	*Nervine, Sedative, Anxiolytic, Anti-Spasmodic*
Vacha	*Acorus calamus*	**Improves**: concentration, clarity of speech, memory **Relieves**: depression, mental dullness, mental stagnation	*Nervine Stimulant, Expectorant, Carminative*
Tusli	*Ocimum sanctum*	**Improves**: mindful awareness, mental clarity **Relieves**: tension or congestive headaches	*Mild Nervine Stimulant, Diaphoretic*
Sarpa-gandha	*Rauwolfia serpentina*	**Improves**: function of brain **Relieves:** insomnia, agitation, mania	*Sedative, Nervine, Cardioprotective, Hypotensive, Tonic for brain*
Arjuna	*Terminalia arjuna*	**Improves**: function of the heart **Relieves**: emotional turbulence and sadness	*Cardioprotective, Alterative, Astringent*

Common Name	Scientific Name	Indications for the Mind	Medicinal Properties*
Bala **Also known as Country Mallow*	*Sida cordifolia*	**Improves**: energy, Ojas **Relieves**: nerve pain, paralysis, neurosis, exhaustion,	*Tonic, Adaptogen, Nervine, Analgesic*
Saffron	*Crocus sativus*	**Improves**: subtle nourishment of the nervous system **Relieves**: depression, nervous debility	*Nervine, Mild Tonic, Digestive Stimulant, Emmenagogue*
Shatavari **Also known as Indian Asparagus*	*Asparagus racemosus*	**Improves**: calm of nervous system and nourishment to brain **Relieves:** pain, spasms, insomnia	*Tonic, Adaptogen, Demulcent (Physical rasayana)*
Amalaki	*Emblica officinalis*	**Improves**: clarity and calmness **Relieves:** agitation, weakness	*Adaptogen, Tonic, Alterative, Antacid*
Rose	*Rosa centifolia/ damascena*	**Improves**: clarity and calmness, patience, compassion, love **Relieves**: depression, anxiety, palpitations, ocular headaches	*Nervine, Alterative, Emmenagogue*

*Related to mental function

The Ayurvedic usage of herbs rests upon its science of the six tastes and herbal energetics through which the basic qualities of botanical medicine can be understood. Note below the six tastes of herbs and their general affects upon the mind.

The Six Tastes

Taste	Elements	Energy	Vata	Pitta	Kapha
Madhura {Sweet}	Earth + Water	Cold	↓	↓	↑
Amla {Sour}	Earth + Fire	Hot	↓	↑	↑
Lavana {Salty}	Water + Fire	Hot	↓	↑	↑
Katu {Pungent}	Fire + Air	Hot	↑	↑	↓
Tikta {Bitter}	Air + Ether	Cold	↑	↓	↓
Kashaya {Astringent}	Air + Earth	Cold	↑	↓	↓

Tastes and the Mind

The mind also produces its own chemicals, flavors and tastes relative to the types of energies it reflects in our sensory, emotional and intellectual activity. These can have positive or negative affects upon brain function.

Taste	Effect On The Mind	In Excess
Madhura {Sweet}	Compassion, love	Attachment, heaviness
Amla {Sour}	Perception, stimulation	Discontent, jealousy, anger
Lavana {Salty}	Conviction, passion for life	Greed, overly ambitious
Katu {Pungent}	Focused, sharp, attentive	Cruelty, hostility, envy

Taste	Effect On The Mind	In Excess
Tikta {Bitter}	Satisfaction, self awareness	Grief, depletion
Kashaya {Astringent}	Quiet	Anxiety, fear

Not only the tastes of herbs, but also their fragrances, affect the mind. Our emotions have their own fragrances as well. There are aromas that are particularly effective for reducing elevated doshas, notably at the level of the mind and nervous system.

Aromatherapy

Dosha	Recommended Essential Oils
Vata	Lavender, Cedar wood, Sage, Geranium, Tulsi, Juniper.
Pitta	Sandalwood, Rose, Lotus, Jasmine, Gardenia, Vetiver, Peppermint, Lemon.
Kapha	Eucalyptus, Tulsi, Basil, Camphor, Sage, Rosemary.

Developing Sattva: Sattvavajaya

The second branch of Ayurvedic therapy that handles psychological well-being is called *Sattvavajaya* or sattva-increasing therapy. Its purpose is to enhance sattva, or mental strength and resilience. We have already discussed this therapy in some detail as it is the main treatment for the mind. The mind's inherent nature is sattvic and only if brought back to that can it be healthy and harmonious. Sattvic therapies of Yoga and Ayurveda show us how to do this. They are largely behavioral in nature and promote a sattvic way of life.

This sattvic therapy uses tools like mantras to dispel fear and anxiety, or yoga and meditation to advance self-knowledge and diminish desire. If you as a counselor are using this treatment modality for your patient, your primary aim would be to enhance their *buddhi*, or proper discrimination and good intelligence. This way, your client can make the right choices in their life.

To encourage this process, simply start by being a reflection of the truth for your patient. Then, offer them tools like pranayama, meditation and positive behavioral changes that will build their mental strength. But remember, as with any treatment, to figure out the precise and correct therapies to administer, you must first thoroughly understand your patient within the context of their lives. It is important you learn to inquire about the details of their daily routines. Then, see if you can observe any destructive, repetitive mental patterns. After that, it is up to you to prescribe therapies that will put the mind along a better course. Usually these are recommendations that involve behavioral and environmental adjustments. As your client begins to make these changes, the current habits of their mind slowly unravel with the input of new, more beneficial sensory information. This is the aim of the sattva-increasing branch of Ayurvedic treatment - to reprogram the mind so that it is can see the Light.

At the level of behavioral medicine, we can give the mind simple, practical tools to use on a daily basis in order to bring it closer to the energy of Spirit. The result of this, as Ayurveda clearly has recognized, is the effortless healing of both mind and body.

The aim within this branch of psychological treatment is to cultivate a state of mind that is *sattvic* in nature. To do this, we must first cultivate a life-style that is *sattvic* in nature. Luckily, Ayurveda outlines practical, every day, cost-free tools that we can use to change our lives! The change will happen gradually but inevitably. There are three stages one goes through to reach a level of *sattvic* being. In the following table you'll see the progression from a *tamasic* mental state to a *sattvic* mental state and how to get there. The psychological maturation that occurs by using sattva-increasing therapy blossoms effortlessly with the incorporation of its simple, basic and practical mechanisms.

Change in Quality of Mind	Therapeutic Goal	Mechanism of Change
1 | **Tamasic → Rajasic**	*Increase Agni, or metabolic strength*	◈ Exercise ◈ Eat more balanced spices ◈ Read spiritual books ◈ Set goals and work to achieve them
2 | **Rajasic → Sattvic**	*Increase element of ether*	◈ Learn how to transcend the ego: meditate ◈ Perform selfless actions: behavioral/achara rasayana ◈ Help others ◈ Eat Sattvic foods ◈ Follow a healthy daily routine
3 | **Transcend Sattva**	*Increase Aware-ness of the Self beyond Prakriti and sattva*	◈ Advanced techniques of Yoga and meditation

Sattvic Diet

Listed in the table are suggestions to eat a sattvic diet and go about a sattvic daily routine. Now let's go into detail about what these recommendations really entail. To begin with, we will examine the nature and qualities of a sattvic diet. Generally, a diet full of mildly spiced, fresh and warm food of organic quality is ideal. Tamasic foods like alcohol, cold, frozen, or leftover foods; red meat, and root vegetables other than carrots, should all be avoided. In addition, it is beneficial to evade rajasic foods like onions, garlic, caffeine and overly spicy or oily food. These will agitate the mind and produce excess heat in the body. Instead, keep your foods fresh, light and simple.

A typical sattvic meal might look something like colorful, freshly cooked vegetables sautéed in ghee with cumin coriander and fennel.

Then, to the side of that, there may be some slow cooked mung dhal simmered in turmeric and ginger served over steamed white rice. Finally, for a special treat, you might have a beautiful lassi made from fresh, homemade yogurt and sweetened with raw honey; or even a simple slice of ripe mango would do nicely. In spite of all this delicious food, the *sattvic* person would still naturally eat less in quantity. Why? Because they are eating mindfully. This person would be tuned into the sensation of being full, and would stop eating just prior to reaching their max. As a whole, they would consume their foods as if they were at a sacred ceremony, smelling, tasting, savoring and chewing every bite fully. Overeating is harder to do when you're in touch with your body and senses.

Sattvic Lifestyle

Next, to cultivate peace and harmony in the mind, it is crucial to have a daily routine. This allows the nervous system, and therefore the mind, to be at rest because it can anticipate what is to come, instead of being thrown around by an erratic schedule. Regulating the timing of meals, bowel movements, bedtimes and wake-times are all important variables that need to be monitored. When these things are regulated, balance in one's circadian rhythm ensues. This is because our bodies' daily activates are finally aligned with the greater cycles of nature. When we move with the force of nature, we are swimming downstream and all of life becomes easier.

To begin with, the start of your routine should be in the morning when you rise. The ancient scriptures dictate that one should arise before dawn; 6:00am is ideal. Meditation, yoga, pranayama, and an early morning walk can all be done before breakfast. If you become tired because of the early wake time, make sure to avoid any daytime sleep. Naps go against nature's cycle and increase *tamasic* energy. Instead, set yourself up for a beautiful day. Dress in clean, light colored clothing and make sure your home is tidy. Consider adding a vase of fresh flowers to the dining room table to brighten the energy of the room. Then, as you go about your day, you may choose to spend the bulk of your time in contemplative work or study.

Finally, at noon, with the height of the sun, it is time to eat your biggest meal of the day. While you cook and eat, consider listening to the beautiful Gandharva Veda music and sharing your meal with loving family members or positive friends.

Later, as your day is drawing to an end, engage in lighthearted activities like gardening or playing with your pets or children. Also, it is essential at some point during the day to incorporate regular, moderate the exercise.

Eventually, in the evening after a light supper, make sure you don't do any work on the computer or Internet. Especially within one hour of bedtime, take extra care to eliminate excessively stimulating work or entertainment, like loud music or dramatic movies. Instead, light a candle and spend your time reading uplifting spiritual scriptures or books before you go to bed. Your day should close with your head on the pillow and lights out by 10:00pm at the latest. Now you have the outline of a day that will balance both the mind and body by orienting them both toward harmony, peace and contentment.

As a side note, although it is logical to think that diet and lifestyle therapies would fall under objectively planned therapies, they are included here under the psychological branch, because their primary focus and aim is on enhancing sattva. In the objectively planned branch of Ayurvedic therapy, diet and lifestyle prescriptions for the mind would be more oriented toward the physiological functioning of the mind rather than its complete behavioral reprogramming. In *sattvavajaya,* the focus is on doing everything possible to bring the mind into a sattvic state of being. Naturally, that includes diet and lifestyle adjustments among others, which we will subsequently discuss.

Spiritual Therapies

The last of the designated Ayurvedic treatment avenues is *daiva-vyapashraya,* or spiritual/divine therapy. This third branch addresses pathologies which are neither psychological nor physical in nature, and which cannot be explained by logic and reasoning alone. It addresses a force which overlays both the psychological and physical realms of existence - Divinity. Practically, its objective is to energetically align a person in the right way, with the cosmological and astrological forces at work in their life - specifically their special karmas. In this way, Ayurveda's spiritual therapy draws upon its sister science of Vedic astrology to interpret astrological natal charts and compassionately guide one toward better timing and more suitable places and people for their lives.

Instances where spiritual therapy might be used are for occurrences in a person's life that are completely out of their control. For example, what if a man is a great worker but loses his job because the business where he is employed goes bankrupt? This is not something he could have ever controlled in any way. Alternatively, take the instance of a woman who is affected by a terrorist attack and loses a limb. She alone could never have predicted or prevented the unfortunate event that fell upon her. She was simply in the wrong place and the wrong time. Both of these people were subject to cosmological forces that were completely beyond their field of vision or control. Ayurveda recognizes that in instances like these, the forces of divinity may need to be invoked to heal psychological wounds and to prevent future traumas from occurring.

If using therapies of such spiritual nature, a Vedic counselor might recommend gemstones, pilgrimage, worship, ritual, fasting, offerings, or any number of other occult practices. In any case, all of these aim to energetically reconcile whatever the inexplicable misfortune may be in a person's life. To be effective though, the exact remedy must be chosen for the corresponding celestial disharmony. At this juncture, it is also wise to take into consideration the person's religious or spiritual background while selecting your chosen therapy.

Perhaps even more important than any prescription, the counselor needs to guide this patient in a Vedantic way. Since the patient's circumstances are outside of their control, they need to learn how to look at their life dispassionately. If not, they will become entangled in the web of their own suffering. Herein lies the primary role of the Vedic counselor – to remind the patient of their true nature. As a result, they will be better equipped to manage, or possibly even transcend their worldly suffering.

To conclude, shedding light on these three branches of Ayurvedic treatment is significant because it demonstrates that the true medicine of Ayurveda is much more than dietary, lifestyle, detoxification and herbal intervention. Ayurveda is a system of medicine that addresses the totality of the mind, body and spirit. This is reflected by each of the three branches of treatment it traditionally offers. Out of these three, two focus entirely on the spiritual and psychological elements of health. This means that two-thirds of Ayurveda's treatment system is dedicated exclusively to repairing one's connection to the divine. In sattva-increasing therapies the concentration is on healing the mental faculties so that they can access the higher Self instead of habitually dwelling in *Maya,* and in spiritual therapies, subtle energies are directly summoned for healing and reconciliation. The point to take away, is that the reason Ayurveda emphasizes clarity of mind and spirit as the majority of its traditional therapies is because of their profound effectiveness in guiding the patient to become 'established in themselves.' This is what Ayurveda defines as the true realization of health.

Yoga, Ayurveda and Behavioral Medicine

Counseling is essentially a form of behavioral medicine. Its prescriptions are mainly life-styled based rather than drugs or surgery. How we communicate and how we live in life, including our work and relationships, sustains either our health or disease. Behavioral medicine is the main focus of psychological treatment, but particularly relative to diet, it is foundational for physical health as well. Behavioral medicine has a special restorative and healing value, bringing peace and calm into our lives.

Behavioral medicine is an interdisciplinary field concerned with the development and integration of behavioral, psychosocial, and biomedical science, knowledge and techniques. It applies this knowledge relative to prevention, diagnosis, treatment and rehabilitation. It addresses the behavioral and social aspects of all medical conditions for body and mind.

A wide variety of health professionals are involved in behavioral medicine research and practice, including cardiologists, counselors, epidemiologists, exercise physiologists, family physicians, health educators, internists, nurses, nutritionists, pediatricians, psychiatrists, and psychologists. Behavioral medicine addresses all age groups and all aspects of society. It addresses the needs of children, teens, adults, and seniors, both individually and in groups. It also accomodates racially and ethnically diverse communities.

Ayurvedic medicine is firmly rooted in behavioral medicine through its life-style changes. In fact, although Ayurvedic medicine can employ any of its three treatment branches to heal a patient, it favors behavioral therapies above the rest. Ayurvedic behavioral medicine is a subset of its sattva-increasing therapy, and is considered to be the ultimate, superior and culminating therapy. Ayurveda values this treatment because it recognizes that positive changes in behavior result in lasting, positive changes in the mind. When behavior becomes *sattvic*, the mind is slowly carved into a perfect key that can unlock the gateway to spiritual knowledge.

Ayurvedic behavioral medicine is a development of its emphasis on sattva guna and its approach to psychological disorders, such as we also find in the system of classical Yoga. The concept of behavioral healing is to change our behavior in order to reverse the disease process and remain in balance with the healing powers of life.

Areas of Behavioral Medicine Research and Intervention

Adolescent Health, Aging, Anxiety, Arthritis, Asthma, Cancer, Cardiovascular Disease (heart disease, hypertension, stroke), Children's Health, Chronic Pain, Cystic Fibrosis, Depression, Diabetes, Disease-Related Pain, Eating Disorders, Environmental Health, Headaches, HIV/AIDS, Incontinence, Insomnia, Low Back Pain, Minority Health, Myofascial Pain, Obesity, Public Health, Pulmonary Disease, Quality of Life, Rehabilitation, Sexually Transmitted Diseases, Social Support, Sports Medicine, Substance Abuse (alcohol, tobacco, and other drugs), Women's Health.

Health and Behavior

Changes in behavior and lifestyle can improve health, prevent illness, and reduce symptoms of illness. More than twenty-five years of research, clinical practice, and community-based interventions in the field of behavioral medicine have shown that behavioral changes can help people feel better physically and emotionally, improve their health status, increase their self-care skills, and improve their ability to live with chronic illness. Behavioral interventions can also improve the effectiveness of medical interventions, help to reduce overutilization of the health care system, and reduce the overall costs of care.

Key Strategies for Successful Behavior Change

Lifestyle Changes	Improve nutrition, increase physical activity, stop smoking, use medications appropriately, practice safer sex, prevent and reduce alcohol and drug abuse.

Training	Coping, relaxation, self-monitoring, stress management, time management, pain management, problem-solving, communication skills, time management, and priority-setting.
Social Support	Group education, caretaker support and training, health counseling, community-based sports events.
New Areas In Development	Integrating behavioral medicine strategies into primary care and managed care. Increasing public awareness of behavioral interventions, including effective behavioral interventions in development of clinical practice guidelines. Increasing use of information technology for behavioral interventions. Improving integration of research and practice.

Behavioral Medicine and Rejuvenation

One of the wonderful and practical sattva-increasing therapies available is called *achara rasayana,* or behavioral rejuvenation. Achara rasayana or the "revitalizing power of our behavior," is a unique concept in Yoga and Ayurvedic medicine. It implies ethical, respectful and harmonious conduct rooted in a higher values or dharma. It employs particular behaviors with the aim of enhancing a person's overall healthy state of mind. Additionally, behavioral rejuvenation employs *sadvritta,* or action in harmony with truth, meaning high ethical principles, truthful or harmonious living. Adherence to these ethical and moral standards naturally produces a clear and clean quality of mind. Behavioral rejuvenation can be likened to an immersion program for learning a new language. You go to the country of the language's origin and constantly practice it in order to become quickly fluent. Behavioral rejuvenation is like a new country with a new language for the mind to learn.

Behavioral rejuvenation means following principles of truth, nonviolence, personal and public cleanliness, mental and personal hygiene, devotion, compassion, and a yogic lifestyle. These types of behavior naturally bring about renewal and rejuvenation in the body-mind system.

One who adopts such conduct gains all the benefits of what is called Rasayana or Rejuvenation therapy without necessarily taking any herbs or formulations (though these can be beneficial along with it as well).

The concept of Rasayana reflects a healing elixir that revitalizes the body, counters the aging process and strengthens both physical and psychological immunity. We should guard it with our highest intentions. Charaka in his ancient Ayurvedic classic text explains this therapy in detail.

Persons who are truthful and free from anger, who do not indulge in intoxicants or lust, who do are free of violence and dissipation, who are peaceful and pleasing in their speech, who practice mantras and cleanliness, who are stable and steady in behavior, who regularly practice charity and self-discipline, who regularly offer prayers to the gods, teachers, preceptors and the elderly, who are free from harsh actions, who are compassionate, whose periods of awakening and sleep are regular, who regularly take milk and ghee, who act in an appropriate manner relative to time and place, who are balanced and rational, who are free from ego, whose conduct is good, who are not narrow minded, who love spiritual knowledge, who have excellent sense organs, who have reverence for seniors, who believe and follow dharma and the words of the wise, persons having self-control and who regularly study spiritual teachings, get the best out of rejuvenation therapy. If persons endowed with these qualities practice rejuvenation therapy, they get all the rejuvenation effects described above. Thus the rejuvenation effects of good conduct and right behavior are described.

Charaka-Samhita, Vi 1/4/30-35

Traditional Behavioral Rasayanas:

A behavioral rasayana is that which deals with the mind's influence on the body in a very concrete, observable way. For instance, when you are happy, your body releases certain feel-good chemicals that promote health. On the other hand, when you are stressed or unhappy the body releases neuro-chemicals that strain and harm the its vital organs, health, and overall well-being. That is why Ayurveda has laid down a comprehensive list of behaviors that a person must cultivate in order to achieve perfect health or *svasthya*. In fact, Ayurvedic sages were so convinced of the mind-body relationship that they emphasized matters such as a doctor's bedside manner as key components in the process of healing. They have recommended certain types of attitudes and behaviors which promote our higher well-being.

Behavior And Attitudes To Maximize:	Behavior And Attitudes To Be Avoided:
◈ Love ◈ Compassion ◈ Speech that uplifts people ◈ Cleanliness of body and mind ◈ Charity and regular donations to good causes ◈ Spiritual practices ◈ Respect toward teachers and elders ◈ Positive attitudes and thoughts ◈ Moderation and self-control, especially with regard to alcohol and sex ◈ Simplicity	◈ Anger ◈ Violence ◈ Harsh or hurtful speech ◈ Conceit ◈ Speaking ill of others ◈ Egotism ◈ Dishonesty ◈ Coveting another's spouse or wealth

Another important Rasayana is "right action according to time and place." In other words, a healthy and regular daily routine is an important behavioral rasayana. Modern science calls it "chronobiology," following the natural rhythms of nature.

> *"For he who is balanced in diet and exercise, in movement and the performance of duties, who is balanced in sleep and waking, Yoga becomes the means of eliminating sorrow. "*
>
> *~ Bhagavad Gita****

Yoga means *yukta* or what is balanced, moderate and harmonious. Such positive behavioral principles are the foundation for Yoga practice, such as the list below.

◈ Truthfulness	◈ Spiritual, Respectful toward Guru
◈ Freedom from anger	◈ Loving, Compassionate, Sensory Control
◈ Non-indulgence in alcohol	◈ Balanced in sleep and wakefulness
◈ Nonviolence	◈ Knowing the measure of time and place
◈ Calmness	◈ Positive attitude
◈ Sweet speech	◈ Devoted to Vedic scriptures
◈ Engaged in meditation	◈ Charitable, living in dharma
◈ Cleanliness	◈ Keeping the company of elders and the wise
◈ Perseverance	◈ Knowing the measure of time and place
◈ Charitable	◈ Using ghee, milk regularly

We can summarize this Vedic behavioral therapy in a few key principles: Using Ayurveda, Yoga, Satsanga, Mantra, Fitness, Nutrition, Emotional Detoxification, Sleep, Spirituality, Laughter, Unconditional Happiness, Guru, Exercise, Support groups, Meditation, Retreats, Relaxation and a Positive outlook towards Life in order to increase sattva - the natural quality of light, clarity, balance, harmony, peace and love in the mind.

Psychological Immunity and Mental Resilience

Most disease and unhappiness begins with a breakdown in our psychological immunity and inner composure. This is our ability to handle stress, strain, conflict, and the other difficulties that are unavoidable in our hectic modern lives. Loss of psychological immunity manifests in many ways like anger, fear, anxiety, irritability or agitation, in which we become emotionally imbalanced for shorter or longer periods.

How do people deal with difficult events and changes that can fundamentally disturb their lives? The death of a loved one, loss of a job, serious illness, natural disasters, terrorist attacks, and other traumatic events are all examples of challenging life experiences. Many people react to such adverse circumstances by falling into negative emotional states that can be very difficult to move out of.

Yet people generally adjust over time to such life-changing situations and stressful conditions and return to their natural equilibrium. What enables them to do so? It involves resilience, an ongoing process that requires time and effort and engages people in taking a number of new steps to improve their condition. This means mental strength, emotional patience and endurance - in short, good psychological immunity. Creating such resilience is an important part of behavioral medicine and its treatment.

Resilience is the process of adapting well in the face of adversity, trauma, tragedy, threats, or significant sources of stress such as family and relationship problems, serious health problems, or workplace and financial difficulties. It refers to our capacity to "bounce back" from difficult experiences.

Research has shown that psychological resilience is ordinary, not extraordinary. People commonly demonstrate resilience in the face of various difficulties. Being resilient does not mean that a person does not experience any difficulty or distress. Emotional pain and sadness are common in people who have suffered major adversity or trauma. In fact, the road to resilience is likely to involve considerable emotional distress. Resilience is not a trait that people either have or do not have. It is the product of behavior, thought and action that can and should be learned and developed in anyone.

FACTORS IN RESILIENCE

A combination of factors contribute to resilience. Many studies show that the primary factor in resilience is having caring and supportive relationships within and outside the family. Relationships that create love and trust, provide role models, and offer encouragement and reassurance, help bolster a person's resilience.

Several additional factors are associated with resilience. All of these are factors that people can develop in themselves:

◈	The capacity to make realistic plans and take steps to carry them out.
◈	A positive view of yourself and confidence in your strengths and abilities.
◈	Skills in communication and problem solving.
◈	The capacity to manage strong feelings and impulses.

STRATEGIES FOR BUILDING RESILIENCE

MAKE CONNECTIONS	Good relationships with close family members, friends or others are important. Accepting help and support from those who care about you and will listen to you strengthens resilience. Some people find that being active in civic groups, faith-based organizations, or other local groups provides social support and can help with reclaiming hope. Assisting others in their time of need also can benefit the helper.

Avoid seeing crises as insurmountable problems	You can't change the fact that highly stressful events happen, but you can change how you interpret and respond to these events. Try looking beyond the present to how future circumstances may be a little better. Note any subtle ways in which you might already feel somewhat better as you deal with difficult situations.
Accept that change is a part of living	Certain goals may no longer be attainable as a result of adverse situations. Accepting circumstances that cannot be changed can help you focus on circumstances that you can alter.
Move toward your goals	Develop some realistic goals. Do something regularly — even if it seems like a small accomplishment — that enables you to move toward your goals. Instead of focusing on tasks that seem unachievable, ask yourself, "What's one thing I know I can accomplish today that helps me move in the direction I want to go?"
Take decisive actions	Act on adverse situations as much as you can. Take decisive actions, rather than detaching completely from problems and stresses and wishing they would just go away.
Look for opportunities for self-discovery	People often learn something about themselves and may find that they have grown in some respect as a result of their struggle with loss. Many people who have experienced tragedies and hardship have reported better relationships, a greater sense of strength even while feeling vulnerable, an increased sense of self-worth, a more developed spirituality and finally, a heightened appreciation for life.
Nurture a positive view of yourself	Developing confidence in your ability to solve problems and trusting your instincts helps build resilience.
Keep things in perspective	Even when facing very painful events, try to consider the stressful situation in a broader context and keep a long-term perspective. Avoid blowing the event out of proportion.

Maintain a hopeful outlook	An optimistic outlook enables you to expect that good things will happen in your life. Try visualizing what you want, rather than worrying about what you fear.
Take care of yourself	Pay attention to your own needs and feelings. Engage in activities that you enjoy and find relaxing. Exercise regularly. Taking care of yourself helps to keep your mind and body primed to deal with situations that require resilience.

There are additional ways of strengthening resilience that may also prove helpful. Some people write down their deepest thoughts and feelings related to trauma or other stressful events in their life. Meditation and spiritual practices help build connections and restore hope, while releasing traumas. The key is to identify ways that are likely to work well for you as part of your own personal strategy for fostering resilience.

Some Questions to Ask about Your Psychological Immunity

Focusing on past experiences and sources of personal strength can help you learn strategies for building resilience. By exploring answers to the following questions about yourself and your reactions to challenging life events, you may discover how you can respond effectively to difficult situations. Resilience involves maintaining flexibility and balance as you deal with stressful circumstances and traumatic events.

◈	What kinds of events have been most stressful for me?
◈	How have those events typically affected me?
◈	Have I found it helpful to think of important people in my life when I am distressed?
◈	To whom have I reached out for support in working through a traumatic or stressful experience?

◈	What have I learned about my interactions with others and myself during difficult times?
◈	Has it been helpful for me to assist someone else going through a similar experience?
◈	Have I been able to overcome obstacles, and if so, how?
◈	What has helped make me feel more hopeful about the future?

Yogic Counseling and the Eight Limbs of Yoga Practice

Veda as knowledge is the theoretical counterpart of Yoga as practice. Yoga therefore can be defined the practice of Vedic counseling. This means that yogic counseling is another name for Vedic counseling. Yogic counseling implies an integrative approach, restoring unity within ourselves and with the universe around us.

Today we regard a Yoga teacher as mainly an exercise teacher, who shows us how to properly align the body, relieve tension, and open up a greater flow of energy. Sometimes the Yoga teacher may teach methods of pranayama, mantra or meditation. Yoga teachers usually give group classes as part of a specific program, as the same defined sequence that may be given to everyone. One-on-one Yoga teaching is less common and usually remains at a general level of exercise modification.

This orientation towards group instruction means that Yoga teachers are not usually trained in one-to-one counseling skills, much less in the approach of Vedic counseling. Bringing in Vedic counseling skills adds a new dimension to the teaching of Yoga. It enables a more individualized instruction and overall life-guidance, such as was originally part of classical Yoga. Yet a Vedic counseling approach requires that we look at Yoga in a broader, more spiritual and psychological light. This reflects the tradition of Raja Yoga, such as taught in the *Yoga Sutras* of Patanjali.

The *Yoga Sutras* form the prime text of Yoga Darshana, one of the six schools of classical Vedic philosophy. Yoga in some form is part of also all six Vedic schools, which are linked together and can be regarded as complimentary. These six Vedic schools accept the authority of the Vedas, Upanishads and Bhagavad Gita in which we find the origins of Yoga. Specifically, the Yoga school is coupled with the Samkhya system that elucidates the prime cosmic principles from gross matter to pure awareness.

YOGA SUTRAS AND VEDIC COUNSELING

We can approach the *Yoga Sutras* as a counseling text, just as it is an important guidebook for psychological well-being. The purpose of Yoga practice as stated in the Yoga philosophy is to end all suffering for body, mind and soul, which Yoga defines owing to the five kleshas or factors of mental affliction. These consist of:

IGNORANCE {AVIDYA}	Lack of knowledge of our true nature, which is pure consciousness beyond the limitations of body and mind. Such ignorance does not consist merely of factual inaccuracies, but of a misperception of the nature of reality. It is not a complete lack of knowledge but a limited or superficial form of knowledge that may reveal the part but not the whole.
EGOISM {ASMITA}	The sense of "I am the body," and self-identification with the external world. This misperception of Self causes us to look externally for happiness, which results in eventual sorrow. Egoism causes arrogance or the thinking that we know all, when in fact we may know little.
ATTRACTION {RAGA} TO OUTSIDE SOURCES OF HAPPINESS.	The separate Self finds certain external factors to be attractive, pleasurable and to provide some degree of happiness. Naturally it seeks to acquire these.
REPULSION {DVESHA} TO OUTSIDE SOURCES OF PAIN.	The separate self finds other external factors to be unattractive, painful and to result in suffering. Naturally, it seeks to avoid these.

Deep seating clinging to the cycle of life experiences {Abhinivesha}.	The separate self gets caught in the dualities of like and dislike, gain and loss, pleasure and pain, happiness and sorrow, along with various sorts of compulsive and conditioned behavior. The ultimate result is sorrow, as we cannot achieve lasting happiness in these transient and dualistic currents of life-experience. Abhinivesha implies addiction and compulsive behavior of all types.

The ultimate source of all our problems from which we seek the resolution, is our own self-ignorance - not understanding who we really are at the core of our own being. From this ignorance we create a wrong idea or image of who we are. The result is that we get caught or enmeshed in a current of life-experience, trying to get what we want and avoid what we do not want. This creates the revolving wheel of samsara that perpetuates this outer seeking not only in this life but into future lives as well.

From these five afflictions arise the karmas that bind us to the realm of samsara as compulsion, sorrow and rebirth. The karmic patterns in our mind get us caught in unwise behavior in which we take what is transient to be lasting, what is unreal to be real and what is bad for us to be good. This is what causes eventual pain.

A Counseling Model Based upon the Kleshas

The five kleshas provide the basis for a good yogic counseling model. The Vedic or Yogic counselor should help the client understand their problems and sorrow according to these five factors. Most clients will have addictions, dependencies, compulsions or fantasies behind their problems in life. They are caught in some negative form of abhinivesha or clinging, to unhelpful patterns in life. They are unable to look at themselves or their behavior in an objective manner. They are victims of their own desires and karmas.

The klesha model helps us recognize the compulsive and unaware nature of our ordinary mindsets. It reveals the addictive patterns of the mind arising from ignorance. The counselor seeks to enlighten the client on the deep-seated nature of our spiritual ignorance. He tries to show the illusions and limitations inherent in our sense of self-identity. He shows how we get caught in dualistic currents of attraction and repulsion. He reveals that our problems are inherent in a wrong view of self and world, and a lack of understanding how our minds work. To counter the problems of the kleshas, the model of Yoga practice arises as the prime therapy, along with other related Vedic disciplines which are also helpful or necessary.

Raja Yoga and Counseling

This means that Raja Yoga is one of the best systems of Vedic counseling and relevant to all true counselors, whatever their background. The *Yoga Sutras* form an excellent manual of Vedic counseling, setting forth its fundamental principles and practices. The eight limbs of Yoga provide a comprehensive life-counseling model that can be further enhanced with the addition of Ayurveda and Vedic astrology. The Sutras are useful for all counseling approaches. After all, the purpose of counseling, like that of the Sutras, is to calm the mind and facilitate a deeper Self-realization.

Yet to apply the counseling model of the *Yoga Sutras*, Yoga teachers will need to study not only the *Yoga Sutras* but also their traditional connections in all the Vedic sciences. The Sutras as a set of short axioms in themselves, are very brief and do not describe their topics in detail (that was more the purpose of commentaries to describe).

The Eight Limbs of Yoga as a Counseling Model

The eight limbs of Yoga are not simply recommendations for Yoga practice but reflect the structure of our lives, action and awareness. They reflect eight prime factors that we all must consider in various ways.

Eight Limbs of Yoga as the Eight Aspects of our Life Orientation

Yamas	Our primary principles and values in life and what they imply.
Niyamas	Our primary attitudes in life and what they imply.
Asana	Our posture and exercise patterns.
Pranayama	How we are using our prana or vital energy, whether we are increasing or decreasing it and where our actions are leading us.
Pratyahara	How we use our senses in life and the consequences.
Dharana	Where we place our attention or focus in life.
Dhyana	Our primary thoughts in life, our most recurring and deep seated mental patterns.
Samadhi	Where we seek our ultimate happiness and peak experiences in life.

Eight Limbs of Yoga as Higher Recommendations

Yoga takes these eight aspects of our natural behavior and shows us how to bring them to a higher consciousness, so that we can develop them in the best possible manner.

Yama	Dharmic principles of right living for both personal and social well-being, what we could call spiritual or eternal values.
Niyamas	Dharmic practices and attitudes of right living, aiming at self-control and self-development.

Asana	Physical health and right orientation of the physical body, along with Ayurvedic dietary and life-style principles. While Yoga provides a good exercise model, Ayurveda provides the corresponding complementary nutritional model.
Pranayama	Right management of energy. Ayurveda shows us the physical use of prana. Yoga shows us the psychological usage of prana.
Pratyahara	Right use of the mind and the senses. Yoga teaches us how to control the mind and senses. Ayurveda shows us the value of sensory therapies like aroma therapy, color therapy and therapeutic touch.
Dharana	Concentration, attention and the right development of intelligence, creating a spiritual and dharmic focus in life.
Dhyana	Meditation therapy to clear out negative karmic patterns down to the subconscious mind.
Samadhi	Achievement of ultimate happiness within, as opposed to the fulfillment of desires externally.

Of these eight aspects of Yoga, the first two, the Yamas and Niyamas, are foundational to Yogic counseling. This is because they set forth the right attitudes and life-style practices for psychological well-being. As such, they also constitute "behavioral medicine" or "behavioral therapy." What we have already discussed relative to Dharma and Karma is relevant to the Yamas and Niyamas.

Yogic Behavioral Principles: Five Yamas

1 | Non-violence – Ahimsa

The Yamas begin with *ahimsa* or an attitude of non-harming as the first principle. Ahimsa is often translated as non-violence, but is much more. Ahimsa is not merely a passive practice of avoiding violence but an active practice of seeking to reduce the amount of harm occurring in the world, starting with reducing harmful activity within our own lives and in our own minds.

We are our own best friends and worst enemies. We raise ourselves up in life or bring ourselves down according to the nature of our own thoughts and actions. And our actions are rooted in our own thoughts. We should strive to be our own best friends and well-wishers, to promote what is positive within us and reduce what is negative. This is to promote sattva guna in all that we do.

Our minds are likely to be the worst terrorist that we must deal with in life. Our own uncontrolled thoughts are the main source of pain for us in life. Unrealistic desires, imaginary fears, unregulated likes and dislikes breed unrest and sorrow. We are often harming ourselves, our bodies and minds, in pursuing enjoyment or seeking wealth.

Ahimsa implies conflict resolution in terms of counseling practices in relationship, work situations and social concerns. Conflict resolution is only possible when we replace seeking to harm others with seeking to promote communication and common well-being, wishing happiness for all. Ahimsa also means not taking pleasure in the pain and unhappiness of others.

2 | Truthfulness - Satya

It is an unfortunate part of our ordinary human behavior and mindset not to tell the truth to others. We may not always overtly lie but we do not always tell the full truth or present things as they really are, if it may not be to our advantage to do so. The realm of advertising is often a good example of this.

Yet if we do not tell the truth to others, we also will not tell the truth to ourselves or be able to determine what is actually true or real. Our thoughts are likely to be filled with illusions, wishful thinking, or distortions born of conflicting emotions. Telling the truth is not just about better social harmony but also about a better ability to understand ourselves and the world in which we live.

We may not want to see the truth about others, particularly if we have various fantasies about them. It is often the people closest to us that we most fail to see the truth about because we have too much invested in our relationships with them. And it is often hardest to see the truth about ourselves. Truthfulness about ourselves is very difficult because we do not really know ourselves. That is where a counselor can be very helpful, like a mirror reflecting back to us who we really are.

3 | Non-Stealing – Asteya

Very few of us actually overtly steal from others. But we do take a lot from other people, much of which we may not acknowledge or express any gratitude for. We often feel entitled for various reasons, which can cause us to use other people. We may think that the world or society owes us something, that our family owes us something, or that we are somehow special and deserving of extra attention.

We may overrate our talents and capacities and expect quick recognition for little actual accomplishments. We may rely on friends and family for financial help or help in our career and not pay such favors back properly. We may take the ideas of others, as is common in the internet age, without giving them proper credit. We may use other people emotionally, while not reciprocating by giving back what they want from us. Such types of misappropriation can take many forms.

For a happy mind it is important that we are karmically clean, that we have no karmic debts. Whatever we take from others creates a karmic debt that can weigh us down in life. We must learn to free ourselves from any type of dependency or using of others for our personal benefit. We must cultivate a sense of integrity, not taking what does not belong to us, which means not taking credit for things we have not actually done. We should cultivate an attitude of giving, in which we give more than we take, and leave no residue or scar upon the Earth for having lived here.

4 | Brahmacharya – Integrity in dealing with our sexuality

Sexuality is probably the most powerful and most potentially disturbing force in our psychology. Many of our emotional problems revolve around sexuality and its related strong emotions. This includes relationship problems or the ability to find the type of relationship that we would like to have. Sexual betrayal or abuse is a major factor in disturbing the mind, particularly if combined with manipulation or violence.

The sexual force can be very creative but also very destructive. It can imbalance the entire psychology. We must respect its power and try to use our sexuality in a responsible and sacred manner, not merely for our own enjoyment. We need to be in control of our sexuality and not let it drive us.

Sometimes Brahmacharya is translated simply as celibacy. Yet celibacy does not necessarily give us inner peace and can be a form of suppression. Brahmacharya means that we must have integrity in dealing with our sexuality and not use it to exploit others. It implies expansion and liberation of our creative energy in a sacred manner. We must learn to move to a greater creativity than physical pleasure to find true love or happiness.

In addition, we must realize that no relationship can be perfect any more than we ourselves are perfect. We cannot find lasting happiness through others, though we can find happiness along with others. We should pursue a path of growth and improvement, not expectation and demand.

5 | Non-hoarding – Aparigraha

Aparigraha means not cluttering our minds with excess thoughts, desires, wants and attachments. Just as we often accumulate unnecessary items in the outer world, so too we do this in our own minds and hearts. Our minds down to a subconscious level are filled with useless memories, impractical desires and fantasies, trivial information, and compulsions and obsessions. We simply have not taken the time to question and remove these things from our mind.

It is not enough to live a simple life outwardly, we must also live a simple life inwardly, with space and freedom in our minds and hearts. To do this we must let go of the past and the burden of knowledge, with an open mind for new experience and realization. We must open ourselves to a new and higher way of life, in which we form thoughts and decisions to make our lives more meaningful and to reflect eternal values, rather than mere transient concerns.

YOGIC BEHAVIORAL PRACTICES: FIVE NIYAMAS

The Niyamas suggest practices for us to do that complement the attitudes of the Yamas.

1 | TAPAS

Tapas is arguably the prime practice for psychological health and well-being. It means to constantly work on ourselves to improve our lives and not to look to others to save us. Tapas means fire and indicates applying heat and energy to change ourselves in a positive manner.

Tapas is opposite to desire. It means seeking to improve ourselves and reach a higher goal, rather than simply indulging ourselves and seeking the fulfillment of our unquestioned wants. It implies a creative and spiritual life-style, in which we seek to develop higher powers of awareness, purify ourselves and remove negativity. Those who have tapas are those engaged in some important research or development, like artists or yogis. They have a purposeful life and use their time wisely.

Tapas implies patience and means that we cannot get quick results in life. We have to work over a long period of time for the best results. We need a long term practice or sadhana to gain what we truly aspire to. When we replace a life of the pursuit of desire with one of tapas and sadhana, our ultimate well-being is assured.

Actually all the Yamas and Niyamas relate to tapas as control of the outer self and energization of the inner or higher Self. Tapas is often a synonym for Yoga as a whole. The entire universe arises through Tapas as developing the inner power through which creation naturally comes forth. Tapas, or turning our energy within, is the basis of all enduring character development.

2 | Self-study - Svadhyaya

Svadhyaya literally means self-study. It implies that our lives are a pursuit of self-knowledge. It means we are actively seeking to learn - not simply studying the external world, but cultivating an inner awareness of our own thoughts and their consequences. Such Self-knowledge is not a fixation on the personal self but an examination of how the mind works. Learning keeps the mind youthful and adaptable, which allows us to continue to develop and grow inwardly as long as we live.

Self-study implies learning about our individual Ayurvedic constitution though the doshas, our specific karmas through Vedic astrology, our spiritual location in the world through Vastu, and the balance of energies of our body, prana, senses and mind through Yoga. It helps us understand our unique nature and capacities in life. Ultimately, it directs us to our true Self through Vedanta.

3 | Surrender – Ishvara Pranidhana

We by our own personal efforts can achieve very little in life. To accomplish anything meaningful, we need to access higher energy sources within and around us. These aids are not just better technology or help from others. We all possess an internal connection to the master force behind the universe, to which we must learn to surrender to. You can call this cosmic energy, God or any other name like Divine Father or Divine Mother, but there is a ruling power that facilitates all higher transformations in life.

There are both higher and lower currents of energy in life. The higher current takes us to greater awareness and peace. The lower current takes us to greater ignorance and agitation. If we learn to surrender to that higher current it will allow us to ascend in life. If we oppose it we will draw ourselves into destruction. We must approach this higher current in an intelligent manner, honoring it as part of our daily activities.

We must learn to access higher universal powers. There is a yogic science to doing this with ritual, mantra and meditation. We are but one current or whirlpool in a vast array of forces that reach beyond time and space. When we make the proper connection to the flow of Divine grace and the abundance of life, magic can occur.

4 | Cleanliness – Saucha

Saucha means cleanliness. Yet purity and cleanliness as yogic principles refer to all aspects of our lives, not simply to cleanliness at an outer level. We need purity in body and mind, as freedom from darkness, toxins and negativity.

The body needs physical purity, which implies a vegetarian and sattvic diet. The senses need their purity, which means emphasizing sattvic and natural impressions, and avoiding the rajasic impressions that are common in the entertainment media. The prana needs its purity, which means pure air and a sattvic expression and action. Purity of speech is very important, which requires avoiding gossip and not denigrating other people. The mind needs its purity, which means purifying ourselves of negative thoughts and emotions.

It is not enough merely to bathe the body everyday, we must bath our entire being with pure vibrations. Such inner bathing is not simply done with water but with natural and spiritual energies. There are various types of yogic bathing or *snana,* where we bathe ourselves in mantra, prana or meditation. We should bathe our minds in positive impressions and intentions. This can be aided by living in a pure natural environment or taking regular spiritual retreats to cleanse ourselves of negative energies.

5 | Contentment - Santosha

Contentment does not mean being complacent with our current state in life. It means having a deeper sense of contentment that provides us with an inner sense of well-being. True well-being does not arise from anything external. It must be intrinsic. Such inner well-being endows us with a natural sense of detachment that causes us to seek inner forms of peace and happiness.

An inner contentment in life, we should note, allows us the maximum outer efficiency, in which we can discharge our duties with a sense of grace. True contentment implies faith in our higher purpose and the patience to allow it to flower in its own time. Contentment is based upon an inner recognition that we will ultimately achieve our goal, because it is already contained in seed form within us. Contentment naturally leads us to bliss and to Samadhi. Inner contentment frees us from running after outer desires and allows us to consistently pursue our spiritual practices.

Yogic Paths and Yoga Types

A good Vedic counselor, particularly with some background in Yoga, can guide the client in Yoga practices. Mantra and meditation are an important part of Yoga and of Vedic counseling. The other aspects of Yoga can come into counseling as well, including asana and pranayama. Vedic counseling recommends Yoga practices and provides for their right application. More specifically, Vedic counseling can help you choose the path of Yoga that is best for you and can help you overcome your problems and issues in life.

Different Yoga paths appeal to different dispositions, which can reflect doshic, karmic and temperamental considerations. Generally speaking, there are four main approaches or types of Yoga, with many subtypes and much overlap, and a fifth approach that combines aspects of all four.

Yoga of Knowledge	*Jnana Yoga*	For knowledge-oriented, intellectual types, philosophical and psychological in nature. Emphasizes contemplation, meditation, Self-inquiry, and study of teachings. Less reliance on techniques, ritual or devotion, and may be formless in nature.
Yoga of Devotion	*Bhakti Yoga*	For feeling-oriented individuals. Relates to devotion, faith and Divine love. Includes rituals of various types, chanting, Divine names, dance, pilgrimage, worship of images or symbols.
Yoga of External Action	*Karma Yoga*	For active temperaments who are service oriented. Helping others, extending to nature and animals. May include performance of rituals. May include social activism, ecological work, healing work, prayers for peace, or charity.

Yoga of Internal Action	*Kriya Yoga*	For those who prefer the use of yoga techniques and exercises, who like to work on themselves and their internal energies. Most of Hatha Yoga comes under this including asana, pranayama and mantra, and techniques aimed at the arousal of Kundalini.
Integral Approach	*Combines all the Yogas*	Much of traditional Raja Yoga is here, though Raja Yoga usually emphasizes the Yoga of Knowledge as the ultimate.

It is important that we discover the appropriate Yoga approach for ourselves. Yet even within one greater Yoga approach several subtypes also exist. And it is possible to change Yoga paths over time as our consciousness evolves.

Determining Your Yoga Path

There are a number of factors that come into play, but it is ultimately based upon your own temperament and inclination. Follow the Yogic path that most resonates with your inner being. If you are in doubt as to what this may be, first experiment with different paths and discover that which is closest to you. The advice of a guru or Vedic counselor is very important in choosing your Yoga path. But you need not be in a hurry and should take time to examine the full range of Yoga practices before settling on one in particular.

Yoga Paths and the Doshas

Ayurvedic Doshic considerations have their relevance in Yoga paths.

Vata	Vata types with their active temperaments incline to Karma Yoga and Kriya Yoga. They like to work with various practices involving the body, senses, prana and mind.

PITTA OR VATA-PITTA	Pitta types or Vata-Pitta types with their perceptive and abstract minds incline to the Yoga of Knowledge. This helps them develop a deeper insight and discrimination.
KAPHA	Generally Kapha people, with their watery and feeling nature, gravitate towards the Yoga of Devotion. This helps them take their emotions to a higher level.

Each aspect of Yoga has its doshic considerations. There are meditation practices more suitable to different doshic types. The same is true of mantras, pranayamas and asanas. An Ayurvedic Yoga teacher can help with these. A good example is the Yoga asanas below.

ASANA AND THE DOSHAS

Postures for Balancing the Doshas

VATA ASANAS	PITTA ASANAS	KAPHA ASANAS
Mountain pose, Tadasana	Downward dog pose, Adhomukha svanasana	Tree pose, Vrikshasana
Triangle pose, Trikonasana	Spread legs forward bend, Padottanasana	Warrior pose, Virabhadrasana
Boat pose, Navasana	Full forward bend pose, Paschimottanasana	Peacock pose, Mayurasana
Shoulder stand, Sarvangasana	Inverted action pose, Viparita karani	Headstand pose, Shirsasana
Head to knee, Janu shirasana	Child's pose, Balasana	Cobra pose, Bhujangasana
Full forward bend, Paschimottanasana	Perfect sitting pose, Siddhasana	Boat pose, Navasana
Sage twist, Marichyasana	Seated spinal twist, Ardha matsyendrasana	Open legs forward bend, Upavistha konasana

Yogic Paths and the Planets

Astrological factors are important indicators of our yogic potentials. These start with planetary types as the prime factors. They extend to specific factors of houses and planetary periods, leading to an extensive system of determining our spiritual potential and the likely timing of its unfoldment. A good Vedic astrologer can help you with these, so that you can know what Yoga approach may be best for you at any particular period of time.

Yoga of Knowledge	*Jupiter, Mercury, Ketu*	Jupiter governs the higher mind and expansive creative capacities. Mercury governs mental focus and insight. Ketu draws our awareness within.
Yoga of Devotion	*Venus, Moon*	The Moon gives a receptive, contemplative nature. Venus gives inspiration and devotion.
Yoga of Action	*Mars, Rahu*	Mars gives power of Agni, Tapas, work, effort and an ascetic nature. Rahu well-placed, gives the ability to influence the public and improve the state of the world.
Yoga of Service	*Saturn*	Saturn gives discipline, detachment and the capacity for work.
Raja Yoga	*Sun*	Sun gives a connection to the higher Self and power of the will.

Certain houses in the birth chart govern spiritual practices, like the twelfth house as the house of liberation or Moksha, the ninth house as the house of dharma, the fourth house as the house of the heart and deeper devotion, and the fifth house as the house of intelligence, insight and buddhi. A Vedic astrologer can help will such detailed determinations.

Yogic Counseling and the Chakras

Yogic counseling as a specific practice has its own considerations and approaches. Perhaps most important among these, yogic counseling aims at helping us develop the higher powers of the chakras or energy centers within us. The chakras connect us to the cosmic mind and prana that help develop our own deeper intelligence and vital energy.

In the ordinary person, these psychic centers are latent or blocked, working under a reduced functioning. They are said to be asleep or dormant in their functioning. The result is that our inner energies do not flow freely and our life force and will power cannot ascend to higher levels of consciousness. We get caught in conditioned patterns of behavior and are unable to link with the greater universal powers.

The chakras as energy centers reflect the powers of the five cosmic elements or earth, water, fire, air and ether, which indicate five different densities of vibrations.

Vedic counseling helps us understand the role of the five elements within and around us, including the action of the five senses and five motor organs. It teaches us how to benefit from the spiritual qualities of the five elements as states of awareness. It helps us move beyond our ordinary emotional blockages of fear, anger and attachment, and awaken a higher peace, love, and receptivity.

The chakras are energy centers in the subtle body whose network of forces underlies the denser physical body. The subtle body has a network of seventy-two thousand nadis or subtle channels through which energy is directed to the physical body like the electric lines and currents behind the equipment that run in your house. As energy centers and electrical forces, we cannot simply reduce the subtle body to the fixed parameters of the physical body. Its pranic currents pervade the physical body as a whole but are closely related to the brain and nerve centers in the body and in the spine.

Connection with the Senses

The chakras are inner counterparts of the senses, reflecting both the cognitive senses like the eyes and ears, and the motor organs like the hands and feet. The chakras are centers of our inner senses and higher consciousness. They reflect subtler energy forces behind the nervous system. Proper use of the senses aids in the healing and higher development of the chakras, including opening the third eye.

The sensory therapies of Ayurveda are useful in yogic healing, such as aroma therapy and the earth chakra, herbal teas and the water chakra, color therapy and the fire chakra, therapeutic touch and air chakra, music and the ether or throat chakra, mantra and the mind or third eye chakra, and meditation and the crown chakra or lotus of the head.

The Senses and the Elements

Elements, sense organs, motor organs, sense qualities

Elements	Sense Organs	Motor Organs	Sense Qualities
Ether	Ear	Vocal Chords	Sound
Air	Skin	Hands	Touch
Fire	Eye	Feet	Sight
Water	Tongue	Genitals	Taste
Earth	Nose	Anus	Smell

The chakras are energy centers in the subtle body that relates to the dream state and is the mental and energetic counterpart of the physical body.

The Subtle Body

Chakras

Name	Petals	Meaning	Physical Location
Muladhara	4	Root	Perineum
Swadhisthana	6	Self-abode	Genitals
Manipura	10	City of gems	Navel
Anahata	12	Unstruck sound	Heart
Vishuddha	16	Very pure	Throat
Ajna	2	Command	Third-eye
Sahasrara	1,000	1,000 petal lotus	Top of head

Name	Vayu	Mantra	Element
Muladhara	Apana	Lam	Earth
Swadhisthana	Apana	Vam	Water
Manipura	Samana	Ram	Fire
Anahata	Vyana	Yam	Air
Vishuddha	Udana	Ham	Ether
Ajna	Prana	Ksham	Mind
Sahasrara	All	Om	Consciousness

The different numbers of petals associated with each chakra, from four at the level of the earth chakra to a thousand relative to the thousand petal lotus of the head, are not literally petals or structures. They indicate vibratory rates. Increasing numbers of petals in the chakras reflect this increasing rate of vibration from the gross to the subtle elements. While the Third eye is usually given only two petals, at a vibratory level it relates to a hundred petals and has a faster rate than that of the throat chakra.

As the chakras are developed their negative emotional energies are gradually transformed into spiritual vibrations. This is an important factor to consider in Vedic counseling. It can be extended to other aspects of chakra functioning. Such Yoga practices as asana, pranayama, mantra, concentration and meditation, help us develop these higher potentials of the chakras. The dharmic values and practices of a Vedic life-style provide the foundation in our behavior for this to occur in a harmonious manner. In working with subtler and higher energies, we need to have a calm mind and heart, as well as a strong nervous system to handle such powerful energy currents.

Specifically there are four main yogic tools of working with chakra energy. These require guidance by a qualified teacher and counselor.

◈	Directing the inner power of the gaze or third eye to the specific chakra. Good for stimulating chakra activity.
◈	Using mantras to energize the chakras, including special bija mantras and Divine names.
◈	Using prana to energize the chakras, including drawing in the prana of nature, with special pranayama practices.
◈	Using meditation to energize the chakras, particularly meditation for developing space, peace and presence.

Psychological Correspondences of the Chakras

The chakras are centers of emotion. They reflect negative emotions when blocked or closed and positive emotions when balanced or open. Emotional balancing is an important part of working with chakra energy. One uses emotions of opposite nature to counter chakra imbalances. For example, one cultivates peace and forgiveness to counter anger and aggression, a third chakra problem. This practice is called *Pratipaksha Bhavana* in the *Yoga Sutras*, meaning opposite therapy at the level of the mind.

Chakra	Emotion when closed	Condition when opened
Earth	Ignorance, fear, ungroundedness	Peace, fearlessness, steadiness
Water	Attachment, emotionality	Devotion, compassion, receptivity
Fire	Anger, aggression, ego	Insight, forgiveness, peace, discrimination
Air	Desire, volatility	Love, wisdom
Ether	Possessiveness, control	Detachment, space in the mind
Third Eye	Narrow mindedness, distraction	One pointed mind, concentration
Crown	Limited awareness	Unlimited awareness, bliss

Generally the three lower chakras hold our life energies when we are not spiritually aware. They relate to our basic vital urges of survival, reproduction and territory that drive the ego. But even these lower chakras are not fully developed except through Yoga practices of pranayama, mantra and meditation. In this way, they connect us to the deeper powers of nature and the healing forces of earth, water and fire.

There are some unusual cases in which people may have access to some of the spiritual energies of the higher chakras without having entirely addressed the worldly energies and desires of the lower chakras. This can lead to various distortions in values and in behavior. It should be guarded against.

General Practices for Harmonizing Chakra Energy

Below are a few key practices for working on the chakras from a yogic perspective. It is good to do some practices for the chakras on a regular basis, just as it is good to exercise the different limbs and faculties of the body and mind.

Chakra	Practices
Earth	Asana, right diet, seva and Karma Yoga
Water	Right intake of fluids, beverages, herbs, receptivity and devotion
Fire	Fixing the gaze, Right intake of light, color, strengthening of the will
Air	Pranayama, devotional practices, contact with the inner Self
Ether	Mantra, mauna (non-speaking, silence), creating sacred space in body and mind
Third Eye	Concentration, unitary mind and prana, deep perception
Crown	Deep meditation, awareness beyond body and mind

Part VI

Specific Approaches of Vedic Counseling - Vedic Astrology & Vastu

The Influences of
Time and Space, Karma and Direction

Vedic Astrology and our Karmic Code

Vedic counseling as a term, often primarily means Vedic astrology. While this can be an oversimplification, it does reflect an important fact. A Vedic astrologer is primarily a life-counselor and Vedic astrology provides the keys to help us understand all aspects and domains of our lives.

Vedic astrology provides a good foundation for integral Vedic counseling, along with which Yoga and Ayurveda can be linked. So too, Vedic astrological practice works best if done according to a Vedic counseling model. Vedic astrology helps us to determine our karma and its unfoldment probably better than any other discipline. Through it we can learn to manage our karma in a way that is in harmony with our own inner being and the Divine purpose of the universe.

Yet this Vedic astrological counseling model is not as well developed as it could be in the field of Vedic astrology today. Not all Vedic astrologers have good counseling skills. The main reason for this is that Vedic astrology in India currently follows a predictive mode, not a counseling model. Rather than providing overall life guidance, much of Vedic astrology revolves around forecasting precise times for the main events likely to occur for us, as if our lives were predetermined. While the counseling model is more proactive and change oriented, the predictive model tends to be fatalistic and can cause us not to take our full initiative in life. The Vedic astrologer comes to resemble a mere fortuneteller forecasting fortune or gloom, rather than a helpful friend and advisor showing us how to better manage our lives. Once a person has their doom forecast by negative predictions they may either give up on life, or reject astrology in order to maintain their sense of well-being!

While knowing what may likely occur for us is helpful, even more useful is to know our true capacities and how we can better unfold them. Approaching Vedic astrology as a form of counseling, and adding to it the concerns and practices of other forms of Vedic counseling, will greatly expand our ability to use astrology in the highest possible manner and for the greatest benefit.

Vedic astrology is a wonderful counseling tool on many levels. It helps us understand our karma in life on all levels, including dharma, artha, kama and moksha, providing helpful and practical information on all of these. There is no other discipline that covers our life and its different domains so completely and specifically. Vedic astrology is particularly important for dealing with psychological issues. It has specific methods for determining the state of our emotions, our intellect, and our spiritual aspiration in life. Yet it is also very helpful with health issues, relationship issues, career guidance and spirituality.

The main difficulty for adding Vedic astrology to Vedic counseling is that Vedic astrology is a complex and intricate study that includes extensive astrological and astronomical concerns, which are not directly related to counseling, including a number of mathematical calculations and correlations. Our purpose in this book is not to teach the details of Vedic astrology, which can be very complex, but to outline its usage and contributions to Vedic counseling, as well as to provide counseling recommendations for Vedic astrologers.

Vedic Astrology and Karmic Management

The soul can be defined as our 'karmic being' as opposed to our human personality that is only its mask during the present life. The soul carries our karmic propensities called *samskaras* from one body and one life to another.

Our karma, we could say, is the DNA of our soul. *Just as the body has its particular genetic code, the soul has its particular "karmic code."* The soul's karmic code is based upon the life patterns it has created—the habits, tendencies, influences, and desires it has set in motion over its many births. These karmic tendencies or samskaras, are like seeds ripening in the soil of our lives, taking root, sprouting and bearing fruit according to favorable circumstances. Our soul's energy is filtered through our karmic potentials, which create the pattern of our lives down to subconscious and instinctual levels.

For the evolution of our species as well as for our own spiritual growth, we must consider both genetic and karmic codes. We cannot understand ourselves through genetics alone, which is only the code of the body; we must also consider the karmic code, the code of the mind and heart. Note how two children born in the same family can share the same genetic pattern, education and environment and yet have very different lives, characters and spiritual interests. This is because of their differing karmic codes.

Fortunately, there is a way that we can discover our karmic code as clearly as our genetic code. Vedic astrology helps us understand the laws of both time and karma. *The Vedic astrological birth chart is probably the best indicator of the karmic code of the soul.* The pattern of the birth chart reveals the "DNA of the soul" behind our current physical incarnation. The positions of the planets in the birth chart —not only relative to the twelve signs of the zodiac but more importantly in regard to the *Nakshatras* or twenty-seven mansions of the Moon — provide a wealth of knowledge through which we can read our karmic code in great detail.

In this regard, *the Vedic astrological chart is probably the most important document that we have in life and is much more important than our genetic code.* Yet like our DNA it is a code written in the language of nature that needs to be deciphered by a trained researcher in order to make sense of its arcane indications. Through the Vedic astrological chart we can determine the purpose of our lives and their potentials, our vulnerabilities and our hidden strengths that can help us fulfill our true destiny.

In addition to showing our karmic code from birth, also of great importance, Vedic astrology can plot this code's unfoldment through the changing course of our lives. This it does according to its elaborate system of astrological timing through the planetary periods (dashas), annual charts (bhuktis) and transits (gochara). That is why Vedic astrologers can be so amazingly accurate both in their delineations of character and in determining the outer events of our lives.

Vedic astrology also has its healing and remedial measures, through the use of planetary gems, mantras, yantras and meditation on planetary deities - its system of remedial measures (upayas). Vedic astrology provides us a number of methods to optimize our karma and take us beyond the limitations of our karmic code, directing us to our inner being and true awareness beyond the karmic constraints of body and mind.

It is imperative that each one of us is aware of our karmic code and learns the tools to modify it. The Vedic system provides us the best tools for this through its many disciplines of Yoga, Ayurveda, Vedic Astrology and Vastu, particularly used together in an integrated manner.

This does not mean that an examination of our Vedic birth chart will quickly answer all our questions, or allow us to avoid all possible suffering or difficulties. We still have to act in life, but the chart will show us how to act in the best and wisest possible manner. In this regard, the Vedic birth chart is our karmic guide to life. The additional branches of Vedic science are complementary tools of karmic improvement and karmic transcendence.

To change ourselves it is not enough to alter the genetic code. We must learn how to alter our karmic code. Changing our karmic code is more important and has more enduring results on our well-being. Fortunately, changing our karmic code is easier than altering our genetics, but is still quite challenging! It requires a great deal of motivation, concentration and expertise. These required efforts must be done within ourselves rather than in an external laboratory. We must change the very way we live, breathe, see and think, such as the methodology of Yoga and other Vedic sciences instructs.

To transform our karma requires that we expand our connections with the conscious universe—that we live the life of the soul that is one with all life. As the soul or our inner being holds the karmic code, only the soul can change it. Once we awaken at the level of the soul or our eternal Self, conscious of ourselves as children of immortality, we can modify our karma in a spiritual direction for the higher evolution of all life. This requires extensive work on ourselves through Yoga and meditation.

Vedic Astrology and Timing

We can choose through Vedic astrology, favorable times for action in order to counter negative karmas in the chart. This is the

Vedic practice of *Muhurta*. It rests upon the Hindu calendar or *Panchanga*, which is a soli-lunar calendar that considers the role of the Moon as the primary factor. The Panchanga outlines the general karmic influences for each day of the year. These five factors are:

◈	Nakshatra or lunar constellation in which the Moon is located.
◈	Tithi or phase of the Moon, fifteen each of the waxing and waning Moon.
◈	Vara or day of the week according to the ruling planet; Sunday as the Sun, for example.
◈	Yoga or Sun-Moon relationship.
◈	Karana, a subtler examination of Sun-Moon relationships.

A Vedic counselor can benefit from a regular examination of the Panchanga. Modern Vedic astrological programs calculate Panchanga information for every day, which varies according to the location in which a person is residing. Knowing the Panchanga information for each day can help us in all counseling ventures and recommending positive actions on a daily basis. It provides a map and a forecast of the karmic currents happening everyday, a kind of karmic weather report. We can use it along with the birth chart to determine how our individual karma interfaces with collective karma.

The Nine Planetary Types

One of the best ways to understand our individual variations is according to planetary types. This is the foundation of deeper astrological studies and provides a good astrological basis for effective Vedic counseling.

Vedic astrology recognizes nine planets. These consist of the Sun and Moon, along with the five visible planets of Mercury, Venus, Mars, Jupiter and Saturn, as well as the two lunar nodes or eclipse causing factors of Rahu (north node or Dragon's head), and Ketu (south node or Dragon's tail).

Generally, people are characterized by one planetary type according to the dominant planet in their birth chart. Individuals will reflect their ruling planet, both in terms of physiology and psychology. A certain spectrum of types does exist under each planet, as each planet has both higher and lower energies. Yet some people may have dual or triple planetary types that combine two or three planets in relatively equal strength, bringing in greater variability.

The nine main planetary types are more specific and complex than the three main Ayurvedic types, which they are related to.

Pitta	Sun, Mars and Ketu types are usually Pitta (fire) in nature.
Kapha	Moon, Jupiter and Venus are usually Kapha (water) in nature.
Vata	Saturn, Mercury and Rahu are usually Vata (air) in nature.

Planetary types are often more psychological than physical in nature and have implications in behavior beyond their physical correlations.

Determination of Planetary Type

We determine planetary types according to the system of Vedic astrology, not western astrology, which is a little different in its calculations and determinations.

The strongest planet in the birth chart usually determines the planetary type. This is usually the lord of the Ascendant, Moon or Sun or the planet that most strongly aspects or influences these three factors.

One planetary type is not necessarily better than another. Higher and lower types exist for each planet. These depend upon the ability of the person to bring in the spiritual energy of the respective planet or only its lower energies. Even spiritually evolved people have their planetary types. An example is the sage Ramana Maharshi. He is said to be an incarnation of Skanda, the deity of the planet Mars, but according to its spiritual energy of knowledge, inquiry and self-discipline.

Planetary types can be evident by looking at a person. For example, Sun types radiate light and warmth through their eyes and face. Moon types are maternal and receptive and may have round luminous faces like the Moon. Besides our individual dominant planetary type, we may reflect the influence of the planets ruling our current planetary period.

To teach our clients their planetary types is perhaps the key to Vedic astrological counseling and remedial measures. It is the foundation of the astrology of self-knowledge. Determining planetary types does not require a strong predictive ability but even prediction is rendered easier by it. We act largely according to our ruling planet and the primary influences upon it. Once we know that planet and its qualities, a person's actions are easier to predict.

We can see all the variations in human behavior in terms of planetary types. We can relate all human problems according to the energetics of the planets. We can understand psychological problems according to the functioning of the planets on a lower level, and spiritual growth as their function on a higher level.

The key to inner growth is to move from the lower to the higher functioning of our dominant planets. This requires becoming conscious of their workings and potentials on both inner and outer levels. It also requires an integration of the planetary influences within us. We must learn to balance not only the solar and lunar forces within us, but all planetary energies.

Sun Types

The Sun represents the positive or healthy side of fire energy and Pitta dosha. Sun types are usually the healthiest of all types because their strong fire energy allows for good digestion, good circulation, and the burning up of toxins. They have strong immune systems and seldom come down with serious diseases. Their appetites and thirst are strong, even excessive. Their bodies run hot and so they like cool foods and cool climates.

Their Sun-ruled complexion is bright, golden or reddish. Their eyes are golden, perceptive or full of light, with round heads and good glow to the skin. Usually they are of moderate build with good muscles. They seldom become overweight or underweight. Though they prefer much sunshine, they are sensitive to direct exposure to the sun. Their main health danger is through overwork or through trying to take responsibility for everything. This can give them heart problems or stomach problems (ulcers).

Psychologically speaking, Sun types are characterized by a strong will and a strong vital energy and Prana. They are independent and proud, sometimes vain. They like to be leaders or authorities and can gain much power over others. They turn others into their satellites and like to be the bestower of light and center of attention. They are highly perceptive, a little critical, and can probe deeply into things. They make good scientists or psychologists. They have strong emotions but are seldom overcome by them.

Usually Sun types have a philosophical or religious disposition and are ethical in their actions, being dominated by sattva guna. This deeper disposition usually comes out later in life, when they often become contemplative. In youth they are largely people of action rather than words and like to command a strong presence in the world. There is something noble or aristocratic about them and they like to associate with people and principles of value. They value character and like to stand above the crowd. They can take upon too much responsibility for themselves.

Yet Sun types do have their vulnerability. If defeated in life, by disease or by failure to succeed, Sun types can lose focus and energy or fall apart quickly. Their death is often sudden, most commonly by heart attacks. Once their period of success is over and they are no longer in the limelight, they suffer from loneliness and regret. They like to have children but are not usually happy with them and try to control them. Their standards are too high and their children tend to revolt against them or disappoint them. They can be domineering in marriage and partnership as well. They need to learn that there are many Suns and stars in the world and that they cannot expect everything to revolve around them.

Moon Types

Moon types are dominated by the water element and Kapha dosha. They show the water element in its greatest flourishing in all aspects of their lives. They have round heads and roundish well-developed flesh or corpulent bodies, particularly later on in life. They have attractive faces and features, particularly when young and can be quite beautiful, possessing a certain luminosity. Their complexion is usually fair or whitish, and the whites of the eyes are pronounced. With age they tend to become maternal types and put on weight and water. For women this excess Kapha often develops after the birth of the first child or after the age of thirty. They possess an abundance of vital fluids and have thick, shiny oily hair and skin. Lunar women usually have a good development of the breasts and thighs and roundness of the figure.

Moon types run cold and damp and can easily accumulate phlegm and mucus, particularly in the region of the chest and upper body. They often develop water retention, including in the lower parts of the bodies, particularly the legs and feet later in life. They have strong lungs and good voices but often suffer from congestion that can weaken them. Usually they live long and are healthy, but may constant minor health problems. Often the kidneys are their weakest organ. They may develop asthma, arthritis or coronary heart disease. They can be prone to laziness or excessive sleep, but they do usually prefer the night time.

Psychologically speaking, Moon types are maternal, loving, caring, nurturing and helpful to others, dominated by the emotional side of sattva guna. They are loyal and dependent and make good friends and marriage partners. They are good cooks and are domestically oriented. Their life is centered in home and family. Yet once they overcome their basic shyness and learn to relate on a public level they can succeed socially or politically and become good and sensitive leaders.

Moon types are highly emotional, romantic and sentimental and cry easily. They are often moody and have their periods of lunar emotional upheavals. Though they are easily hurt, they easily forgive and forget. Their emotional sensitivity is not always a real sensitivity to the emotions of others, however; sometimes they may be so caught in their own emotional responses that they cannot really see what others are feeling. Yet their emotional sensitivity may give them artistic talents, particularly for the performing arts, but sometimes poetry and literature as well.

Yet we should remember that if the Moon is isolated or afflicted in the chart, the person will not be like a typical Moon type. That disturbed Moon may reflect a number of psychological and emotional problems like anger, anxiety or depression.

Mars Types

Mars represents the negative side of the fire element and Pitta dosha and its excesses and diseases. While Sun types run hot and dry and maintain a good digestive power, Mars types run hot and wet or a little oily. They suffer from excess bile and acidity that can weaken what is often a strong digestion in their early years. Their blood runs hot and they easily accumulate toxins and come down with infectious and febrile diseases or inflammatory conditions. They suffer from excess heat and dampness.

Physically, Mars types possess moderate build with good muscles. Their complexion tends to be red, with oily skin and they bruise or bleed easily. Their eyes are often red and they tend towards eye diseases. They are sensitive to the sunlight and often wear glasses or sunglasses.

Generally, Mars types possess strong energy and have periods of good health, often going in for sports and athletic activity. But owing to bad living habits, they can come down with acute diseases. They suffer from overuse of alcohol, cigarettes, meat, hot spices, oily and fried foods, overdrinking and overeating. Fiery emotions like anger, jealousy and hatred damage their physical constitution as well. Usually the liver is their weakest organ and they tend towards hepatitis, cirrhosis and herpes.

Mars types are the most prone to injuries, accidents and traumatic diseases, generally from their own rashness or violent behavior. They often have surgeries or even organs removed. Disease comes to them from outside factors; their basic vitality is usually good. Their health problems are often due to their own excessive or blind actions.

Psychologically, Mars types are perceptive, critical and argumentative, and can easily move into rajasic aggression or tamasic violent. They are persistent, bold, daring, rash and adventurous. They often get into arguments and conflicts, which dominate their thoughts. They make good debaters, speakers, policemen, and lawyers. Their sense of logic is strong but often follows their anger more so than a real sense of justice. They love to win and hate to lose.

Mars types are very loyal to their friends and like to form alliances, teams and hierarchies, though usually as opposed to an external threat. They have strong passions and are possessive and controlling. Their sexual energy is strong but not always refined. They tend to overindulge and burn themselves out.

Mars types possess a good sense of mechanics and make good scientists, research workers and are good at working with tools and weapons. They need a practical outlet for their energy to prevent it from going to excess. A higher Mars type exists as well. This is the highly perceptive and self-disciplined yogi, psychologist or social activist. They seek to work on themselves and control their lower nature. Or outwardly they seek to arouse society to greater achievements and harmony.

Mercury Types

Mercury represents the positive side of the air element and Vata dosha. Mercury types are airy, intellectual, sensitive and nervously sensitive. They are congenial, communicative and compassionate. They are very friendly and talkative but can be introverted from an excess of thinking. As Mercury is a mutable planet, they often take the physical appearance of the planet strongest to aspect or influence Mercury. Yet overall they have youthful and Mercurial or changeable appearances.

Yet more defined Mercury physical types do exist. They are a little tall or short, thin in build, and generally attractive. Their eyes are often greenish and their skin is a little moist, unlike other air types that tend to be dry. They run on the cool side and often have sensitive lungs. They are susceptible to allergies and hay fever as well as to bronchial disorders. Their digestion is often weak or variable, nervous in nature. Their heart is sensitive and they are prone to palpitations. They may have difficulty sleeping or feeling calm and grounded.

Mercury types possess good prana or life-energy, live long, and have a certain glow, if they can protect their nervous systems. They make good runners or basketball players but their endurance is not always high. Often they are athletic when young but shift over to more intellectual pursuits after puberty. Their nervous sensitivity can also make them very sexual, and they can be experimental in their relationships as well.

Psychologically, Mercury types possess quick minds, a good sense of information and fluent powers of speech. They are good at languages and at statistics but may get their minds caught in trivia. They are witty and have a good sense of humor. They are helpful, service oriented and often take background or dependent roles. They are good at the mass media and make good moderators and interviewers. They may have powers of acting and are good at imitation.

Mercury types with their verbal skills make good secretaries, teachers and writers. With their strong sense of consideration and their desire to create harmony in life, they also make good doctors and nurses. They love nature, particularly plants, and are good at gardening. They have a refined sense of taste usually free of sensuality. They can develop a deep spirituality once they learn to turn their minds inward. The buddhi or higher mind is well-developed in higher Mercury types who have strong powers of discernment and discrimination. While they can easily become rajasic or changeable, they can learn to control this tendency and develop higher sattvic qualities.

Jupiter Types

Jupiter represents the positive side of the water element and Kapha dosha. Jupiter is the planet of positive health and longevity. Jupiter types possess strong constitutions, with good muscles. All their body tissues are well developed but with strength. They tend towards corpulence later in life, but are seldom overweight when young. Their complexion is tinged yellow or golden. They often have great strength and endurance and love physical work, exercise and trips into the wilderness. Generally they are very healthy and long-lived, with good Ojas and strong immune systems. Their most weak organ is their spleen-pancreas. They suffer mainly from overeating sweet, rich and oily foods. Excessive sugar consumption can lead them to diabetes.

Psychologically speaking, Jupiter types are joyful, jovial and content. They are friendly, generous and enjoy being with people. They have a strong sense of play and enjoyment, yet seldom become vulgar. They are kind and compassionate and always try to be just. Yet their sentiments and ideals may be too grandiose at times. They love music, enthusiasm and the display of energy. They are more active and athletic than the other watery types. They tend toward overindulgence or self-complacency. They can have much good karma in life, but this can make them materialistic as well.

Generally, Jupiter types are highly moral and ethical people and can be devoutly religious. They are naturally sattvic and dharmic in their nature, activities and values. However, they can tend towards conventionality in their beliefs and do not like to offend anyone. They have a strong devotion, are the most calm of all types, and can easily be at peace within themselves. They do like to accumulate and can be possessive. Many people in the business realm have such a dominating Jupiter energy.

Jupiter types often become teachers, gurus, ministers, or counselors and are good at working with people and helping others. They can be very creative either in the mind or in the external world. They develop a contemplative or philosophical bent, as they love to find the larger forces at work in life and join the energy of expansion. Their spirit is positive, optimistic and helpful. They seldom worry and tend towards over optimism or excess expansion. They have a natural interest in the spiritual life and in promoting higher causes.

Venus Types

Venus types represent a combination of the water and air, or Kapha and Vata temperaments, a more refined form of lunar energy. They are often beautiful, in form and appearance being the most attractive of all planetary types. They possess beauty of face, hair and eyes and a general sexual charm and feminine grace. Their tissues are roundish and well developed but they seldom become overweight. Their hands are well formed and delicate, without deep lines. Their sexual vitality is strong and steady and they have somewhat feminine features, even in the men. Yet they have a certain strength and power as well.

Venus types are generally healthy in constitution but lose this as they tend to over indulge themselves. In this case, they may suffer from weakness of the kidneys, reproductive organs, lungs and heart, including conditions like diabetes and sexual exhaustion. This may come later in life.

Psychologically speaking, Venus types are romantically inclined but not really sentimental, using their charm to control others. They feel the complementary nature of all forces in life. They have a strong sense of refinement, if not elegance. They make good artists, are highly creative, and possess a good sense of form and design and are often actors, performers and dancers. They possess good imaginations and have vivid dreams, including a strong connection to the astral plane.

Their disposition is generally ethical and they possess love and devotion, though jealousy easily disturbs them. They are strongly socially minded and can be very diplomatic, courteous and formal. Rajas or the quality of passion predominates in them and they have many emotional dramas in life.

Venus types love beauty, comfort and color. They like to adorn things, including, first of all, their own bodies. They enjoy jewelry and like beautiful clothing, homes, courtyards and gardens. As such, they can become addicted to luxury but are seldom really greedy. They love to display the wealth they possess to charm and influence others. They like to draw the attention of others and have a special charisma that allows them to dominate others by their moods. They have a good spiritual potential once they learn the meaning of Divine love and can develop the power of devotion. They can develop a good occult or astrological insight through appreciating the beauty of natural law. Their minds are intuitive and inspiring. They are children of the Goddess or Shakti.

Saturn Types

Saturn types are often the least attractive of planetary types. They may be unusually tall or short, thin and bony. They may have large noses or large teeth, with bones prominent. Their hands and feet tend to be large, as are their bones overall. Their skin is dry, rough or cracked and tinged brown or black. Their hair is brittle or scanty. Their nails may be cracked. A more attractive Saturn type does exist, usually as an artist with some Venus influence. The person is dark, elusive, gaunt and striking in appearance, with an aura of mystery and enigma.

Saturn is the overall planet of disease, of Vata dosha and the aging process. Saturn types are the most disease-prone of all planetary types. They have usually low vitality, poor endurance, and cannot handle much stress. They run cold and dry and have poor digestion and weak circulation. They tend towards constipation and to accumulate waste materials in the body. They are often chronically ill and may not live long.

Psychologically, Saturn types are saturnine, or inclined toward melancholy. They are overly serious, even morbid at times. They are usually pessimistic and may suffer from depression. They are generally introverted, solitary, independent and sometimes selfish. The many difficulties that they face in life make them insensitive to the needs of others. They may be miserly and overly calculating, as what they gain only comes through much effort so they are unwilling to share it. They tend toward worry, fear or anxiety, seldom smile and are rarely really happy. They are practically-minded, self-protective, and seldom good dreamers or inventors. They are willing to serve and work hard, though they do not always get the proper rewards for their efforts. They like to stand outside of normal society and may suffer from poverty. They may be rebels or outcasts.

Higher Saturn types are yogis, ascetics or monks who renounce the world. They possess detachment and are free of emotional fluctuations. They have inner peace, calm, composure and self-contentment. They are aligned with the powers of eternity. They are beyond the cares of the world and can reach the higher realizations, letting go of ordinary desires. Lower Saturn types, on the other hand, may be criminals, underworld figures or tyrants (particularly when the influence of Saturn combines with that of Mars). They are suspicious and paranoid, greedy and selfish, and can be strongly caught in the ego or body consciousness. The duality of Saturn types is probably more pronounced than any of the other planetary types.

Rahu Types

Rahu and Ketu are the nodes of the Moon, the so-called Dragon's Head and Dragon's Tail of western astrology. As Rahu and Ketu are not really planets, one may think that planetary types for them do not exist. Yet they can be delineated at least as secondary types. Their influences are shadowy and indicate something hidden or secretive about the person. They tend to reflect the influence of the planet ruling the sign in which they are located but have some characteristics of their own as well.

Rahu types are dark in features and mobile, moody and changeable in temperament. There is a kind of cloud around them, a dark shadow. They have deep-seated psychological problems from the past haunting them. They are either a little ghostly in their manners and appearance or they can be veiled and mysterious, sometimes with a certain beauty and allure. They enjoy foreigners, foreign lands or living on the fringes of society.

Rahu types possess very sensitive nervous systems and often suffer from insomnia or bad dreams. They are prone to drugs and addictions. On a psychic level, they are often possessed by something, either another entity, curses, unfulfilled longings from past lives, or the influences of other people. While they easily gain psychic, occult and astral sensitivities, it can be dangerous for them and make them unstable. They may become mediums or do channeling but are easily caught by illusion.

Rahu type women are clinging but at the same time willful and like to control their men through crying, hysteria or threats. They exert a strange fascination that often proves destructive. They are tempting, strangely fascinating and alluring. They can have unusual artistic or performance based talents.

Rahu individuals possess grandiose desires or cravings, but may be incapable of accomplishing ordinary things. When they do have success in the world, even on a grand scale, it is unfulfilling and may cause mental breakdowns or other psychological problems. Their egos are inflated but weak. They are either dominating or dominated. They suffer from a certain vanity and have unrealistic fantasies. Spirituality comes to them only after a great deal of self-examination and learning of self-control. Then they can become empathic and gain healing powers.

Ketu Types

Ketu types are introverted and individualistic often to the point of eccentricity. They go their own way and rebel against the social order, becoming isolated and alienated from the society. Often they debase themselves by following lower social influences. They possess self-doubt and even while they go their own way, they are confused about what it really is. They are very sensitive to criticism and react in a strongly defensive manner, if questioned. They often suffer from neuromuscular disorders and have a lack of coordination in their movement. They are prone to accidents, surgery, or violence, and suffer in wars and other mass catastrophes.

Ketu types are perceptive but their focus can be narrow. Their minds are critical, negative and highly discriminating. They tend to be overly serious and are seldom really happy. They are often fixated on the past and may make good historians or archaeologists. They are probing, searching and examining so make good research scientists. Once a problem enters their minds they will go over it endlessly until they find an answer. Often they are so doubting that they never arrive at an answer, or if one comes, they do not trust it. They are best at research and are able to find the light in darkness, though they may miss the light of day.

Higher Ketu-types are yogis (Jnanis) and possess much spiritual knowledge and insight. They see the illusory and transient nature of the world and go their own way regardless of circumstances. They are free of karma and desire. They are able to see through and go beyond the ego. They are a law unto themselves. They may not be recognized or appreciated but they are beyond the praise or blame of the world. Ketu can give the knowledge of astrology and other deeper wisdom.

Mixed Types

For people who have two planets of equal strength, a mixed type will emerge. For example, a Sun-Moon type will have a strong personality, both in its active and receptive, solar and lunar sides. A Mars-Jupiter type will give a Jupiterian expansiveness to the Mars work and action principles. A Mercury-Jupiter type will have an expansive but detailed and strong intelligence. A Mars-Venus type will have a strong sexuality, passion and vital will.

Sometimes higher and lower planetary influences combine as well. For example, a person may have a higher Jupiter influence with a lower Mars energy. They may have much expansiveness, faith and a philosophical disposition but allied with a lower Martial will to impose it upon others.

Other Astrological Typologies

There are several other important planetary typologies that we will mention briefly.

Ascendant Type	First is the Ascendant type. It is determined by one of the twelve zodiac signs which is present and rising at the time of birth. Ascendants are connected to their ruling planets, like Aries and Mars for instance.
Sign of Moon or zodiac	Second is the Moon sign or sign of the zodiac in which the Moon is located, including its ruling planet (much like the Ascendant).
Nakshatra or lunar constellation	Third is the birth Nakshatra or lunar constellation, of which there are twenty-seven. This is an extension of the Moon sign. Each Nakshatra has its specific energies and qualities delineated in Vedic texts.

Such additional typologies are part of advanced astrological counseling, important for an in-depth psychological profile of a person.

Broader Planetary Influences

Vedic astrology teaches us the planetary influences relative to each domain of our lives as defined by the twelve houses (bhavas) of the birth chart. These can be very important for counseling purposes as well. Each house governs certain factors of life and has a general planetary influence, as well as a specific planetary influence. The specific planetary influence is relative to the ruler of the sign marking that house, which is relative to the rising sign or Ascendant.

1 |	Self, body, prana, birth	Sun and ruler of first house in the birth chart
2 |	Speech, vocation, livelihood, childhood	Jupiter and the ruler of the second house in the birth chart.
3 |	Brothers and sisters, friends, activities, interests	Mars and ruler of the third house in the birth chart.
4 |	Mother, emotions, home, property, vehicles	Moon and ruler of the fourth house in the birth chart.
5 |	Children, intelligence, creativity, past life merit	Jupiter and ruler of the fifth house in the birth chart.
6 |	Disease, enemies, distant relatives, work and service	Saturn and ruler of the sixth house in the birth chart.
7 |	Partnership, social influence, marriage	Venus for men, Jupiter for women and the ruler of the seventh house in the birth chart.
8 |	Death, mystery, secret knowledge, research, power	Saturn and ruler of the eighth house in the birth chart.
9 |	Father, dharma, higher education, grace	Jupiter and ruler of the ninth house in the birth chart
10 |	Career, social success, and karma	Sun, Mercury and ruler of the tenth house in the birth chart.
11 |	Gains, public influence, recognition, income, rewards	Jupiter and ruler of the eleventh house in the birth chart.
12 |	Losses, liberation, spirituality, service	Saturn and Ketu, and the ruler of the twelfth house in the birth chart.

Specific planetary influences relative to the different houses can be examined in relation to particular counseling issues. For instance, the tenth house can give information about career counseling, and the seventh house works well for relationship counseling. Much precise information can be gathered accordingly.

Vedic Astrology and Psychology

The Vedic astrology chart is perhaps the best indicator of a person's overall psychology. It shows deeper karmic currents not necessarily visible in the outer life or even entirely known to the person, or which may manifest at later time in life.

As per general rules in Vedic astrology, one examines the Sun, the first house or Ascendant, and its influences for issues of personality, ego, outer bodily identity and self-projection relative to the outer world. One looks at the Moon and the fourth house for issues of feeling and emotion, and for deeper personal and social relations. One judges Jupiter and the fifth house for issues of judgment, insight, values, and creative intelligence. Mercury relates to speech, perception, communication and mental acuity.

Such different angles of approach help us understand the different areas and aspects of psychological energetics in a person. This astrological knowledge is very important for advanced psychological counseling. It grants us a great deal of specificity both in terms of delineations and timing factors. For example, if Mars is transiting the fourth house a person may be having issues with anger or emotional conflict.

Primary Planetary Correspondences

Rahu is generally like Saturn but subtler in energies, and Ketu is like Mars. Yet as shadowy planets, we must always look at Rahu and Ketu according to the planets ruling the signs in which they are located in the birth chart.

Planet	Sun	Moon	Mars	Mercury	Jupiter	Venus	Saturn	Rahu	Ketu
Dosha	P	K/V	P	VPK	K	K/V	V	V	P
Tissue	Blood	Plasma	Muscle	Nerve	Fat	Reproduc-tive	Bone	–	–
Element	Fire	Water	Fire	Earth	Ether/ Water	Water	Air	–	–
Exalted in	Aries	Taurus	Capricorn	Virgo	Cancer	Pisces	Libra	–	–
Debilitated in	Libra	Scorpio	Cancer	Pisces	Capricorn	Virgo	Aries	–	–
Aspect	7	7	4/7/8	7	5/7/9	7	3/7/10	–	–
Friends	Mo/Ma/Ju	Sun, Me	Su/Mo/Ju	Su/Ve	Su/Mo/Ma	Me/Sa	Me/Ve	–	–
Enemies	Ve/Sa	None	Me	Mo	Me/Ve	Su/Mo	Su/Mo/ Ma	–	–
Group	Malefic	Benefic *(when bright)*	Malefic	By association	Benefic	Benefic	Malefic	Malefic	Malefic
House Strength	10	4	10	1	1	4	7	10	12
Day	Sunday	Monday	Tuesday	Wednesday	Thursday	Friday	Saturday	Saturday	Tuesday
Gem	Ruby	Pearl	Red coral	Emerald	Yellow Sapphire	Diamond	Blue sapphire	Gomedha	Cat's eye
Deities	Agni/Shiva	Shakti/ Parvati	Skanda/ Bhumi	Vishnu	Ganesh/ Indra	Lakshmi	Brahma	Durga	Ganesh

V – Vata P – Pitta K – Kapha

Vastu Based Vedic Counseling

Vastu is the Vedic science of directional influences, somewhat like Feng Shui in the Chinese systems. Vastu shows us how to orient our dwellings to bring in the right and most beneficial directional influences. Its importance extends to the house, the work place and the right orientation of public buildings. Vastu also brings in further considerations of the right direction to face for meditation or the right way to set up an altar or meditation room.

Vastu experts guide us to the proper orientation of houses, buildings and plots of land relative to the forces of nature. Once this is done, they also help us orient the rooms within buildings, including elements of utility and design. Relative to existing structures, Vastu experts may recommend certain adjustments to improve the Vastu, or flow of energy in your dwelling. These may involve changing or adding windows, doorways, colors of the walls, placement of water or heat sources, furniture and related factors. Recommendations can extend from personal homes to office complexes and urban planning. The same Vastu concerns are there for clinics, treatment rooms and counseling rooms.

Directional influences are subtle and can affect both the subconscious mind and the prana of a person, impacting perception and decisions at a subliminal level. Wrong Vastu in the house or workplace can cause physical or psychological problems, or set in motion difficult karmas or relationship problems. It can weaken the immune system, disturb our thoughts or disrupt our sleep, as well as promote conflict with others.

Bringing Vastu into Vedic counseling may not be as essential as Yoga, Ayurveda or Vedic astrology, but it does have its importance. Vastu can also stand on its own as a counseling practice. Similarly, a Vastu based counselor should be aware of the relevance of Vedic counseling overall. A Vastu expert should have good counseling skills and understand the psychological issues of the client as well as the objective factors of building structure and orientation.

Honoring and sanctifying the directions of space with mantras or rituals is another important way of assuring that higher divine energies enter into our lives. Many traditional cultures have prayers and chants to the four directions. Vedic counseling may recommend such practices as well.

Our purpose here is not to explain the fundamentals of Vastu, which is a complex subject in its own right, but to indicate the value of Vastu as a counseling tool. Note below the main correlations of Vastu with other Vedic disciplines. A good Vedic counselor should be aware of these.

Directional Deities and Cosmic Principles

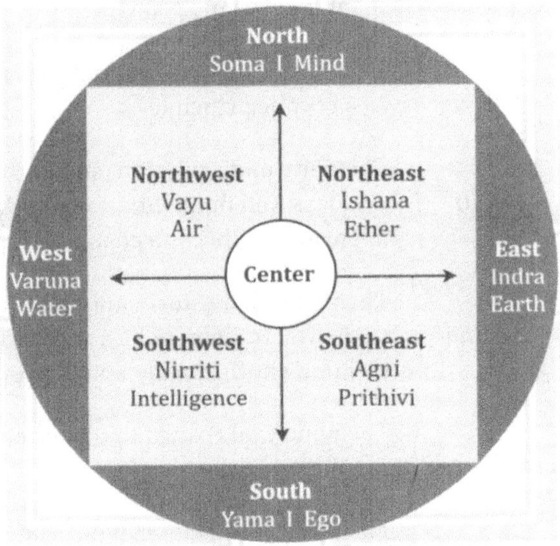

Each direction has a deity or cosmic principle, which protects us from the negative energies and promotes the positive energies. The central direction is not counted in the sequence as it represents the place that we are seeking to protect.

Directional deities grant control of both the external and the internal elements and aspects of the psyche that they relate to: the five elements of earth, water, fire, air and ether, mind (manas), ego (ahamkara), and intelligence (buddhi).It is good to strengthen the direction whose corresponding influences we wish to increase. The directions are usually counted off starting in the east.

Direction	Deities	Cosmic Principles
East	*Indra*	The deity of light and the Sun, relates to the earth as an element and cosmic principle.
Southeast	*Agni*	The deity of fire and relates to fire as an element and cosmic principle.
South	*Yama*	The deity of restraint and death, relates to ego as a cosmic principle.
Southwest	*Nirriti*	The deity of dissolution ,similar to the Goddess Kali in qualities, who relates to intelligence (buddhi) as a cosmic principle.
West	*Varuna*	The deity of the storm and the rains, relates to the water element as a cosmic principle, including both earthly and heavenly waters.
Northwest	*Vayu*	The wind God relates to the air element as a cosmic principle.
North	*Soma*	The deity of the Moon, who relates to the mind as a cosmic principle.
Northeast	*Ishana*	The supreme Lord, who relates to the element of ether or space as a cosmic principle.

Two other important directional influences are also recognized:

Direction	
Upward direction or above.	This corresponds on a horizontal plane with East-North-East, the intermediate point between East and North East. It is the place of *Brahma* or the Divine Creator, who represents the ruling spiritual energy coming from above.
Downward direction or below	This corresponds on a horizontal plane with West-South-West, the intermediate point between W and SW. It is the place of *Ananta*, the serpent that upholds the worlds, represents the supportive energy coming from below.

Doshas and Directions

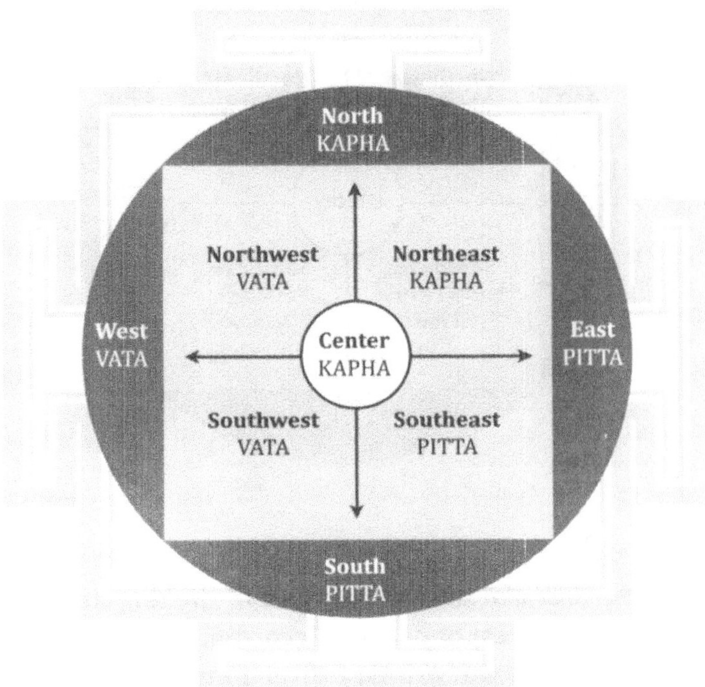

Each direction has its doshic influences according to Ayurveda. Kapha, or the water humor, dominates north, northeast and center. It governs directions of rest and darkness, in which moisture usually increases. Pitta, or fire, dominates east, southeast and south. It governs directions of increasing light and heat. Vata, or air, dominates southwest, west and northwest. It governs directions of declining light, dryness and dispersion. Kapha directions are overall most helpful and nourishing and also bring in spiritual influences. Vata directions expose us to the influences of decay and disease.

Planets and the Directions

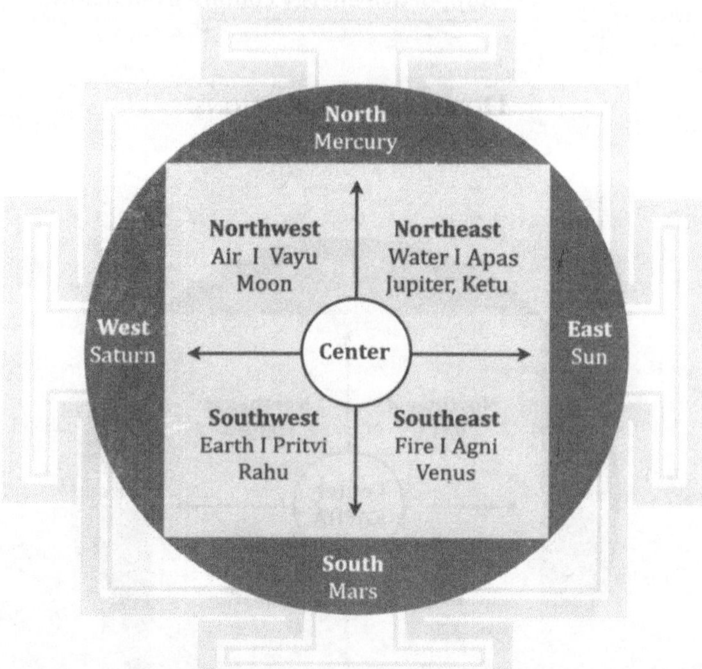

We can further classify the energies of the directions according to their planetary correspondences. According to Vedic astrology, the planets correspond to the primary directions from which they cast their influences. These correspondences are a little different than those between the planets and the elements, reflecting subtler energies.

Northeast	The Northeast direction has a positive or benefic Jupiterian energy and is good for spiritual and religious practices and influences.
North	North has a positive Mercury energy and is good for learning, study and education.
East	East is the direction of the Sun and is good for work, action, healing and spiritual practices.
Southeast	Southeast has a Venus energy and is a place of power, connection, relationship and expression.
South	South has a Mars energy and inclines us to work, action, assertion and conflict.
Southwest	Southwest has a negative Rahu energy and is a place of rest, control and subtle influences.
West	West has a Saturn energy and brings about decay and decline, but also maturity and detachment.
Northwest	Northwest has a lunar energy, but one that tends to be sensitive, vulnerable, changeable and unstable.

Vastu Principles

Basic Applications of Vastu – for reference purposes

Examples for Construction or Site	◈ Plots/sites in Southwest, South and West directions are more advantageous than others. ◈ Rectangular or square shapes are more advisable. ◈ North should be lower than South, so the site should be sloping towards North. ◈ It is advisable to have equal open space on all four sides. ◈ South and West should have less open space and be at a higher elevation.

Entrance	◈ The most beneficial entrances to the house are those in the Northeast, East or North directions. ◈ The width of the door should be half of its height. Square and automatic doors should be avoided.
Living room	◈ The best locations are North, Northeast, East or West directions. The center area of a living room ◈ (Brahmasthana) should be free of obstructions such as pillars, fixtures, or staircases.
Bedroom	◈ It can be located in any quadrant except Southeast direction.
Kids' bedroom	◈ Northwest is recommended; avoid Southeast and Southwest.
Guest bedroom	◈ It is best if located in Northwest or Northeast directions.
Study room	◈ All directions are good except Northwest, which is the direction of dispersion and decay. It is best to sit facing East or North, which bring in energy and light.
Kitchen	◈ The most ideal location is the Southeast direction.
Bathroom	◈ Northwest, West or South directions are recommended.
Sleep	◈ Never sleep with the head in the North quadrant; all other directions are positive.

Part VI

Summary - Vedic Laws of Right Living

In this section we will highlight the key principles of Vedic living relative to Vedic counseling in the form of special axioms or sutras.

Being aware of such "Vedic laws" helps us develop our Vedic counseling skills and harmony of life overall.

Vedic Laws of Right Living Principles of Dharma

Right living implies living in harmony with the universal life and allowing it to express itself through our individual lives. Right living implies sacred living, accepting the divine nature of all life. A Vedic life is a life in harmony with karma, dharma, nature and Self on all levels outer and inner.

Who we are and what we will become in life depends upon how we live, which means upon what constitutes our life style. To have a conscious life-style is the foundation of a Vedic life. Right living implies recognizing the unity and interdependence of all existence.

Prime Principles of Right Living:

Be true to your Higher Self	Not just to the desires and opinions of others.
Honor the whole of life	Not just your personal or social concerns.
Cultivate Sattva Guna, Reduce Rajas and Tamas	Develop peace, harmony and respect for all.
Follow Your Dharma	Adhere to your deeper soul's mission over any outer demands.
Understand Your Karma	Know what forces you have set in motion in life and how these are likely to shape your future.
Be in Harmony with Your Mind-body Constitution	Follow your Ayurvedic type as Vata, Pitta or Kapha, and the state of your Prana or primary life-energy.

Balance of Intake and Output - Ahara and Vihara

As organic entities our lives are built around intake and output, our factors of nutrition and expression. We must balance both what we take into ourselves (our sources of nourishment), and how we act and express ourselves (what we give back to the world). This is the foundation of a proper Ayurvedic life-style.

◈	Right nutrition on all levels of our being: regulating intake of food, air, impressions, ideas, and experiences.
◈	Right expression and exercise on all levels of our being, body, prana, senses, motor organs, and mind.
◈	Honor the sacrament of food. Food is the basis of our existence in the physical world. Eating should be a sacrament. Aim at freshly cooked home meals.

Honor the Senses as Sacred

Seeing	Honor what you see as Divine light
Hearing	Honor what you hear as Divine Music
Touch	Honor what you touch as Divine feeling
Taste	Honor what you taste as the nectar of immortality
Smell	Honor what you smell as Divine fragrance

Proper Vihara

Regular Exercise and Expression

◈	Keep body and mind healthy with regular activity, but done without stress or aggression.
◈	Exercise prana as well. This is the role of pranayama.
◈	Exercise your senses in developing greater acuity.

◈	Exercise in nature as much as possible.
◈	Take time not only to work but also to relax and retreat.

CLEANLINESS

◈	Need for physical, psychological and spiritual cleanliness.
◈	Cleansing body, mind, emotions and psychic environment.
◈	Seasonal purification regimens through Pancha Karma, including oil massage and steam (sweating) therapies.

MOVE WITH THE RHYTHMS OF LIFE, NOT SIMPLY WITH CHRONOLOGICAL TIME

Be conscious of the on-going rhythms of nature and adjust your behavior accordingly.

◈	Follow the rhythms of time through the day, honoring, sunrise, noon and sunset.
◈	Follow the rhythms of time through the month, being aware of the new and full moon, waxing and waning phases.
◈	Follow and honor the seasons of the year.

Understand the four stages of life – These mark around 20-25 years each but vary by individual.

YOUTH	Period of learning, maintaining innocence.

Maturity	Caring and providing for others.
Middle age	Greater responsibility for family and community, taking on the role of an elder.
Renunciation/ Old Age	Letting go of worldly responsibilities and dedicating yourself to an inner life of meditation.

Proper Self-expression

◈	Be polite and courteous to all.
◈	Speak kind, pleasant and truthful words.
◈	Be silent and do not speak unnecessarily.
◈	Do not give advice unsought for.

Right relationship on all levels

◈	Right relationship with oneself as the basis of all relationships.
◈	Right relationships with others.
◈	Right relationship with nature.
◈	Right relationship with the Being of all.

Vedic Laws of Psychological Well-Being

Most of us do not know how our mind works and so we often end up creating the opposite of what we really wish to achieve. The mind has its own dynamics that we need to be aware of. The mind as an energetic system has its own organic patterns that must be respected. The mind requires proper nutrition and proper exercise as well.

The mind has its own nature and functions, its tendencies towards harmony and disharmony, happiness or sorrow. We need to comprehend these in order to achieve optimal psychological well-being. As it is most of our mental activity is harmful to ourselves, even if it does not affect other people. We should learn to develop the Soma or nectar of the mind, and to let go of the poison of negative emotions, urges and compulsions. Your mind can be either your best friend or your worst enemy. For most of us, our mind functions like an inner terrorist instilling fear and anger and reducing the other good qualities or powers we may have.

Develop the Higher Mind:

Develop your power of attention	Whatever you give your attention to can control you. If you are in control of your own power of attention, you are capable of independent action and direct perception.
Learn the art of right intention	Consciously seek to promote your higher goals and values in life, letting go of what is not relevant.
Develop ability to concentrate and focus	Learn to use your mind like a focused light to examine what you need to know.
Learn to harness the Shakti or power of the mind	Let your mind release its creative and perceptual powers for the benefit of all.

Promote the positive aspects of your mind's functioning.

◈	Develop positive thinking, opening yourself up to positive outcomes and solutions.
◈	Give up negative thoughts, emotions, opinions and desires. Do not be attached to your sorrow.
◈	Learn to see the good in others and the benefic nature of all existence.
◈	Send out good wishes and blessings to all.
◈	Practice the art of prayer or prarthana, for promoting good wishes for all.

Give up the Two Greatest Sins or faults in the mind

Give up worry	The main sin against yourself. Have faith in your Self and your destiny as a divine and cosmic being.
Give up gossip	The main sin and violence to others. Respect the Divine in others and stop harming others with your mind.

Maintain your sense of humor

◈	Meditate upon the world as a dream or magic show lasting only a few days.
◈	Do not take yourself or the world too seriously.
◈	Bring humor into your communication.

OPPOSITE TREATMENT AT THE LEVEL OF THE MIND

CULTIVATE HIGHER EMOTIONS TO COUNTER THE LOWER.

Counter **anger** *with* **calm**. *Counter* **fear** *with* **daring**. *Counter* **pride** *with* **humility**.

~ *Pratipaksha Bhavana* of the *Yoga Sutras*

MOVE FROM LESSER DESIRES TO GREAT FEELINGS

◈	Move from personal desires to universal compassion.
◈	Move from individual love to love of all.

PRINCIPLES OF A HAPPY MIND

OBSERVATION	Learn to observe things and see what they are; do not prejudge.
DETACHMENT	Accept what things are, see them as they are, and let them reveal to you their essence.
SURRENDER	Submit to reality, do not seek to change it; let it guide you.
LOVE	Be One with all, not against anyone
FAITH	Have faith in the supreme consciousness, not in any outer forms or personalities.

PURIFICATION OF THE MIND OR *CHITTA PRASADANA* OF THE *YOGA SUTRAS*

Cool, clear and cleanse the mind, let the mind flow like water and purify itself.

◈	Learn to cleanse your mind every day, particularly before sleep, letting go of memory and sensation.
◈	Discover the transformative power of silencing the mind and your inner stillness.
◈	Cultivate receptivity rather than reactivity.
◈	Avoid self-negativity and affirm your higher potentials; do not be an enemy to yourself.
◈	Turn emotion into devotion.
◈	Value inner clarity and peace.

Vedic Laws of Right Intention

We are the product of our intentions, called *samkalpas* in Sanskrit. As is our intention, so is our action or karma, and so is what we will ultimately become. As we desire, so we act; as we act, so we become, not only for this life but for future lives as well. This means that we must understand our intentions and motivations and all that they imply, if we want to make our actions optimal and transformative.

We need to cultivate right or higher intentions and goals and let go of those that are lower. View life as ascending a series of steps and ever seek to move upward.

Examining our intentions and motivations

We need to examine our intentions and motivations, so we know in what direction we are steering ourselves in life. This involves investigating the type of motivations we are creating, consciously or unconsciously, including several important life decisions.

◈	Choose the right path for yourself, which implies knowing your dharma.
◈	Choose the right partner and associations to succeed in your endeavors. Very little can be done single-handedly. We have a natural need and desire to unite with others.
◈	Choosing the right vocation and occupation that supports your path and your dharma.

The Art of Right Intention or True Wishes

Knowing how to form proper intentions and develop them consistently over time is crucial for success in whatever we do. Usually we follow changing desires that keep us moving in several directions, generally at the surface of life, and so we are unable to achieve anything consequential.

Form Proper Intentions

Be the Master of Your Desires.	Learn to be content without desire to disturb you.
Develop a strong will power and do not let others dominate you.	Be in control of your faculties and master of your mind.
Do not be swayed by your senses.	Do not let your senses control your power of attention. This also means do not let the mass media dominate your mind.
Develop a capacity for endurance.	Be in projects for the long run and do not get distracted by short term difficulties.
Establish a dharana or concentration born commitment.	Hold to a primary intention or motivation throughout the day.
Make sacred your power of attention.	Do not give your power of attention away idly, carelessly or without forethought.
Seek your highest goals and wishes.	You can achieve what you wish, so aim at what is highest. Do not waste your time on petty desires.

Understand the Principle and Law of Tapas

Tapas is the yogic process of holding our focus on a particular object. It is a sustained but steady and flexible concentration, like a mother thinking about her child when she goes about her activities during the day. Whatever we hold to in our hearts at a deep level must eventually come to us by the law of karma. Tapas means holding an inner flame on our highest goal.

◈	Learn the value of patience, waiting, preparation and receptivity. You must first prepare the vessel in order to receive.
◈	Beware of premature action or action without the proper preparation. Let things come to fruition before taking action.
◈	Let your inaction become a determined preparation for decisive action at the optimal time and place when you are ready.

Empowering Your Higher Intentions

There are many ways to empower our intentions. There are special Vedic rituals for this purpose, particularly Yajnas or fire offerings. In fact, every ritual or spiritual practice should begin with the formation and stating of the intention involved. Meditation, mantras and prayers are very important as well. Note the time and make a record of your intentions. A good astrologer can help.

Laws of Yoga for Spiritual Well-being

Yoga is a path of spiritual well-being, but for it to work we need to understand the laws of Yoga through which our deeper nature can unfold. Yoga in the broader sense, is the application of Vedic counseling. It is its main method of self-knowing and self-improvement.

Yoga is an art of reducing stress, negativity and entropy through turning within. It shows us how to use conserve our energies for inner transformation through the core of our awareness. Below we have taken the main factors of Yoga and provided the key principles for their proper development.

◈	Relax out of body consciousness through your Yoga asana.
◈	Asana is not an exercise but a way of internalizing our awareness.
◈	Contact the Unitary Breath behind inhalation and exhalation, the inner life-force.
◈	Pranayama is not simply exercising the breath but contacting the inner life-force or power of consciousness behind the breath. Use Prana to calm the mind.
◈	Turn Your Senses Within and awaken your inner Senses, to the inner light and sound. Our senses have a higher and inner potential that we should cultivate. Learn to discover the inner eye, inner ear and inner voice.
◈	Develop the Power of Attention so that you can learn whatever you wish
◈	Attention is a sacred power to create and alter our sense of reality. Use your power of attention to shape your life towards your highest aspirations.

◈	Have Key Mantras to develop your highest potential. Energize your Mantra with right intention and aspiration. Let your mantra become the ground of your psyche, the music of your soul.
◈	Inquire and investigate the core of your being. Let your life be an adventure in consciousness!
◈	Meditate. Be what you are in essence, when the mind is still.
◈	Learn that through being what you are, you can become all that you truly wish to be. Provide your mind a regular space of meditation for its rest and renewal.

Need for Daily Sadhana, Spiritual Practice, Yoga and Meditation

Vedic counseling helps us develop our personal spiritual practice or sadhana. A Vedic counselor is a sadhana guide. All life should be a sadhana for us, meaning done with awareness. A regular sadhana is the main means of removing all of our psychological afflictions.

Vedic Divine Laws for Total Harmony

The following Divine Laws are keys to higher awareness and universal harmony, which is the ultimate goal of all that we seek. They help us understand how Self and universe reflect the workings of higher Divine, cosmic and spiritual energies.

The universe reflects Divine laws and intentions that we can only benefit from if we take a Divine attitude in life. We need a Divine view of ourselves, recognizing the Divine presence in all beings, particularly in our own minds and hearts.

Balance Being and Becoming

Law of Being	You are all, you are everywhere, you are free.
Law of Becoming	You can become all that you wish by being what you truly are.

Law of Increasing Awareness

Law of Awareness	Whatever you give your consciousness to will grow in power within you; only give your consciousness to that which is higher.

Laws of Action

Law of Inaction	Everything comes to those are receptive and willing to prepare the way for it to happen. Learn the art of non-being, waiting, being patient, still, content and prepared.
Law of Decisive Action	Learn how to prepare your action, to wait carefully, and act with strength at the most decisive moment.

Law of Manifestation

◈	Law of Manifestation – whatever you wholeheartedly and consistently follow and attempt to do, you will succeed at.
◈	Whatever you pursue in a half-hearted manner or expect others to get for you will never come to any positive fruition.

Laws of Unity and Diversity

Law of Unity	All in essence is one. Unity underlies and supports all other states and conditions. Dare to be one with all!
Law of Diversity	All in manifestation is manifold like the leaves, flowers and fruit of a single tree. Let yourself unfold from pure unity to unbounded infinity.
Law of Unity in Diversity	You need not seek to be the same or different than others. You only need to be yourself. That unity of inner Self will provide you the greatest scope of diversity in your expressions and interactions.

Vedic Ecology:

Harmonization with the Greater Universe

Another primary Vedic principle is proper harmonization with Nature both externally and internally. This is the key to universal well-being and to optimal ecological living. Vedic counseling includes ecological counseling, or how to cultivate our own inner and outer natural ecosystems so that they can bear the fruit of higher awareness. Vedic counseling teaches us to manage the ecosystem of our own lives, which is to honor the laws and processes of the nature of our own body, mind and consciousness.

Harmonize Your Environment

To live happily we must learn how to harmonize ourselves with our environment. Harmonizing your environment begins with harmonizing your home. Here the Vedic science of Vastu comes into play, teaching us the right placement of our dwelling relative to the Earth and the directions of space. Along with this we should bring beauty and a spiritual presence into the house. This is can be created by a special altar or meditation room.

We must also learn to harmonize the environment around the home. Gardens are important if you have outdoor land. In an apartment, flat or urban environment, it requires that you take journeys into nature, forests or mountains to renew your ties with Mother Nature. You can also keep plants and natural decorations inside the home.

Honor the Five Great Elements and Ecological Living

Vedic living is ecological living and begins with honoring the five great elements of Earth, Water, Fire, Air and Space. Earth is most important and fundamental. We should learn to contact, honor, perceive and experience the different aspects of the Earth element.

Harmonization with the soil, rocks and mineral kingdom	Be aware of the ground and landforms around you as the ground of your being
Harmonization with Plants, Leaves, Trees and Flowers	Be aware of the plants around you as the source of Prana for all life
Harmonization with the Animal Kingdom	Feel the animal forms as part of your own greater life. See the wisdom and cosmic powers each creature represents
Harmonization with the Waters	Be aware of the waters in your environment, whether the ocean, lakes, rivers or fountains
Harmonization with the Atmosphere	Be aware of the wind and clouds in the atmosphere around you as part of the planetary life
Harmonization with the Sky	Be aware of the cosmic space as the space of your own deeper awareness

Vedic Harmonization with All Humanity

◈	Learn to respect all human beings
◈	Honor diversity in human culture extending to art, religion and spirituality
◈	Promote global peace and well-being
◈	Embrace the spiritual origins of our species
◈	Embrace our ultimate spiritual goal to bring peace, love and wisdom to the planet

Part VI

Appendix

Traditional Aspects of Vedic Knowledge

The Tree of Vedic Knowledge

It is important to examine the traditional aspects of Vedic knowledge in the context of Vedic counseling. This information provides a good reference for the background, complexity and antiquity of Vedic knowledge.

Four Vedas and Four Aspects of Each Veda

There are four collections of Vedic teachings, of which the *Rigveda* is the oldest and most primary. *Samaveda* consists almost entirely of Rigvedic mantras put in a special chanting style. *Yajurveda* has a number of original mantras as well as many from Rigveda in a more ritualistic application. *Atharvaveda* provides a collection of supplementary mantras on many topics.

Each Veda has four aspects. The *Samhita* consists of the foundational mantras. The *Brahmanas* consist of ritualistic applications. *Aranyakas* are contemplative teachings. *Upanishads* comprise the secret, philosophical and spiritual meanings. These older Vedic teachings are quite ancient and esoteric, used mainly for their special mantras like the Gayatri mantra.

Ayurveda and Vedas/ Upavedas

There are four *Upavedas* or supplementary Vedic approaches.

1 |	**Ayurveda**	Healing arts
2 |	**Dhanur Veda**	Martial arts
3 |	**Sthapatya Veda**	Architecture, sculpture and geomancy
4 |	**Gandharva Veda**	Music, poetry and dance

The Upavedas supplement the Vedas with specific applications of the Vedic teachings. Ayurveda is perhaps the most important Upaveda, with the specific goal of health and well-being for body and mind, and Vedic therapies (Chikitsa) of all types.

Ayurveda is closely connected with all the Upavedas. It relies upon Dhanur Veda, or the martial arts, for exercise recommendations and styles of massage and body work, particularly the treatment of the marmas or sensitive points on the body. Ayurveda employs Gandharva Veda for its subtle therapies of music and art, which are very important in healing both mind and body. Yogas of music and sound develop out of Gandharva Veda.

Sthapatya Veda, more commonly called *Vastu*, shows the right design of structures to bring in wholesome earth and spatial energies. This is essential for the proper orientation and construction of clinics, hospitals, and healing rooms.

The Vedangas/ Jyotish

There are six *Vedangas* or limbs of the *Vedas*. These are closer to the *Vedas* than the Upavedas. Being part of the *Vedas* themselves, they are the main tools used to interpret them.

1	**Jyotish**	Astrology
2	**Kalpa**	Rules of ritual
3	**Shiksha**	Pronunciation
4	**Vyakarana**	Grammar
5	**Nirukta**	Etymology
6	**Chhandas**	Meters

Of the six Vedangas, Jyotish or Vedic astrology is the most important. For Ayurveda it helps determine the basic health potential of the person, their disease tendency and possibility of recovery. This is particularly important for patients suffering from severe illnesses and for illnesses that are not responding to normal treatment measures. Vedic astrology is also used for the timing of treatment and for preparing medicines. Even the right therapy done at the wrong time may not bring good results. Astrology helps us understand psychological problems, which are often evident from the birth chart. It is useful in Ayurvedic therapies, particularly for showing what gems are best for a person to wear.

Four of the six Vedangas deal with language. They are the basis of the Sanskrit language and its precise terminology for both yoga and Ayurveda. They are part of the path of mantra yoga, which is very important in both yoga and Ayurveda. Ayurveda uses mantra as the main tool for healing the mind. Yoga uses it as the main tool for purifying the mind and unfolding its inner powers and faculties. Mantra is the most important tool of yoga, Ayurveda and Jyotish and is the foundation of Vedic science.

The Six Schools of Vedic Insight

Out of the *Vedas* arose six schools of philosophy, *shad darshanas*, which literally means six ways of seeing or insight. These were designed to show the logical, metaphysical and cosmological implications with the Vedic mantras. Classical yoga as expounded by Patanjali in the *Yoga Sutras* is one of these six schools of Vedic philosophy. Hiranyagarbha, a name for the sun god as the cosmic Creator, was the traditional founder of the Yoga system.

The Six Schools of Vedic Philosophy and Their Founders			
1	**Nyaya**	Logic School	*Gautama*
2	**Vaisheshika**	Atomic School	*Kannada*
3	**Samkhya**	Cosmic Principle School	*Kapila*
4	**Yoga**	Yoga School	*Hiranyagarbha*

The Six Schools of Vedic Philosophy and Their Founders			
5 |	**Purva Mimamsa**	Ritualistic School	*Jaimini*
6 |	**Uttara Mimamsa/ Vedanta**	Theological or Metaphysical School	*Badarayana*

Nyaya and Vaisheshika are schools of logical philosophy, similar to the system of Plato in Western thought. All Vedic schools, including Ayurveda and yoga, insist upon the development of strong rational skills, which comes about through training in Nyaya-Vaisheshika. Both the yogi and the Ayurvedic doctor must support their conclusions with the proper logic, though this is made subordinate to a higher intuitive perception.

Samkhya provides the background philosophy and cosmology both for yoga and Ayurveda. It has a scientific view, examining both internal and external reality. The Samkhya system outlines the tattvas or cosmic principles that yogic practice seeks to realize.

Yoga adds a theistic view to Samkhya and could be called a theistic form of Samkhya. Yet the approach of yoga is more practical and so more of a technology than a philosophy. It thus can be used with various philosophical systems.

The ritualistic school, Purva Mimamsa, emphasizes proper performance of rituals for both individual and social welfare. It uses special prayers and offerings to link us with the beneficent forces of the universe. These rituals are good for purifying body and mind and prepare us for meditation. This is the field of Karma Yoga or the yoga of service.

The term Vedanta is used specifically for the Uttara Mimamsa School, which is the most concerned of the six systems with the proper interpretation of Vedic texts (though all the six systems share this concern). Vedanta or the theological/metaphysical school, discusses the nature of God, the soul, the Absolute and their relationship. There are several schools of Vedanta, which became in time, the most important and extensive of the Vedic philosophical traditions.

Non-dualistic (Advaita) Vedanta, taught by the great philosopher Shankara (seventh century), makes both God and the soul to be manifestations of the Absolute, which constitutes their real Self. It emphasizes Jnana Yoga or the yoga of knowledge. Dualistic (Dvaita) Vedanta, like that taught by Madhva (fourteenth century), makes God and the soul to be different but eternally related. It teaches devotion to God and the subordination of the soul to His grace. It emphasizes Bhakti Yoga or the yoga of devotion. An intermediate school, the qualified non-dualist Visishtadvaita school of Ramanuja (twelfth century), is also important. It is largely devotional like the dualistic school.

Yoga is closely aligned with Vedanta of one of these schools or another. Yoga in some form, is part of all six Vedic schools, which are integral parts of the same Vedic Darshana or way of seeing. Yoga provides the practical foundation for the insights that the other systems seek to develop — preparing body, prana and mind to become tools of inner inquiry. In this regard, yoga is probably the most universal of the six systems and is the main link between them. Ayurveda provides the foundation of right living for yoga and for all the six systems. Its worldview and practices are thus shared among all of them.

Putting together this entire system of Vedic knowledge — combining Ayurveda, Yoga and related disciplines — we have a tremendous resource that can transform ourselves and our planet if we apply it in our daily lives. This is the background through which we can approach Vedic counseling and use it in the optimal manner.

Glossary of Terms

A

Abhinivesha - clinging to the cycle of life experiences

Achara rasayana - therapies for behavioral rejuvenation

Achara - behavior

Advaita - non-duality

Agni - fire, inner flame, and the power of transformation

Ahamkara - ego.

Ahara - nutritive factors

Ahimsa - non-violence

Ama - toxicity

Ananda - bliss

Anandamaya kosha - layer of the inner body made of bliss and love, unity consciousness

Anna - matter, food, physical reality.

Annamaya kosha - physical body that is made of matter, food, physical reality.

Apana - downward moving prana

Aparigraha - non-hoarding

Aranyakas - aspect of Vedic scriptures that shares contemplative teachings

Arogya - physical and psychological health and well-being

Artha - one of the four great goals, the pursuit of the goals and resources of life

Asana - Yoga posture; seat

Asmita - egoism, arrogance

Asteya- non-stealing

Asuric - violent, egoistic nature

Atharvaveda - One of the four primary Vedas

Atman - individual soul; immortal spirit

Avidya - ignorance

Ayurveda - Vedic branch of medicine for healing and medical treatment

B

Bhakti Yoga - Vedic approach to union with the Divine through inner surrender

Bhakti Yoga - Yoga of devotion

Bhasmas - ashes of the sacred fire

Bhoga - desire and enjoyment

Brahma - Divine Creator

Brahmacharya - integrity in dealing with sexuality

Brahmanas - Vedic text that offer commentaries of Vedic ritualistic applications

Buddhi - innate, spiritual intelligence that exists at a subtler level than the outer mind

C

Chakra – energy centers in the subtle body
Chikitsa – Vedic therapies
Chit – consciousness
Chit-Shakti – the power of consciousness
Chitta Prasadana – purification of the mind
Chitta– The net effect throughout time of both nature and nurture on the temperament the mind.
Chronobiology – following the natural rhythms of nature

D

Daiva Chikitsa – Branch of Ayurvedic treatment that handles or spiritual/divine therapy
Deva – Divine
Dhanur Veda – Vedic martial arts (upaveda)
Dharma – the order of the universe; duty, natural law
Dharana – concentration.
Dhatu – tissue in the body; seven types total
Dhyana – meditation
Dinacharya – cycle of the day
Dosha – fault or impurity; bioenergetic principal of Vata, Pitta or Kapha
Dvaita – dualism
Dvesha – repulsion

G

Gandharva Veda – Vedic music, poetry and dance (upaveda)
Gayatri Mantra – mantra to the solar Godhead. Most commonly used Vedic mantra.
Guna – attribute or quality, three primary as sattva, rajas and tamas

H

Hatha Yoga – Vedic discipline of psycho-physical integration

I

Ishvara Pranidhana – surrender to the Divine

J

Jivatman – individual soul
Jnana Yoga – Yoga of knowledge, direct approach to Self-realization
Jnanendriya – sense organ
Jyotisha – Vedic science of astrology, time and karma

K

Kama – one of the four great goals of life, the pursuit of enjoyment, happiness, well-being
Kapha – One of three fundamental biological humors, expressing the qualities of water and earth.
Karana sharira – innermost causal body

Karma Yoga – Yoga of action, service and rituals
Karmas – actions done by mind or body and corresponding consequences
Karmendriyas – organs of action
Ketu – descending lunar node, dragon's tail
Kleshas – mental afflictions
Koshas – sheath or covering; five comprising the individual
Kriya Yoga – Yoga of internal action and energy

M

Mahat – cosmic intelligence
Majja Dhatu – nerve tissue
Manas sattva – acquired mental strength
Manas – mind, particularly in its outer orientation relative to the senses
Manasika Prakriti – mental nature
Manomaya kosha – mental sheath among the inner bodies
Manovaha srotas – channel of the mind
Mantra Yoga – Yoga of mantra and sacred sound
Mantra – sacred sound or words with sacred, transformative qualities
Marma – specific energy points on the body
Maya – illusion
Medhya – herbs that the mind
Medhya rasayanas – herbs that are psychological rejuvenatives
Moksha – one of the four great goals of life, the pursuit of liberation and higher spiritual knowledge

N

Nakshatra – lunar constellation in which the moon is located
Niyamas – positive duties and observances of Yoga

O

Ojas – subtle bioenergetic substance of reserve, immunity and energy in the physical body

P

Pancha Mahayajna – five great sacrifices, offerings or duties
Pancha Karma – five primary Ayurvedic detoxification measures
Pitta – one of three fundamental bioenergetic constituents, expressing the qualities of fire and water
Prajna – life wisdom
Prajnaparadha – cause of disease as the failure to adhere to internal wisdom
Prakriti – nature, mind-body or doshic constitution

Prana Yoga – Yoga of higher life energy, pranic practices and pranic healing
Prana – breath, spirit and vital energy
Pranamaya kosha – layer of the inner body made of breath energy, the vital force
Pranavaha nadis – subtle channels of prana or life force energy within the body
Pranayama – yogic breathing exercises along with other ways of enhancing or monitoring internal energies
Prarthana – prayer
Pratipaksha Bhavana – opposite treatment at the level of the mind and emotions
Pratyahara – control of the senses
Purusha – pure consciousness, unmanifest
Puja – ritual worship
Purusharthas –four primary goals of life (dharma, artha, kama, and moksha)

R

Raga – attraction
Rahu – ascending lunar node, dragon's head
Raja Yoga – Yoga of mental and will power
Rajas – one of the three gunas characterized by movement, transformation and turbulence
Rasayana – rejuvenation
Rigveda – oldest and most primary Vedic text out of the four
Rishi – seer to whom the wisdom of the Vedas was revealed
Ritucharya – cycle of the year and seasons
Roga – disease

S

Sadhana – spiritual practice
Sadvritta –ethical principles, truthful and harmonious living
Samadhi – unity consciousness
Samana – balancing prana
Samaveda – One of the four primary Vedas with mantras put into special chanting style
Samhita – Vedic scripture that contains foundational mantras
Samkalpa – intention, motivation and will-power
Samkhya – cosmic principle school of Vedic philosophy founded by Kapila
Santosha – contentment
Sat – Being
Satsanga – spiritual association
Sattva – one of the three Mahagunas characterized by peace, harmony and Divine connection, can also refer to the mind

Sattvavajaya - branch of Ayurvedic treatment that handles psychological well-being
Saucha - cleanliness
Shakti - female principal of Divine energy
Shankara - philosopher of the seventh century who taught nondualistic Vedanta
Shanti - peace
Sharira - body
Sharirika Prakriti - nature of the body and its energy
Shiva - masculine principal of Divine energy
Shuddha Sattva - pure in sattva guna, Pure Mind
Sthapatya Veda - Vedic architecture, sculpture and geomancy (upaveda)
Sthula sharira - The physical body
Sukshma sharira - subtle body
Svadhyaya - power of self-examination
Svastha - health

T

Tamas - One of the three Mahagunas characterized by the qualities of inertia, darkness and ignorance
Tapas - power of concentration, austerity
Tejas - subtle expression of Pitta dosha or fire
Tithi - phase of the moon; thirty per month

U

Udana - upward moving prana
Upanishads - Vedic teachings that enumerates the philosophical and spiritual meanings of life
Upavedas - supplementary Vedic sciences including Ayurveda, Dhanur Veda, Sthapatya Veda, and Gandharva Veda

V

Vaidya - physician or doctor
Vastu - Vedic science of space and directional influences
Vata - one of three bioenergetic constituents of a human being; expressing the qualities of space and air
Vayu - air
Vedangas - limbs of the Vedas
Vedas - prime Vedic scriptures of mantric knowledge, and sacred wisdom
Vedanta - Vedic philosophy of Self-awareness
Vedic Yoga - Vedic tools of self-unfoldment and Self-realization
Vichara - mind's ability to perform inquiry and examination.
Vihara - lifestyle

Vijnanamaya kosha – layer of body made of buddhi or intelligence, discernment, and wisdom
Vikriti – disease and disharmony
Vyana – outward moving prana

Y

Yajna – sacred offering or mode of worship
Yajurveda – One of the four primary Vedas
Yama – Yoga limb of self-control
Yantra – meditation designs
Yoga (Vedic philosophy) – Yoga school of Vedic philosophy founded by Hiranyagarbha
Yoga – Vedic system of practice and discipline in which the physical and mental bodies seek to attain oneness with the Divine
Yukti Vyapashraya – branch of Ayurvedic treatment based on objectively planned therapy

Bibliography

RELEVANT BOOKS BY DAVID FRAWLEY

ASTROLOGY OF THE SEERS
- *Twin Lakes WI: Lotus Press, 2000.*

AYURVEDIC ASTROLOGY: Self-Healing Through The Stars
- *Twin Lakes WI: Lotus Press, 2005.*

AYURVEDA AND THE MIND
- *Twin Lakes WI: Lotus Press, 1997.*

AYURVEDIC HEALING: A Comprehensive Guide
second edition - *Twin Lakes WI: Lotus Press, 2001.*

MANTRA YOGA AND PRIMAL SOUND: Secrets Of Bija (Seed) Mantras - *Twin Lakes WI: Lotus Press, 2010.*

SOMA IN YOGA AND AYURVEDA: The Power Of Rejuvenation and Immortality - *Twin Lakes WI: Lotus Press 2001.*

VEDIC YOGA: THE PATH OF THE RISHI
- *Twin Lakes WI: Lotus Press, 2014.*

YOGA AND AYURVEDA: Self-Healing and Self-Realization
- *Twin Lakes WI: Lotus Press, 1999.*

YOGA FOR YOUR TYPE by David Frawley and Sandra Kozak.
- *Twin Lakes WI: Lotus Press, 2001.*

THE YOGA OF HERBS by Frawley, David and Vasant Lad
- *Twin Lakes WI: Lotus Press, 1986.*

Relevant Books, Audio Titles and Courses by Dr. Suhas and Dr. Manisha Kshirsagar

THE HOT BELLY DIET
- *Simon & Schuster, 2014*

AYURVEDA: A quick reference handbook
- *Lotus Press, 2011*

ENCHANTING BEAUTY: Ancient Secrets for Inner, Outer & Lasting Beauty - *Lotus Press, 2015*

THE ART & SCIENCE OF VEDIC COUNSELING
by David Frawley & Suhas Kshirsagar - *Lotus Press, 2016*

AYURVEDIC WELLNESS: The Art & Science of Vibrant Health
Audible & Audio CD set - Sounds True 2014

EFFORTLESS WEIGHT LOSS: The Ayurvedic Way
Audible & Audio CD - Sounds True 2014

Other books by **DAVID FRAWLEY**

Astrology of the Seers : A Guide to Vedic/ Hindu Astrology

Ayurveda and The Mind : The Healing of Consciousness

Ayurveda Nature's Medicine (with Author Subhash Ranade)

Ayurvedic Astrology : Self Healing Through the Stars (In Press)

Ayurvedic Healing A Comprehensive Guide

From the River of Heaven : Hindu and Vedic Knowledge for Modern Age

Gods Sages and Kings : Vedic Secrets of Ancient Civilization

In Search of the Cradle of Civilization : New Insight on Ancient India Georg Feuerstein, (In Press)(with Author Subhash Kak)

Inner Tantric Yoga : Working with the Universal Shakti (Secrets of Mantras, Deities and Meditation)

Mantra Yoga and Primal Sound : Secrets of Seed (Bija) Mantras

Neti : Healing Secrets of Yoga and Ayurveda

Planetary Herbology : An Integration of Western Herbs into the Traditional Chinese and Ayurvedic System (with Author Michael Tierra) (In Press)

Soma in Yoga and Ayurveda : The Power of Rejuvenation and Immortality

Tantric Yoga and the Wisdom Goddesses : Spiritual Secrets of Ayurveda

Tantric Yoga and the Wisdom Goddesses : (Spiritual Secrets of Ayurveda)

The Oracle of Rama : An Adaptation of Rama Ajna Prashna of Goswami Tulsidas with Comm. David Frawley (In Press)

The Yoga of Herbs : An Ayurvedic Guide to Herbal Medicine (with Author Vasant Lad)

Wisdom of the Ancient Seers : Mantras of the Rigveda

Yoga for Your Type : An Ayurvedic Approach to your Asana Practice (with Author Sandra Summer- Fields & M.S. Kozak)

Yoga and Ayurveda Self Healing and Self Realization

Yoga and the Sacred Fire : Self-Realization and Planatary Transformation

Author's Resources

Dr. David Frawley (Pandit Vamadeva Shastri)

Dr. David Frawley is the author of more than forty published books and several distance learning courses. His books are available in twenty different languages and include important publications in the fields of Ayurvedic medicine, Vedic astrology, Raja Yoga, Veda, Vedanta, and Tantra. His books are noted for their depth and specificity and serve as textbooks in their fields.

Vamadeva is one of the most respected Vedacharyas or teachers of the ancient Vedic wisdom in recent decades and one of the main pioneers to bring Vedic knowledge to the West. He has a D .Litt from SVYASYA in India and a special Padma Bhushan award from the president of India for "distinguished service of a high order to the nation." He is an advisor for Sanchi University in Bhopal, India and a Master Educator for the Chopra Center.

American Institute of Vedic Studies

The American Institute of Vedic Studies is an internationally recognized center of Vedic learning, with affiliated organizations worldwide. Directed by Dr. David Frawley (Pandit Vamadeva Shastri) and Yogini Shambhavi Devi, the Vedic institute serves as a vehicle for their work, books, programs, and activities. The institute, which is primarily web-based, offers in depth training, including several distance-learning programs:

1. Ayurveda Healing Course in Ayurvedic Medicine
2. Yoga, Ayurveda, Mantra and Meditation Course
3. Vedic Astrology and Ayurveda Course
4. Integral Vedic Counseling Course
5. Mantra Yoga Course and Training
6. Yoga Shakti Training Program with Yogini Shambhavi Devi
7. Yoga Shakti Retreats
8. Vedic Astrology Consultations with Yogini Shambhavi Devi

The institute conducts regular retreats in India and USA to bring in students for a deeper level of instruction. It participates in international programs, events and conferences, particularly in India. The institute website features extensive on-line articles, books, and a full range of Vedic resources for the serious student.

American Institute of Vedic Studies – www.vedanet.com

Dr. David Frawley Facebook - drdavidfrawley

Dr. David Frawley Twitter - @davidfrawleyved.

Yogini Shambhavi Devi Facebook – yogini.shambhavi

Dr. Suhas Kshirsagar BAMS, MD (Ayurveda), Jyotisha Brihaspati:

- *Founder and Director: Ayurvedic Healing Inc. CA*
- *Faculty & Consulting Ayurvedic Physician, Chopra Center, CA*
- *Best Selling Author: The Hot Belly Diet*

Dr. Suhas Kshirsagar is a world-renown Ayurvedic physician & Educator from India born of a traditional Rig-Vedic family. He holds a M.D. in Ayurvedic Medicine, with a Gold Medal from the prestigious Pune University in India.

Dr. Suhas is one of the most academically accomplished Ayurvedic physicians in US, Who has traveled worldwide popularizing Ayurvedic Medicine, setting up clinics, offering courses for both medical professional and laypersons, and has provided Ayurvedic consultations for thousands of patients.

He is an internationally acclaimed motivational speaker and a visiting Professor at various Ayurvedic Schools & Universities, worldwide. He is an Adviser and Consultant for the Chopra Center University. He has featured in numerous radio and television shows like Dr OZ, NBC and many more. He is an experienced Clinician & an insightful Vedic Counselor, who adds tremendous value to his clients and students alike.

He is an internationally acclaimed Researcher, Best Selling Author, Medical Astrologer, Formulator and Consultant to various nutritional companies.

He is the lead formulator of Zrii, Achieve, Accell, Zrii Rise & Purify.

He is currently the Director of "Ayurvedic Healing" an Integrative Wellness Clinic in Santa Cruz, California.

Ayurvedic Academy of Healing Arts (AAHA): Ayurvedic Academy of Healing Arts is an internationally acclaimed educational institute offering workshops, classes and seminars on various Vedic disciplines like Ayurveda, Jyotish, Vaastu, Yoga and Sanskrit. It is affiliated with numerous organizations worldwide. The school offers web based as well as in person, advanced classes at our Santa Cruz, CA location.

- Hot Belly Diet Webinar Series
- Hot Belly Diet Audio Course
- Women's Health by Dr. Manisha - Course
- Pancha-Karma Training workshop – Practicum Course
- Vedic Medical Astrology by Dr. Suhas - Course
- Ayurvedic Skin & Beauty workshop by Dr. Manisha – Course
- Ayurvedic Herbal Formulations by Dr. Manisha- Practicum Course
- Ayurveda Wellness Counselor Series: 2016 - Course

AFFILIATED ORGANIZATIONS:

NAMA (National Ayurvedic Medical Association) BOD since 2011
AAPNA (Ayurvedic Association of Professionals in North America)
Mount Madonna College of Ayurveda: Faculty since 2008
Kerala Ayurveda Academy: Adviser & Faculty since 2007
Chopra Center for Well Being: Faculty & Consultant since 2007
"Zrii": Scientific Adviser and Chief Formulator since 2007

Index

HINDU TRADITION SERIES

General Editor

JOHANNES BRONKHORST

The Hindu Tradition Series aims to bring together books of the highest academic standard that critically interrogate Hindu tradition in the widest sense. Its focus is on cultural and religious history, including relevant political and social developments. The interaction with other traditions, whether originally from inside or outside the Indian subcontinent, will figure prominently among its volumes.

1. *The Mahābhārata and Greek Mythology* — **FERNANDO WULFF ALONSO** [978-81-208-3791-1]
2. *Viraha-Bhakti : The Early History of Kṛṣṇa Devotion* — **FRIEDHELM HARDY** [978-81-208-3616-1]
3. *Classical Hindu Mythology : A Reader in the Sanskrit Purāṇas*— Ed. and Tr. by **CORNELLA DIMMITT** and **J.A.B. VAN BUTTENAN** [978-81-208-3972-4]
4. *India and the Hellenistic Word* — **KLAUS KARTTUNEN** [978-81-208–4100-0]
5. *Engaged Enancipation : Mind, Morals and Make- Believe in the Mokṣopāya (Yogavāsiṣtha)* —Edited by **CHRISTOPHER KEY CHAPPLE** and **ARINDAM CHAKRABARTI** [978-81-208–4093-5]
6. *The Pātityagramanirnaya : A Purāṇic History of Some Brahman Communuties* — **STEPHAN HILLYER LEVITT**
7. *Mythology of Brahma* — **GREG BAILEY**

INDIA'S SCIENTIFIC HERITAGE SERIES

Founder Editor : Late L.M. Singhvi,
Gen. Ed. : S.N. Bhavsar,
Guest Ed. Murli Manohar Joshi
ISBN : 978-81-208-3364-7

1. **Vedic Mathematics** (Revised & Enlarged)—*Bharati Krsna Tirthaji*
ISBN: 978-81-208-0163-9 (C); ISBN: 978-81-208-0164-6 (P)
2. **Discover Vedic Mathematics :** A Practical system Based on Sixteen Simple Formulae from the Vedas—*Kenneth R. Williams*, Foreword by *L.M . Singhvi.*
ISBN: 978-81-208-3096-7 (C); ISBN: 978-81-208-3097-4 (P)
3. **The Cosmic Calculator:** A Vedic Mathematics Course for Schools (3 Books+Teacher's Guide & Answer Book)—*Kenneth Williams & Mark Gaskell*
ISBN: 978-81-208-2014-2 (Set) (C); ISBN: 978-81-208-1871-2 (Set) (P)
4. **The Natural Calculator:** Using the Natural Processes of the Mind for Mental Calculation—*Kenneth R. Williams*
ISBN: 978-81-208-1961-0 (C); ISBN: 978-81-208-1962-7 (P)
5. **Triples:** Applications of Pythagorean Triples—*Kenneth R. Williams*
ISBN: 978-81-208-1957-3 (C); ISBN: 978-81-208-1958-0 (P)
6. **Vertically and Crosswise:** Applications of the Vedic Mathematics Sutra—*A.P. Nicholas, Kenneth Williams & J. Pickles*
ISBN: 978-81-208-1960-3 (C); ISBN: 978-81-208-1982-5 (P)
7. **Astronomical Applications of Vedic Mathematics**—*Kenneth R. Williams*
ISBN: 978-81-208-1959-7 (C); ISBN: 978-81-208-1983-2 (P)
8. **Paratattvaganitadarsanam:** Egometry or Principles of Transcendental Philosophy of Mathematical Truth—*G.S. Murty*
ISBN: 978-81-208-1821-7
9. **Vedic Mathematics Teacher's Manual (3 Vols.)** (Elementary Level/ Intermediate Level/Advanced Level)—*Kenneth R. Williams*
ISBN: 978-81-208-2773-8 (C); ISBN: 978-81-208-2785-1 (P)
10. **Sunya and Nothingness in Science, Philosophy and Religion**—*Jayant D. Burde* ISBN: 978-81-208-3343-2
11. **Rituals, Mantras and Science :** An Integral Perspective—*Jayant Burde*
ISBN: 978-81-208-2053-1
12. **Vedic Mathematics for All Ages :** A Beginner's Guide—*Vandana Singhal* ISBN: 978-81-208-3211-4 (C); ISBN: 978-81-208-3230-5 (P)
13. **Vedic Physics**—*Keshav Dev Verma* ISBN: 978-81-208-3270-1
14. **Changing Minds**—*Michele Mari Desmarais*
ISBN: 978-81-208-3328-9 (C); ISBN: 978-81-208-3336-4 (P)
15. **Buddhist Logic and Quantum Dilemma** —*Jayant Burde*
ISBN: 978-81-208-3552-8
16. **Jaina Relativism and Relativity Physics** —*Jayant Burde*
ISBN: 978-81-208-3815-4